Claiming Citizenship

Claiming Citizenship is an authoritative and vital series published by Zed Books in partnership with the Citizenship Development Research Centre (CDRC).

Each high-quality volume features thoroughly peer-reviewed research from senior experts in their field, which examines the multifaceted issues of citizenship, rights, participation and accountability. The books are global in scope and packed with empirical and original case studies, largely from Southern contexts, bringing voices and materials to debates that have often been dominated by the North. While essential reading for development studies students and researchers, the series will be of interest to a broad range of scholars, activists and practitioners concerned with issues of citizenship.

Available titles

Inclusive Citizenship: Meanings and Expressions, edited by Naila Kabeer

Science and Citizens: Globalization and the Challenge of Engagement, edited by Melissa Leach, Ian Scoones and Brian Wynne

Rights, Resources and the Politics of Accountability, edited by Peter Newell and Joanna Wheeler

Spaces for Change? The Politics of Citizen Participation in New Democratic Arenas, edited by Andrea Cornwall and Vera Schattan Coelho

Citizenship and Social Movements: Perspectives from the Global South, edited by Lisa Thompson and Chris Tapscott

Citizen Action and National Policy Reform: Making Change Happen, edited by John Gaventa and Rosemary McGee

Globalizing Citizens: New Dynamics of Inclusion and Exclusion, edited by John Gaventa and Rajesh Tandon

Forthcoming titles

Mobilizing for Democracy: Citizen Action and the Politics of Public Participation, edited by Vera Schattan P. Coelho and Bettina von Lieres

About the editors

John Gaventa is a research professor and fellow in the Participation, Power and Social Change Team at the Institute of Development Studies, University of Sussex. A political sociologist by training, he has written widely on issues of power, citizen action, participation and democracy, including the award-winning *Power and Powerlessness in an Appalachian Valley* (1980) and *Global Citizen Action* (co-editor, 2001). He also has been active with a number of NGOs and civil society organizations internationally, including the Highlander Center in the United States and Oxfam in the UK. He is the director of the Development Research Centre on Citizenship, Participation and Accountability and served as co-convenor of the working group on globalizing citizen engagements.

Rajesh Tandon is the founder and executive director of PRIA (Society for Participatory Research in Asia), and has been an activist-scholar for the past three decades, focusing on issues such as citizenship and participatory governance, participatory research and building civil society alliances. In addition to his writing and scholarship, he has served as a civil society leader in India and internationally, including serving as a founding member and chair of CIVICUS, programme director of the Citizens and Governance Programme of the Commonwealth Foundation and chair of the Montreal International Forum (FIM). He has been an active participant in the Development Research Centre on Citizenship, Participation and Accountability and served as co-convenor of the working group on globalizing citizen engagements.

Globalizing citizens
new dynamics of inclusion and exclusion

edited by John Gaventa
and Rajesh Tandon

Zed Books
LONDON | NEW YORK

Globalizing citizens: new dynamics of inclusion and exclusion was first published in 2010 by Zed Books Ltd, 7 Cynthia Street, London N1 9JF, UK and Room 400, 175 Fifth Avenue, New York, NY 10010, USA

www.zedbooks.co.uk

Editorial Copyright © John Gaventa and Rajesh Tandon, 2010
Copyright in this collection © Zed Books 2010

The rights of John Gaventa and Rajesh Tandon to be identified as the editors of this work have been asserted by them in accordance with the Copyright, Designs and Patents Act, 1988

Set in OurType Arnhem and Futura Bold by Ewan Smith, London
Index: ed.emery@thefreeuniversity.net
Cover designed by Andrew Corbett.
Printed and bound in Great Britain by MPG Books, Bodmin and King's Lynn

Distributed in the USA exclusively by Palgrave Macmillan, a division of St Martin's Press, LLC, 175 Fifth Avenue, New York, NY 10010, USA

All rights reserved. No part of this publication may be reproduced, stored in a retrieval system or transmitted in any form or by any means, electronic, mechanical, photocopying or otherwise, without the prior permission of Zed Books Ltd.

A catalogue record for this book is available from the British Library
Library of Congress Cataloging in Publication Data available

ISBN 978 1 84813 471 3 hb
ISBN 978 1 84813 472 0 pb
ISBN 978 1 84813 473 7 eb

Contents

Acronyms | vii Foreword | x

PART ONE Introduction

1 Citizen engagements in a globalizing world 3
   JOHN GAVENTA AND RAJESH TANDON

PART TWO From global to local: the impact of global governance on everyday citizenship

2 Mediated health citizenships: living with HIV and engaging with the Global Fund in the Gambia 33
   REBECCA CASSIDY AND MELISSA LEACH

3 Mobilizing and mediating global medicine and health citizenship: the politics of AIDS knowledge production in rural South Africa 56
   STEVEN ROBINS

4 Enhancing everyday citizenship practices: women's livelihoods and global markets 79
   JULIE THEKKUDAN

5 The politics of global assessments: the case of the IAASTD . . 96
   IAN SCOONES

PART THREE From local to global: the dynamics of transnational citizen action

6 Campaigns for land and citizenship rights: the dynamics of transnational agrarian movements 119
   SATURNINO M. BORRAS AND JENNIFER C. FRANCO

7 Spanning citizenship spaces through transnational coalitions: the Global Campaign for Education 140
   JOHN GAVENTA AND MARJORIE MAYO

8 Citizenship and trade governance in the Americas 163
ROSALBA ICAZA, PETER NEWELL AND MARCELO SAGUIER

9 Mobilization and political momentum: anti-asbestos struggles in South Africa and India 185
LINDA WALDMAN

10 Hybrid activism: paths of globalization in the Brazilian environmental movement 211
ANGELA ALONSO

11 Caught between national and global jurisdictions: displaced people's struggle for rights 232
LYLA MEHTA AND REBECCA NAPIER-MOORE

About the contributors | 253

Index | 258

Acronyms

ACTSA	Action for Southern Africa
ART	antiretroviral therapy
ARV	antiretroviral
BANI	Ban Asbestos Network India
CAFTA-DR	Central America Free Trade Agreement – Dominican Republic
CBO	community-based organization
CCM	Country Coordinating Mechanism
CEDI	Centro Ecumênico de Documentação e Informação/ Ecumenical Centre of Documentation and Information
CEF	Commonwealth Education Fund
CGR	Committee of Government Representatives on the Participation of Civil Society
CI	Conservation International
COPA	Confederación Parlamentaria de las Américas/Parliamentary Confederation of the Americas
CPAA	Concerned People against Asbestos
CSO	civil society organization
CSR	corporate social responsibility
EFA	Education for All
EPH	Environmental Public Hearings
ESIS	Employers State Insurance Scheme
FAO	Food and Agriculture Organization
FBCN	Fundação Brasileira para a Conservação de Natureza/ Brazilian Foundation for Nature Conservation
FTA	free trade agreement
FTAA	Free Trade Area of the Americas
GCE	Global Campaign for Education
GCS	global civil society
GFATM	Global Fund to Fight AIDS, Tuberculosis and Malaria
GM	genetically modified
GoAP	government of Andhra Pradesh
GWA	Global Week of Action
HARRP	HIV/AIDS Rapid Response Project
HSA	Hemispheric Social Alliance
HUL	Hindustan Unilever Limited

IAASTD	International Assessment of Agricultural Knowledge, Science and Technology for Development
IBAS	International Ban Asbestos Secretariat
ICARRD	International Conference on Agrarian Reform and Rural Development
ICCO	Interchurch Organization for Development Cooperation
IFAD	International Fund for Agricultural Development
IFAP	International Federation of Agricultural Producers
ILC	International Land Coalition
IMF	International Monetary Fund
INGO	international non-governmental organization
IPC	International Planning Committee for Food Sovereignty
IPCC	Intergovernmental Panel on Climate Change
ISA	Instituto Socioambiental/Socioenvironmental Institute
KMP	Kilusang Magbubukid ng Pilipinas/Peasant Movement of the Philippines
KSSM	Kamdar Swasthya Suraksha Mandal
MAP	Multi-Country AIDS Programme
MBOD	Medical Bureau of Occupational Diseases
MDG	Millennium Development Goal
MNC	multinational corporation
MSF	Médecins Sans Frontières/Doctors without Borders
NACP	National AIDS Control Programme
NAFTA	North American Free Trade Agreement
NAS	National AIDS Secretariat
NCDRLD	National Campaign on Dust-Related Lung Diseases
NGO	non-governmental organization
NIOH	National Institute of Occupational Health
NUM	National Union of Mineworkers
PAKISAMA	Pambansang Katipunan ng mga Samahang Magsasaka/National Council of Farmers' Associations
PANNA	Pesticide Action Network of North America
PEPFAR	President's Emergency Plan for AIDS Relief
PPTCT	prevention of parent-to-child transmission
PR	Principal Recipient
PRIA	Participatory Research in Asia
PWA	person living with AIDS
SANAC	South African National AIDS Council
SHG	self-help group
SR	sub-recipient
TAC	Treatment Action Campaign
TLP	treatment literacy practitioner

TNC	transnational corporation
UDHR	Universal Declaration of Human Rights
UNAIDS	Joint United Nations Programme on HIV/AIDS
UNCED	United Nations Conference on Environment and Development
UNHCR	United Nations High Commissioner for Refugees
UNORKA	Pambansang Ugnayan ng Nagsasariling Lokal na mga Samahang Mamamayan sa Kanayunan/National Coordination of Autonomous Local Rural People's Organizations
USAID	United States Agency for International Development
VCT	Voluntary Counselling and Testing
WHO	World Health Organization
WTO	World Trade Organization
WWF	World Wildlife Fund

Foreword

In a globally interconnected world, changing patterns of authority and power pose new challenges to the ways in which ordinary citizens exercise their voices, claim their rights and share solidarities with others. While much has been written on these shifting patterns of global governance, very few studies have taken a 'vertical view' to focus on the interrelationships of the local and the global, and their consequences for the practices and identities of citizenship.

The case studies in this volume respond to this challenge, taking a citizens' perspective to look upwards and outwards from everyday experiences and struggles to the changing local, national and global landscapes of governance and authority. They tell the stories of how these changing landscapes affect diverse groups of citizens, be they those grappling with HIV in the Gambia or South Africa, women affected by global markets in India, or farmers affected by international expert-led assessments of agriculture. They tell other stories of how citizens are collectively responding to new global actors and forces, as seen in campaigns for land rights in the Philippines, educational rights in India and Nigeria, occupational health in South Africa and India or protection of the environment in Brazil. They tell other stories of struggles for voice and recognition, whether it be in the governance of trade policy in Latin America or in the treatment of displaced peoples, who are no longer are seen as 'citizens' in the localities to which they have been relocated.

In sharing and analysing these case studies, the book engages with and contributes to a number of significant debates. To the large body of work on changing global governance, the case studies will add concrete insights into how these global architectures affect everyday lives and actions. To the normative and conceptual literature on global citizenship, the volume offers empirically grounded insights into debates on whether shifting global configurations are in fact giving rise to new forms of global solidarity and identity. To the growing work on transnational citizen activism, global social movements and global civil society, this work takes a different, more vertical view. The focus is less on how citizens mobilize internationally, and more on how global power extends to local and national forms of citizen action, and conversely how locally held rights claims are extended to international institutions. By bringing in-depth case studies to bear on these larger questions, important implications emerge for the possibilities and processes of securing inclusive and active citizenship in a global age.

This volume, like the others in this series, has emerged from the work of the Development Research Centre on Citizenship, Participation and Accountability (Citizenship DRC), an international network of researchers who have worked together for almost a decade to explore themes of citizen action across some twenty countries. (For further information see www.drc-citizenship.org). The volume is the seventh in the Zed Books series on *Claiming Citizenship*. While previous volumes focus primarily on the dynamics of citizen engagement at the local and sometimes national levels, this is the first to explore the global and international links so explicitly. The work emerged to fill gaps felt in the previous inquiries, as even in these earlier volumes international actors, norms, agreements, funds and discourses always seemed to be somehow part of the local story. (See, for instance, the second volume in this series, *Science and Citizens: Globalization and the Challenge of Engagement*, from which evolved some of the themes explored in this volume.)

As with other projects in the Citizenship DRC, the researchers involved came together in a working group, representing differing disciplines, backgrounds and institutions. Also as in the other projects, our approach was an iterative one. Rather than starting with broad propositions which we sought to 'test' in local case studies, we chose a set of cases which we thought would illuminate the tensions and questions we sought to consider. Many of these reflected issues or contexts in which the researchers were already to some degree involved. By researching the cases further, and through meeting to discuss and reflect together on our findings over the course of three years, cross-cutting themes and propositions were developed. In many of the research projects, our approach was not that purely of outside observers. Rather, the findings often emerged as well through dialogue, engagement and participation with the groups or campaigns involved.

As series editor, as well as one of the co-convenors of the volume, I want to thank many who made this work possible. We have been privileged throughout the history of the Citizenship DRC to have long-term funding from the Department of International Development in the UK, as well as additional support from the Ford Foundation and the Rockefeller Foundation. We have benefited greatly from the comments and critiques of several other researchers along the way, including Jan

Aart Scholte, Lisa Jordan and Fiona Wilson, as well as from editing assistance by Karen Brock. We were aided by an excellent literature review by Nicholas Benequista and Tamara Levine, later updated by Greg Barrett. The members of the Global Citizen Engagements Working Group (who are the contributors to this volume) gave generously of their time through meetings and emails, responded patiently to comments on their work from the editors, reviewers and from one another, and through their discussions helped to shape the overall findings of the volume.

I am also grateful to the co-convenor of this group and co-editor of the volume, Rajesh Tandon, who brought to the project not only his great synthesis skills, but also the insights from his vast experience as a civil society leader in linking across local, national and global arenas. Most importantly, however, we want to thank the activists, community leaders, government staff, scientists and others in the many sites around the world where this work was done – who allowed us to engage, who shared their experiences and views and who often gave feedback on our findings. We hope we have done justice to your knowledge.

John Gaventa
Director, Development Research Centre on Citizenship, Participation
and Accountability, Institute of Development Studies
June 2010

PART ONE
Introduction

1 · Citizen engagements in a globalizing world

JOHN GAVENTA AND RAJESH TANDON[1]

Introduction

From Cancún to Copenhagen, from trade debates to climate debates and from financial crises to food crises, the impacts of global forces on everyday life are becoming increasingly apparent. With globalization have come changing forms of power and new realms of authority, and with these, new spaces for public action. From local to global, fields of power and landscapes of authority are being reconfigured, affecting the lives and futures of citizens across the planet, while simultaneously reshaping where and how citizens engage to make their voices heard. If we believe in the ideals of democracy, in which citizens have the right to participate in decisions and deliberations affecting their lives, what are the implications when these extend beyond traditionally understood national and local boundaries? If we are interested in the possibilities of citizen action to claim and ensure rights, and to bring about social change, how do citizens navigate this new, more complicated terrain? What are the consequences for an emerging sense and experience of global citizenship, and for holding governments and powerful supranational institutions and authorities to account?

While a great deal of attention has been paid in the literature to these changing patterns of global governance, we know remarkably little about how they play out, or their consequences and implications for ordinary citizens. In this volume, this theme is explored through empirical research in Brazil, India, the Gambia, Nigeria, the Philippines and South Africa, as well as in cross-national projects in Latin America and Africa. The case studies focus on a number of sectors: the environment, trade, education, livelihoods, health and HIV/AIDS, work and occupational disease, agriculture and land.[2] They document different types of engagement, ranging from transnational campaigns and social movements to participation in new institutionally designed fora. Taking a citizen's perspective, they look upwards and outwards at shifting global forms of authority and ask whether, in response to these governance changes, citizens themselves are expressing new rights claims on global duty holders, and whether they are expressing new forms of global solidarity with citizens in other localities.

There are a number of possible responses to these questions. On the one hand, some scholars have argued, globalization has led to changes in governance and emerging transnational social movements which are creating new spaces and opportunities for citizen engagement. In the process, as citizenship has become delinked from territorial boundaries, it has also become more multilayered and multi-scaled, while governance increasingly involves both state and non-state actors, many of which are transnational. The new global configuration, some optimistically argue, provides the conditions for the ascendancy of a new sense of global citizenship, which deepens and expands democratic participation and the realization of human rights.

The case studies in this volume, however, collectively present a somewhat more sombre picture. While shifting landscapes of global authority create new spaces and opportunities for citizen engagement, they also carry with them new possibilities for and forms of power, which interact with deeply embedded local practices. For some citizens, there are new opportunities for participation in transnational processes of action, resulting in the emergence of a new sense of global citizenship and solidarity. Yet for many other ordinary citizens, changes in global authority may have the opposite effect, strengthening the layers and discourses of power that limit the possibilities for their local action, and constraining – or, at least, not enabling – a sense of citizen agency. Even in these cases, however, one can see localized patterns of resistance to global forces, motivated by immediate issues of survival and fragility, rather than a virtuous sense of global solidarity and citizenship.

In the first section of this introductory chapter, we bring together empirical insights from the case studies on how changing global governance patterns affect the possibilities for and arenas of citizen engagement. Sometimes they create new spheres for engagement beyond the nation-state; at other times they bring global factors to bear on national and local forms of action. Contrary to some assertions made in the literature, we find that globalized governance does not necessarily imply a diminishing role for the nation-state. Rather, globalization adds new layers, arenas and jurisdictions of governance, often bringing contestation and competition across them rather than the replacing of one arena with another.

We move on to discuss ways that the multi-tiered and multipolar character of global authority simultaneously creates new multilayered and multidimensional identities of citizenship, which in some cases create new possibilities for inclusive citizen voice, while in others serve to reinforce axes for greater exclusion, contributing to the weakening of already fragile forms of citizen expression. In sum, there are winners and losers in this process.

In the next section we argue that explaining the difference in these outcomes involves exploring forms of mobilization, the role of mediators and the politics of knowledge which shape the possibilities and practices of citizenship in response to the changes in the global landscape. By examining these intervening factors, we can gain insights into the paradox of why, for some, globalization offers possibilities for a new sense of solidarity and new opportunities for engagement, while for others it offers little real opportunity for expanded solidarity, and weakens the possibilities for citizen agency.

We end this chapter by arguing that taking a 'vertical' approach – one that looks at the *interrelationships* of levels of authority along a scale running from local to global – has important strategic implications for citizen action and social movements. In this interdependent world, more inclusive citizenship, and with it more effective forms of citizen engagement, will not be realized by a focus on one arena or layer of political authority alone. Rather, more promise is found in new forms of engagement which recognize the layers of authority and employ strategies that build citizen solidarity vertically and synergistically across them.

The changing nature of governance: new spaces for citizen engagements?

It is now commonplace in emerging literature on globalization and governance to argue that authority is moving beyond singular nation-state systems and power is increasingly dispersed along a scale from local to global, and across state and non-state actors. In this new emerging global order, governance is seen as a) multilayered (cutting across global, regional, national and local institutions), b) polyarchic or pluralistic (in the sense that no site of governance has unilateral, supreme and absolute authority), c) geometrically varied (in that regulatory systems vary across issues and geographies), and d) structurally complex (made up of diverse state and non-state agencies and networks) (Held and McGrew 2002: 9). Such shifts in global governance have important consequences for grassroots actors. They reshape the possibilities for extending their action to the international arena, as well as for citizen action more locally (Della Porta and Tarrow 2005; Edwards and Gaventa 2001; Keck and Sikkink 1998; Appadurai 2000).[3]

In every case in this volume, we see examples of how this shifting political authority affects where and how citizens engage on a range of issues including education, HIV, occupational health, environment, land, agriculture, livelihood, trade and 'forced' displacement. While much of the literature on the consequences of global governance focuses on the emergence of *transnational* citizen action, our first group of chapters present a number of examples of how new global actors and factors are brought to bear on *national and local* decision-making processes. In Chapter 2, Cassidy and Leach outline how changing patterns of power and governance are unfolding in relation to HIV/AIDS in the small West African country of the Gambia. Here, a new globalism in public health has led to an array of international initiatives and funding mechanisms contributing to a shift from authority based on the nation-state towards global public–private–philanthropic partnerships. We see how powerful global funding mechanisms – such as the Global Fund, the US President's Emergency Plan for AIDS Relief, and the World Bank's Multi-Country AIDS Programme – affect the decision-making and dynamics of citizen engagement at the national and local level, with little or no downwards accountability to the people affected. Continuing in the field of global health, in Chapter 3 Robins investigates how global funding in South Africa is mediated downwards through international NGOs and local health activists, and with it the extension of global ideas, discourses and technologies that affect patterns of local action and resistance.

In Chapter 4, we shift from Africa to India, and from health to the arena of livelihoods. In this chapter, Julie Thekkudan focuses on Project Shakti, an initiative promoted by the Indian government in collaboration with Unilever, a multinational corporation, to fund women's self-help groups at the grassroots level. This initiative represented a new public–private partnership arrangement, but with little accountability downwards, despite great consequences for local identities and the actions of local participants. Moving to agricultural livelihoods, in Chapter 5 Ian Scoones examines the dynamics of engagement in new global fora, in this case the International Assessment of Agricultural Knowledge, Science and Technology for Development (IAASTD), an ambitious attempt to encourage local and global debate on the future of agricultural science and technology through 'cross-stakeholder dialogue'. Responding to critiques of top-down, Northern-dominated expert assessments of the past, the IAASTD aimed to be more inclusive and participatory in both design and process, in a way that became inevitably 'fraught and flawed'.

In the next section of the book, we move from cases that examine the impact of global actors on everyday citizenship to those which explore the dynamics of transnational action as citizens attempt to mobilize upwards from their local spaces to put pressure on global decision-makers. In so doing, these case studies also reveal, they must deal with an increasing complexity of levels and types of authorities.

In Chapter 6, Borras and Franco focus on the case of Vía Campesina, one of the largest transnational agrarian movements, examining how rural agrarian movements have responded to the growing forces of globalization, especially in relation to land rights. Drawing on Fox (2001), the authors describe how nation-states have been affected by a 'triple squeeze': 'from above' through the growing regulatory power of international institutions; 'from below' through the decentralization of some authority to local actors; and the 'from the sides' through the ceding of some functions to private or quasi-public actors. As a result, the peasant movement has begun to focus much more on international institutions as duty bearers that must be accountable for upholding local land rights.

The diffusion of authority across layers and actors is also found in Chapter 7, which examines the Global Campaign for Education (GCE). Gaventa and Mayo outline how the global right to education is now affected by a multiplicity of players at different levels. As a result, they argue, citizen action must span a variety of new spaces in order to reach the universal goal of education for all. In Chapter 8, Icaza et al. illustrate how shifting patterns of trade governance, as seen in the North American Free Trade Agreement and other similar accords, create new rights for private actors, which affect where and how citizens can exercise their voice. From traditionally holding their own state to account for the provision of basic services and the fulfilment of social and economic rights, citizens must now engage private actors and defend their rights in the regional and international arenas where key decisions are increasingly made.

In Chapter 9, Waldman describes how the area of occupational health is governed increasingly by a dizzying array of global regulatory actors that exercise an array of hard and soft regulatory powers, and the consequent effects on citizen mobilization on asbestos disease in South Africa and India. In Chapter 10, Alonso shows how challenges of linking from the local to the global on environmental issues in Brazil create new types of 'hybrid activists', with new sets of skills required for effective engagement. In Chapter 11, Mehta and Napier-Moore describe how even displaced people – who are in some cases effectively stateless and do not have access to full citizenship rights in their host countries – in fact find themselves regulated and governed by an array of international frameworks and agencies.

Thus each of the chapters in this book illustrates a concrete example of how the shifting landscapes of global authority affect the possible terrain of spaces in which citizens may engage. In each of the important policy issues illustrated, the responsible actors and authorities are found not only at the national and local levels. Such new governance regimes are driven by a number of factors, many of which are associated with global economic forces. In India, increased engagement with global market actors reshapes public and private contours of power at the national and local level, while in the Philippines and elsewhere a growing international land grab affects the traditional structures that regulate land reform. In other cases new quasi-public entities such as the Global Fund or large environmental foundations – what Edwards (2008) calls the philanthrocapitalists – play an increasing role in the governance of social policies across a range of sectors. In some cases, these actors exercise power through formal authority. More often than not, however, they illustrate the 'soft powers' that characterize global authority (Nye 2004; Lukes 2007), through their effect on knowledge and discourses, or through the creation of cross-cutting networks of actors, which link public and private, governmental and non-governmental, in visible or sometimes less visible ways.

In all of these changes, the nation-state increasingly becomes squeezed between the rights and needs of its citizens, and the demands and expectations of global forces and actors, many of whom are non-state or international actors who bring a different set of pressures and accountabilities (Scholte 2005). While some scholars argue that the growth of global governance effectively diminishes the role of the nation-state (Rosenau 2002), these cases suggest in fact that the capacity of the nation-state to mediate between the local and the global is critical to how global pressures enhance or weaken the rights and claims of local citizens. From a citizen's perspective, the internationalization of authority means negotiating additional layers of governance, characterized by increasing complexity and opaqueness, in which the local, national and global constantly mingle. Mobilization for rights and accountability, if it is to be effective, must look beyond the national and the local to the global arena, as well as to interactions across the entire spectrum of governance. Movements themselves, as we shall explore later, are faced with the challenge of becoming multi-scalar, as well as becoming able to deal with a wide variety of actors and authorities.

The implications of changing authorities for the meanings and practices of citizenship

To raise the question of the impact of global governance on citizen action is to immediately enter into voluminous and enduring debates on the possibilities of 'global', 'world' or 'cosmopolitan' citizenship. While there is much debate on the meanings of these terms,[4] at its most basic level the concept of global or cosmopolitan citizenship challenges the conventional meaning of citizenship as exclusive membership and participation within a territorially bounded political community. The notion is not necessarily new: it has existed in political thought since early Greek thinking on citizenship, and as such even pre-dates notions of citizenship linked to the nation (Schattle 2008). Since the 1980s, however, in the face of globalization and the associated transnationalization of markets, communications and civil society, the term 'global citizenship' has become increasingly common in public and academic discourse, while views on its normative importance and practical possibilities remain deeply divided.

On the one hand, there are those who argue normatively that the expansion of global citizenship is critical in today's world. It is a path for promoting global democracy (Archibugi 2008; Held 1995) and overcoming global governance deficits (Scholte 2002), for ensuring ecological sustainability (van Steenbergen 1994) and for realizing universal human values (Falk 1993; Heater 2002). Shifts in global authority, the arguments go, require the possibility of new practices of global citizen action (Edwards and Gaventa 2001), a democratizing and regulatory role for global civil society (Scholte 2008; MacKenzie 2009), the extension of global rights frameworks through citizen engagement and social movements (McKeon 2009; Stammers 2009), the development of new forms of global accountability (Ebrahim and Weisband 2007) and new identities and possibilities of global citizenship (Schattle 2008). 'Global citizenship, in the present day,' Schattle argues, 'is rich, complex and tangible. In this new millennium, global citizenship has become much more than an abstract ideal espoused mainly by philosophers and visionaries. Now, more than ever, the practices of global citizenship are upon us' (ibid.: 6).

On the other hand, sceptics argue, such notions of global citizenship are at best an aspiration and at worst ill founded. As Heater argues, 'the essence of citizenship is the individual's relation to the state. Yet there is no *world* state' (2002: 6); therefore there are few prospects of meaningful forms of global citizenship. To argue for such, some suggest, is to risk weakening and undermining the legitimacy of existing nation-states and the frameworks of human rights implemented through them. Moreover, others propose, meaningful participation and deliberations can only best occur at the smaller-scale, community level (Schattle 2008). Others argue that while the aspiration of a global identity or community of citizens is admirable, it is deeply contradicted by rising national and ethnic allegiances (Heater 2002). Even where transnational identities and communities are emerging, Fox argues, these 'involve boundaries, rights and responsibilities that are too amorphous to warrant the term citizenship, especially when ideas such as membership, standing or human rights will do' (Fox 2005: 194).

While the views are highly divided, the position one takes within them often turns on two other definitional issues. First, those who take a sceptical view often define citizenship in relation to states, to the exclusion of other widely recognized understandings which recognize that citizenship identities are more complex and multidimensional than those which are simply state-conferred. These broader concepts include seeing citizenship in terms of solidarity and belonging to a broader community (Ellison 1997), and seeing one's rights and duties in relationship to non-state institutions and actors as well as states (e.g. corporations) (Hoffman 2004; Mohanty and Tandon 2006). At the international level, this broader, more multidimensional view arguably increases in importance, and exists side by side with the statist view. As Schattle (2008: 3-4) observes, 'the legal institution of national citizenship might well remain firmly in the hands of nation-states, and nation-states might well remain a principal but not exclusive basis of political membership and allegiance, but these realities no longer keep global citizenship from flourishing in other ways. Like it or not, individuals all over the world are choosing to think of themselves as global citizens and to shape their lives as members and participants in communities reaching out to all humanity.'

Second, differences in views on global citizenship often hinge on whether one is defining the status quo, or whether one is defining an emergent notion – in Falk's view, whether one is looking at the 'axis of feasibility' or the 'axis of aspiration' (1994: 140). He goes on to argue that 'global citizenship in its idealistic and aspirational expression, if mechanically superimposed on the present reality of geopolitics, is a purely sentimental, and slightly absurd notion. In contrast, if global citizenship is conceived to be a political project, associated with the possibility of a future political community of global or species scope, then it assumes, it seems to me, a far more constitutive and challenging political character' (ibid.: 139). From this latter perspective, citizenship can be understood as an emergent and historically evolving concept, rather than something which is fixed at a given point in time.

While both intense and voluminous, these debates on the possibilities of global citizenship remain normative and theoretical in nature. Very few studies have looked empirically at how citizens themselves actually engage with and respond to the changing landscapes of global authority, and what this means for their own understandings and practices of citizenship. Those that have done so have focused more on global citizenship identities through personal narratives[5] than on what these mean for collective citizen action. The case studies in this volume, therefore, give us a unique insight into how citizens at the grassroots level actually experience changes in global authority, and what in turn that implies for the meanings of citizenship and the possibilities of global citizen action.

Consistent with other volumes in this *Claiming Citizenship* series, these cases take a citizens' perspective (Eyben and Ladbury 2006), looking upwards and outwards at how citizens see and experience global institutions, rather than the other way around. In such an approach, we understand citizenship through the lens of how it is understood and practised, rather than whether it is legally or institutionally ascribed. Such an actor-oriented approach (Nyamu-Musembi 2005) also puts more emphasis on how citizens perceive their own agency, and whom they hold accountable for their rights, than on whether global institutions and legal frameworks that can uphold such rights already exist.[6] In other words, we are interested in whether and how the shifting nature of political authority in global governance has creating lived experiences of citizenship which have a transnational, trans-state character, even if these are yet to be acknowledged explicitly by such political authorities in global governance. By focusing on whether there is an emergent sense of global citizenship, we also take a historical view of citizenship as being under construction over time, through social movements and social action, not only 'given' from above through more elite reforms.[7]

In taking such a view, we agree with the approach of Heater, which suggests that citizenship operates both 'vertically' and 'horizontally'. As he puts it, 'the world citizen needs to relate in that capacity both to global institutions and to human world community [...] For example, a world citizen may wish to concentrate on campaigning for reform of the UN or on supporting organisations devoted to relieving world poverty' (2002: 5).

The vertical view has to do with the perceived relationships of citizens to the state, and potentially to other authorities. Historically, this is the most prevalent view at the national level. Rights are conferred to citizens by the state, through constitutions, laws and policies, and, in turn, citizens can claim these rights and acccountability from the concerned state agencies, which are duty bound to respond. Transposing this pattern of conferring, claiming and responding to the international

.a, we can ask how the changing configurations of global authority affect the spaces in which citizens can claim their rights and their perceptions of duty holders. We argue that if citizens have a subjective sense of rights vis-à-vis global duty holders, this may be evidence of an emerging sense of global citizenship.

The second dimension, the horizontal view, has to do with how citizens perceive themselves as part of a broader global community. In earlier studies in this series, as well as in the broader literature on citizenship, this has also been found to be an important dimension of shifting patterns of authority. As Kabeer (2005) found in her volume on *Inclusive Citizenship*, which focused on the meanings of citizenship at local and national levels, 'what emerges from these narratives is what might be called a "horizontal" view of citizenship, one which stresses that the relationship between citizens is at least as important as the more traditional "vertical" view of citizenship as the relationship between the state and the individual' (ibid.: 23). How, then, we may ask, is such a meaning of citizenship played out across borders? Is there a sense of solidarity with others? Does this horizontal solidarity contribute to strengthened citizen action, whether locally or globally?

Using the vertical and horizontal views of citizenship, we explore what these chapters say about the possibilities for an emergent global citizenship offered by the new configuration of global authorities. Our empirical interrogation leads us to somewhat contradictory conclusions, suggesting that global governance is Janus-faced, simultaneously opening and constraining new meanings and practices of citizenship.

Our first question is whether and how shifting global authority has opened up new perceptions and possibilities for citizens to claim rights and accountability from those institutions perceived to be responsible for them. On the one hand, we see a number of examples where this has been the case. In the example of Vía Campesina, for instance, Borras and Franco show how the movement has reframed land rights as citizenship rights, projecting themselves as 'rights holders' and targeting global institutions as 'duty bearers' that must be held accountable. In so doing Vía Campesina has advocated, created and occupied a 'new citizenship space' that did not exist before at the global governance level – a distinct space for poor peasants and small farmers. Similarly, Gaventa and Mayo show that the international 'Education for All' campaign is seen as a relatively successful example of how to negotiate a multilayered terrain in order to put pressure on international authorities to realize the right to education. Icaza et al. explore how changing patterns of trade governance affect the meanings and practices of citizenship in the

Americas, finding new solidarities and expressions of citizenship being articulated 'from below' in defence of rights and livelihoods. These are voiced, in multiple governance arenas, to a range of duty holders, including governments, regional and intergovernmental organizations and multinational corporations. By contrast, Mehta and Napier-Moore demonstrate how displaced people exercise their agency and participate in protest and mobilization vis-à-vis perceived duty holders, despite their stateless status. In so doing so, they challenge conventional understandings of citizenship in relation to the nation-state and make the need for new concepts of global citizenship even more compelling.

Other chapters, however, show cases where the emergence of global actors and forces did not necessarily open up new possibilities for engagement, and arguably in some cases even weakened the terrains for action at the national and local levels. In the Gambia and South Africa, global donors have become dominant players on the HIV/AIDS agenda, on the one hand bringing funding, but on the other adding a new layer of governance to already fragile states and communities. Asking whether the new global configurations offer the possibilities for those living with HIV in the Gambia to express new forms of citizenship, Cassidy and Leach write, 'for people so extremely poor and vulnerable, in these power effects such global initiatives sweep them up into a vortex of discourse and procedure that may look like local–global citizen engagement but are perhaps better cast as subjection to (global) governmentality' (this volume: page 51). Similarly, Robins illustrates how global health programmes, and their local NGO and social movement mediators in South Africa, often encounter considerable 'friction' not only from powerful national state actors, who may view such programmes as challenges to national sovereignty, but also from the most marginalized village-level actors, who may resist globalizing discourses on health in complex and yet often hidden ways.

Another example is provided by the IAASTD process described by Scoones. While IAASTD was designed to open up more inclusive and participatory spaces in global dialogues on the future of agriculture, Scoones questions the extent to which it was able to do so, and notes the absence of the voices of local farmers – those most directly affected – in the process.

In each of these cases, then, while global spaces for engagement were in theory opened up to citizen action from below, in fact other global actors also stepped into these spaces, often driven by other interests, and affecting and constraining the possibilities for local action. On the one hand, these spaces create new possibilities and identities for rights-claiming from below; yet on the other, they can add new levels of power and discourse, which are difficult for local citizens and even nation-states to transcend.

The degree to which the new spaces offer opportunities to exercise citizenship through claiming rights or accountability 'vertically' from global institutions affects and is affected in turn by new horizontal identities and solidarities, and whether they help to strengthen citizen action and claims from below. Here again the cases provide us with mixed, somewhat contradictory evidence.

On the one hand, in the examples of the transnational movements on land, education and trade, we gain a sense of strong horizontal connections among those facing common issues across borders. Territorial boundaries were overcome by the strength of mobilizations created around the shared identities of peasants, poor parents or fellow activists. In the case of the GCE, in particular, the construction of a Global Week of Action created a new space for concerted simultaneous action on education in localities around the globe. With this came an empowering sense of connection with others, one which extended rather than replaced a sense of national citizenship.

By contrast, the women members of Unilever-sponsored self-help groups in India, the grassroots asbestos factory workers in Gujarat and people living with HIV/AIDS in the Gambia and South Africa were unable to access or demand their rights in the global sphere, and as a result, trans-border solidarities were not developed or mobilized. In the Indian case local women's self-help groups become partners with Unilever, a large multinational company, in a project aimed at linking them to the global economy and contributing to their economic empowerment as *Shakti Amma* (empowerment mothers). In reality, however, the integration of the self-help groups into the global value chain through the sale of soap, detergents and cosmetics gradually affected the identities of the rural women involved, who instead of 'empowerment mothers' came to be seen as 'beauty agents'. Identities of cleanliness and Western beauty, the chapter argues, helped to undermine the strength and potential of the self-help groups that were meant to be transformed. In all of these cases, in the absence of horizontal solidarity networks, global duty bearers were subtly able to deflect their obligations towards others.

Across these cases, looking both vertically and horizontally, we gain a paradoxical view of the possibilities that changing global landscapes offer citizen action. By way of summary, the contrasts are perhaps most clearly illustrated in Chapter 9, in which Waldman gives two very different pictures of struggles over asbestos-related diseases in South Africa

and India. In South Africa, a global campaign was grounded i
roots and supported by the South African state, not only lea(
cessful claims, but also shaping a new sense of empowered
at the local level. In India, by contrast, a more professional campaign, facing the hostility of the Indian state, was able to mobilize globally, but with little impact either on national policies or on the sense of global solidarity of the asbestos workers affected. In fact, the chapter argues, the Indian workers became more distant from the discourses and debates that affected them.

For scholars of citizenship, these results are perhaps unsurprising. Historically, the concept of citizenship has always been about both inclusion and exclusion (Kabeer 2005; Yashar 2005). To define and enrol some as citizens has often meant shaping boundaries that exclude others, be they migrants, youth, the illiterate, indigenous peoples, sexual minorities or other groups that are marginalized at particular historical moments. Struggles over citizenship have always been not only about the progressive expansion of rights and identities, but also about counter-pressures or trends which serve to limit the rights and identities of others. This is perhaps most clearly seen today in the simultaneous trends of emergent interests in global citizenship, alongside the increased backlash and restrictions affecting global migrants.

Navigating the global terrain

In the previous section, we gave some examples of how changing patterns of global authority had very different effects on citizenship identities and practices, offering the possibilities of a strengthened sense of inclusive citizenship for some, while serving to create new forms of exclusion for others. How can we explain these differences? While we cannot make causal assertions, in discussions and analysis of the case studies among the authors[8] three important factors emerged: the politics of mobilization, the politics of intermediation, and the politics of knowledge. It is these intervening factors – which sit between citizens and global authorities – to which we now turn.

The politics of mobilization As we have argued throughout this chapter, changing patterns of globalization create new opportunities for both inclusion and exclusion, across increasingly complex multi-tiered and multi-scalar forms of governance. What are the implications of this complexity for the politics of mobilization, and for the strategies and tactics that are used for collective citizen action?

For Tarrow, the new internationalization opens the possibility of scale shift': 'an essential element of all contentious politics, without which all contention that arises locally would remain at that level. Such a shift can operate in two directions: *upward*, in which case local action spreads outwards from its origins; or *downward*, when a generalized practice is adopted at a lower level' (2005: 121).⁹ Navigating the international system can be particularly challenging for activists because it both 'opens conduits for upward shift and can empower national, regional and local contention with international models of collective action. But by the same token, as new forms of contention move downward, their original meanings may diffuse and the forms of organization they produce may domesticate' (ibid.: 121).

Certainly, in our cases we see examples of both upward and downward scale shifts. Upward shifts are illustrated by the global campaigns on agrarian reform, education rights, trade and occupational health, where we see examples of well-built transnational advocacy networks, largely arising from and involving actions from below. As well as these, we see examples of where the origins of scalar shift are located 'above', and involve the intervention of new actors or discourses, such as the Global Fund in the Gambia and NGO mediators in South African AIDS politics; or the creation of the IAASTD as a global forum; or in Unilever's intervention into local women's self-help groups. What is also clear, but has been less explored by Tarrow and other analysts, is that the origin of the scalar shift – whether from 'below' or 'above' – has an effect on the dynamics of the mobilization and action which consequently occur.

This is illustrated, for instance, in the two contrasting cases of Brazilian environmental activism examined by Alonso. Borrowing a concept from Tilly, she argues that in the case of SOS Rainforest, in moving from global to local one sees a politics of 'emulation' or local reproduction of global modes of operation. By contrast, in the case of the Instituto Socioambiental, a local Brazilian organization which moved from local campaigns to global ones, one sees a politics of 'adaptation', in which mobilization adapted to new realities.

Though perhaps not as neatly as in the Brazil example, other cases illustrate ways in which the direction of the scalar shift had a dramatic effect on the types of mobilization strategies that were available. In those cases originating from below and seeking international attention, campaigners sought to gain public recognition of their grievances, using a wide variety of tactics. Sometimes, as in the cases of the agrarian movements and trade movements, they mobilized in 'invited' or formal consultative arenas, usually organized 'from above' by regional or international bodies. Yet such engagements, the cases remind us, risk legitimizing the very global structures the movements sought to challenge, so they were often also supplemented by strategies to create new public spaces – globally, nationally and locally – that could give visibility to their demands. For the GCE, the 2008 Global Week of Action was one such space, in which 7.5 million activists participated simultaneously in actions in 120 countries. For the trade campaigns, popular plebiscites created similar spaces for mobilization: in Paraguay, a citizen-organized consultation in 2003 led to the participation of over 160,000 people, putting the issue on the national agenda. Borras and Franco note that the Vía Campesina campaign used a combination of mobilization tactics, from 'protests in international venues, participation in some official conferences, and non-participation in others, combined with continuing land-related actions "from below" in national and local settings' (this volume: page 123), while for the South African anti-asbestos campaigners, a combination of grassroots action, national lobbying and international legal challenges was used. In all of these cases, though the focus was on bringing grassroots challenges upwards to global attention, mobilization continued to involve multiple, simultaneous strategies across levels.

When the scalar shift moves in the other direction – when global actors or institutions attempt to enlist the engagement of the grass roots, or construct their identities from above in such a way as to provoke local resistance – we see another type of engagement. In the case of the interventions from above by the Global Fund in the Gambia, the injection of large pools of funds and resources created a perverse dynamic, in which engagement in the global project was not necessarily a sign of collective mobilization for citizenship rights, but primarily a form of accessing and competing for material resources. In South Africa, reliance on local cultural and religious beliefs in Pondoland, part of the rural periphery, is cast by Robins as a way in which citizens contest or circumvent 'globalizing and biomedicalizing' governance initiatives. In both cases, the planned interventions from above to enrol citizens into forms of global–local engagement prompted unforeseen responses, in which even the very poor resisted, ignored or adapted global initiatives to their own ends rather than mobilize publicly upon them.

In the case of displaced peoples, even those without formal citizenship rights in their host states still found ways to mobilize – sometimes by acquisition of rights through informal means, sometimes by quiet subversion and resistance to identities ascribed to them by their refugee status, and at other times by highly visible symbolic protest. In Egypt, while Sudanese refugees could not take their protest to the global stage, they could protest in front of the local offices of the UNHCR, giving visibility to their claims. In the UK, an asylum seeker sewed his eyes, ears and lips closed, dramatically symbolizing the failures to be seen or heard, and in so doing gained international media coverage as well as the attention of national and global authorities.

The point of all of these examples is that global citizen engagement may take place in a number of ways. In some of the better-known cases, now well documented in the literature on global citizen action, it occurs through transnational action. But in other cases, it occurs through local, rather than transnational, forms of resistance to global forces and actors as they are manifested within the locality. Citizen action in response to global forces can be *on* the global *in* the local, as well as *from* the local *to* the global – though the tactics and strategies of each may vary.

But if, as we saw in the previous section, governance and authority are multilayered, then one would expect that the most effective forms of citizen engagement would be those that are able to mobilize across all levels simultaneously. In some of our cases, we catch glimpses of how this can occur. In the case of the GCE, for instance, deliberate attempts were made to construct linked action across multiple 'citizenship spaces'. But other cases illustrate the complexities of doing this. In the Indian anti-asbestos campaign, as national-level professional campaigners moved to build global pressure, they lost their roots and connection to the local. The capacity and ability of movements to navigate this local–global terrain depends therefore on two other very important factors – the nature of the intermediation between the local and the global, and the politics of knowledge that affects the framing and legitimacy of key issues and actors across levels.

The politics of intermediation If mobilization increasingly moves from the local to the global, and vice versa, a factor of growing importance is the nature of the mediation across and between actors and authorities at different levels. As most mobilizing groups are not able to speak directly to power in their own locale, the politics of representation, of who speaks for whom, and of accountability, becomes more important. And without effective mediating mechanisms which link the scales and arenas of engagement, various writers argue, transnational forms of action risk floating 'free in a global ether' (Florini 2000: 217), unaccountable and disconnected from the grass roots (Batliwala 2002).

In our case studies, it becomes clear that the nature and quality of mediation across levels or scales of power and action are critical for determining the nature and quality of the impact which emerges. As is best illustrated by the case study of environmental movements in Brazil, 'hybrid activism' – the ability to maintain a local identity and connection simultaneously – can have a big impact on the success of mobilization. By direct contrast, in the Indian case, it was the absence of effective mediation which was a key factor in a programme aimed at creating women's empowerment, but which resulted instead in 'the making of "vulnerable salesgirls" unable to empower themselves' (Thekkudan, this volume: page 92). In the Gambia, a new 'nexus of governmental and non-governmental institutions' became an important mediator between the Global Fund and people living with HIV and AIDS, while in the case of the Vía Campesina, the struggle was to bypass mediation by government and NGO agencies, and for peasants to have more direct representation in the global arenas themselves.

Who are these mediators? In these cases, they range enormously, from individuals to NGOs and social movements to the state itself. In many cases, mediators emerge as highly skilled individuals who are able to move across spaces of engagement and interpret between actors. At the international level, Tarrow describes these individuals as 'rooted cosmopolitans' or 'transnational activists' (2005: 29). In her work on the biographies of two environmental leaders in Brazil, Alonso prefers to use the term 'hybrid citizens': those who maintain deep rootedness to the local, even while moving within and across global arenas. Hybrid citizens are constantly juggling to maintain multiple identities, sometimes more successfully than others. In the IAASTD process, for instance, Scoones discusses the role played by 'international experts' who also held other identities – based on gender, regional origin, family background – which affected how they were seen and how they spoke. In the anti-asbestos campaigns in South Africa, the local–global links were mediated by professional doctors and human rights specialists who were able to link to the international while remaining rooted in South Africa; in India, Delhi-based professionals who were drawn into international science and regulatory circles were less able to maintain their local connections. In the HIV/AIDS case in South Africa, Robins describes the representatives of international NGOs, as well as local AIDS activists and practitioners, as the 'brokers of biomedicine' who encountered perhaps unexpected contestation from those living with HIV/AIDs themselves. In the Gambia, some local actors found that the ability to sit in user, NGO and state committees, and to be able to speak 'the language of funders and intermediary NGOS', was 'the key to having productive engagements with them', be those the per diems they received, or other in-kind benefits.

In other cases, the hybrid activism and the politics of intermediation were reflected more at the group or organizational level than through individuals. In the Gambia, for instance, local-level treatment support groups and national-level NGOs became critical new intermediary actors between the Global Fund and those living with HIV/AIDs. In other examples, such as Brazil, India and South Africa, the role of national-level civil society actors proves critical, yet still illustrates the challenges of remaining connected to local constituencies while simultaneously trying to influence global actors. In the case of the GCE, strong and preexisting national campaigns, some of which received direct support from dedicated international sources, became a key building block and connector between global and local actors.

Both individual and organizational mediators, in turn, become critical in linking the local to the international effectively. Even when movements and campaigns occur only at one level – for example, within a local community – there are always questions of legitimacy, representation and accountability which arise about who speaks for whom and with what authority.[10] When mobilizations attempt to link across levels, these questions become even more important. In the case of IAASTD, international civil society representatives were placed in the powerful and very responsible position of speaking *for* farmers whose lives would be affected by the agricultural policies being discussed, but there was little direct consultation *with* the farmers themselves. Many chose to deal with this pragmatically – to try to enter the space, despite their problematic position, to push the agendas to which they held strongly, perhaps deeply rooted in earlier experiences, but all done on behalf of others. On the other hand, in the case of the transnational agrarian movements, Vía Campesina challenged the legitimacy of the NGOs and the International Federation of Agricultural Producers which had traditionally represented peasant voices in global fora, and advocated a distinct space where peasants and small farmers could speak for themselves. In the case of the GCE, an attempt was made to overcome some of the hierarchies and sense of exclusion of local voices which have beset many other NGO-led international campaigns. In this case, Gaventa and Mayo argue, five factors were important for mediating between the local and the global through a single campaign movement. These included: a) strong pre-existing organizations at the base; b) inclusive and representative organizational structures; c) collective and intentional framing of the issues to link local and global concerns; d) recognitions of and sensitivity to the importance of the different roles of actors in each arena; and e) attention to the material base of the campaign, so that international and national NGOs were not competing for the same funding.

While much of the literature, as well as examples in this book, shed light on the importance and identities of civil-society-based mediators in local–global citizen engagements, the state also emerges as a critical actor in shaping the politics and outcomes of intermediation. This is perhaps most clearly seen in the comparative study of the anti-asbestos campaigns in South Africa and India. While both have democratic states, the South African state supported the anti-asbestos stance of the citizens' movement, and promoted its engagement in international arenas. In India, on the other hand, the state tended to ally with the asbestos industry, and to put in place processes that discredited or weakened activist voices. In land struggles in the Philippines, despite the neoliberal pressures for the state to leave land issues to the market, it has continued to play a strong mediating role. What emerges, then, is that the role of the nation-state, rather than being weakened in local–global citizen engagement, remains critical, not only in state-to-state relations, but in how it allies with and supports civil society in dealing – or failing to deal – with global market or other forces.

While we thus see multiple types of mediators – hybrid individuals, organizations, international networks and movements, even states – the nature of mediation is also affected by the origins of the mobilization. In more 'global–local' mobilizations, mediators were often experts, professionals and international NGOs, as seen primarily in Part Two of this volume. In more 'local–global' movements, illustrated in Part Three, the mediators were more likely to be 'hybrid activists', deeply rooted in the local identities and associations. In turn, where there are effective mediators – be they individuals, organizations or states – who remain deeply rooted and connected to local citizens, there appears to be a stronger likelihood of effective rights-claiming strategies and a sense of empowered citizenship emerging among movement participants. Where mediation is weak, claims may falter, and the 'global' may become an arena for greater exclusion, rather than giving rise to any new sense of global citizenship or solidarity.

The politics of knowledge Just as the origins of the mobilization affect the nature of mediation within it, so too does the mediation itself depend a great deal on the ability to navigate the politics of knowledge effectively. The role of knowledge in shaping and challenging power has long been considered in relation to citizen action at the local level (Tandon 1981; Leach and Scoones 2006). When we move to the global arenas, many argue, the politics of knowledge becomes even more important. In the absence of the clear and widely accepted authority of global governance institutions, the production of and deliberations over knowledge become a critical path to establishing legitimacy (Adler and Bernstein 2005; Miller 2007) and regimes increasingly based on soft power and knowledge networks become more important (Nye 2004; Lukes 2007). As Miller puts it, there is therefore a need to give further attention 'to *knowledge-making* as well as *decision-making* processes' of international institutions' (Miller 2007: 327, emphasis added).

For Miller, there are three important mechanisms through which international institutions 'contribute to the epistemic ordering of world affairs' (ibid.: 328), each of which is seen in the cases in this book. The first mechanism involves setting international knowledge standards and rules for monitoring and regulating global issues, as seen in these cases, for instance, in the role that asbestos standards played in shaping debates on occupational disease, or on educational standards in monitoring national level educational performance. A second mechanism has to do with 'making global kinds, that is by bringing into being new ontological frameworks, classifications, and mappings that frame the conceptual underpinnings of global deliberation' (ibid.: 328). The ways in which global biomedical knowledge is used to frame debates on HIV/AIDS in the Gambia and South Africa, or the numerous ways of labelling and classifying categories of 'displacement', are examples of this phenomenon. The third mechanism involves constructing new deliberative spaces, in which claims to knowledge and expertise become increasingly important, as seen, for instance, in the global deliberative experiment of the IAASTD. While recognizing the risks that their potential will not be realized, Miller argues for the relatively optimistic possibility that together the new global knowledge institutions 'signal the struggle to deploy scientific knowledge and expertise as the basis for a global civic epistemology [that will emerge] out of deliberation rather than exclusion' (ibid.: 350).

While affirming the importance of the global knowledge mechanisms, the cases in this volume suggest restraint on such an optimistic view for a number of reasons. First, as a number of cases suggest, rather than constraining global power, such knowledge mechanisms and institutions can themselves become new arenas for the exercise and contestation of power. As Scoones warns in the case of the IAASTD, the desire to create a universally deliberative space, driven by science and reason, can in fact serve to disguise the power differences and diversities that exist within the process itself. As he points out, 'there is an interesting contradiction in the simultaneous talk of engagement and involvement of diverse, multi-stakeholder perspectives and its confrontation with the ideal of consensus and an appeal to a universalized objectivity of science and expertise: the ultimate global vision' (this volume, page 105). Where these tensions are not addressed, then underlying issues of power may also remain unresolved.

Second, these cases suggest that knowledge legitimacy cannot be constructed through deliberation at the global level alone. Rather, it involves interaction with the local as well, which often brings into competition opposing framings and discourses between claims to universal 'truths' and locally understood realities. Within such interactions, write Jasanoff and Martello, what is particularly of interest is 'the reassertion of local knowledge claims and local identities against the simplifying and universalising forces of global science, technology and capital' (2004: 4). In this volume, the Gambia and South African cases on HIV/AIDS powerfully illustrate how global biomedical discourses are met with deep suspicion by differently situated actors, who draw on plural forms of knowing and interpreting their illness, resulting, as Robins observes, 'in complex citizen responses and contested forms of knowledge politics' (this volume: page 76).

In an era of 'soft' power, with often loose accountabilities, the ability to gain political legitimacy depends in turn on whose knowledge is seen as most legitimate and how an issue is framed. Mobilization not only involves action, but also knowledge (Keck and Sikkink 1998), particularly persuading or enrolling others within a particular knowledge frame. How issues are framed, and around whose views, often depends on the source of mobilizations and direction of travel. To establish broad framing and gain broad acceptance 'from above', knowledge is often presented as 'neutral', as objective science (as in the case of asbestos) or as growing from deliberative multi-stakeholder consultations (as in the cases of trade and agriculture). As the cases show, however, both the science and the deliberations are shaped themselves by powerful special interests or particular world-views. To establish framing 'from below', much emphasis is on the importance of local voices and on knowledge based on indigenous experiences. We see this in struggles over land rights, where the peasant movement documented and mobilized its own knowledge to challenge the homogenizing discourses and definitions of the problem organized by the World Bank. As Borras and Franco remind us, who produces knowledge is not inconsequential to the world-view and perspective which it represents.

In the Brazil case study, we see two differing strategies for linking across the local–global knowledge issue. In the strategy of emulation, local activists worked to develop their own global expertise in order to engage within global debates; in the strategy of adaptation there was greater emphasis on shifting the global discourse to a local context. The GCE pursued yet another strategy: to establish its own legitimacy as a global campaign, it created the global week of action discussed above, but was at pains to be very inclusive in the process of framing the themes for this space, and thus able to transcend global–local divides more successfully. Whatever the dynamics of mobilization around knowledge politics, it is clear that knowledge mediators – be they 'hybrid activists', citizen scientists or activist experts – gain growing power if they are able to link multiple discourses and forms of knowledge effectively. Whether the new global knowledge institutions will lead to a more inclusive 'global civic epistemology' depends much on who controls and uses them.

Conclusions and implications

This introductory chapter has explored the impact of changing global governance on the meanings and identities of citizenship and the related practices of citizen action. The case studies that follow bring more detailed and nuanced accounts to these debates. What is clear throughout these pages is that for many key issues of global concern – whether they concern health, education, livelihoods, trade or gender – solutions will not arise from action at a single level of governance. Increasingly, global, national and local actors and arenas connect and interconnect, reshaping the contours of power, redefining the nature of governance. Global governance, we have argued, does not mean the replacement of one level of authority with another, but an increased complexity of power, which requires the ability to span spaces and arenas if more inclusive citizenship and effective citizenship action are to be attained.

In this view, we argue that one cannot understand the possibilities of global citizenship by asking simply whether there is a global state that can confer it. The absence of a singular political authority is a challenge but not a constraint for citizen action. In many instances, citizens understand and mobilize around multiple surrogate duty holders who take on new powerful roles, whether they be multinational corporations, private donors or an array of intergovernmental regulatory agencies. At the same time, not only does globalization have consequences for transnational forms of citizen action, but the shifts in global authority also reshape local identities and practices of citizenship. New global authority has implications as citizens move from the local to the global, but the opposite is also true: new forms of power move from the global to the local as well, opening and constraining possibilities of local action.

In addition to vertical relationships between state and citizen, horizontal solidarities among fellow citizens also define people's sense of who they are, where they belong, and what meanings of citizenship they carry. For those citizens whose state-conferred meaning of citizenship is blurred or ambiguous, or for those who are so discriminated against as to not be able to realize their state-conferred citizenship rights, such horizontal solidarities are major sources of survival and sustenance. Yet neither can these be simply conferred from above, by social movements or other actors.

Taking such a view has given us a complex and somewhat contradictory picture of what is occurring. In some cases, largely in Part Two, the evidence of emerging solidarities and mobilization to hold global duty holders to account is weak, and global power may serve to enfeeble an already fragile citizenship status, even vis-à-vis the national and local state, and increase a sense of exclusion. In others, especially in the cases of campaigns for land rights, education, trade, occupational health and the environment – largely in Part Three – we see a different picture, in which new forms of mobilization, solidarity and claim-making have arisen and, in some cases, succeeded (though, as the case on asbestos reminds us, even within the same movements one can have differential outcomes). In the last chapter, we see some examples of how even among 'orphaned citizens', those without states, a sense of solidarity and appeal to global authority is emerging, challenging us to think even more literally about citizenship beyond the nation-state. In these latter cases, globalizing citizenship can be inclusive and empowering.

What contributes to these differences? Three factors emerge from the case studies as critical. First, the new layers and complexities of authority require mobilization strategies which are able to cut across local–global spaces in a linked and simultaneous way. For many local actors, the reach to the global is difficult; for many global actors, the reverse is also true. Yet, challenging multi-tiered and polycentric forms of power requires multi-tiered and networked forms of action to be effective.

Whether such strategies can be achieved in turn depends on two further factors, the nature and quality of mediation and the dynamics and use of knowledge. As actors and identities span multiple spaces, the role of mediators who can act within and link across spaces becomes ever more important and ever more challenging. Similarly, effective action, linked across actors and arenas, requires being able to use and link multiple forms of knowledge, and to communicate simultaneously with multiple and disparate audiences. In each of these factors – mobilization, mediation and knowledge – the origin and direction of travel of 'scale shift' – whether from global to local, or from local to global – have important impacts on the strategies used.

All of this is of consequence for policy-makers, practitioners and activists alike. Most intervention strategies – be they by donors, governments, NGOs or social movements – still operate in worlds divided by scale. This approach tends to place policies, programmes and interventions that focus at the international level in one department or strategy, the national in another and the local in yet another. While there may be important work linking each of these horizontally to the others – for example, through networks which cut across countries to share experiences or build alliances – rarely do they link vertically in coherent and inclusive ways.

Our analysis would suggest the need for a different approach. Whether led by grassroots activists or high-level policy-makers, by donors, NGOs or social movements, to be effective in the global world, change must link simultaneously and synergistically across levels. Whether intervention from above or mobilization from below, the key challenge is how global power translates to local practice, not how to bring about change in one arena or at one level alone. In this process, close attention must be paid to the capacities and quality of the mediating structures which cut across spaces and levels of action – be they individuals, NGOs or even states – and to forms and framings of knowledge which are genuinely inclusive of multiply positioned perspectives. Success must be understood not only in terms of the change at one level of governance, but in terms of its consequences for power and inclusion in other interconnected arenas as well.

To focus on the changing spatial dimensions of global governance does not imply an undermining of the importance of the nation-state or state-conferred meanings of citizenship. In fact, in this approach, the nation-state has been found to play a critical role, opening or closing the possibilities of effective linking of rights and claims, upwards and downwards, from local to global. The state plays an important role in either assisting or resisting the process of claim-making. Where citizens have kept state agencies in their sights and included them deliberately in their mobilization strategies, the support lent by the state has positively contributed to the realization of such claims.

While the nation-state continues to be important, it is, as we have seen, but one layer of multiple levels of authority. And just as we understand authority as multi-tiered and complex, so also can we understand sites of change and the expressions of citizenship as multidimensional. Rather than argue either for national or global, statist or societal, identities of citizenship, it is possible in a global world to imagine these as multiple identities held by the same citizen, who simultaneously may engage with local, national and international forms of authority, and also link with local neighbours or global communities in a range of ways. It is where globalizing forces ignore, or assume to dominate or override, other dimensions of citizenship that they are experienced as exclusionary. On the other hand, as some of the case studies that follow demonstrate, where these multiple senses and identities of citizenship are linked across spaces to engage with multi-tiered and complex forms of global authority, the possibilities of inclusive global citizenship are most likely to emerge. In the twenty-first century, where interconnected global problems will increasingly require multidimensional forms of citizenship to respond, it is these more inclusive forms of citizenship and citizen action which we must seek to foster.

Notes

1 This introduction draws heavily on the conversations and contributions of members of the Global Citizen Engagements Working Group of the Development Research Centre on Citizenship, Participation and Accountability, whose chapters are found in the remaining portions of the book. Our thanks for comments also go to Greg Barrett, Jan Aart Scholte, Fiona Wilson and members of the writers' circle of the Participation, Power and Social Change team at IDS.

2 The range of case studies in this volume is quite broad, but we recognize that there are significant gaps in terms of groups that are challenging nation-state concepts of citizenship (see, for instance, Yashar 2005), and studies in the global North or other significant regions of the world.

3 While in the fields of international relations there is much discussion on the multilayered or multi-scaled nature of local, national and global governance, others, such as those coming from the field of critical geography, challenge such vertical conceptions of scale and the notion of a 'nested hierarchy' that the local–national–global continuum implies (Marston et al. 2005). While aware of these academic debates, we have nevertheless used the terms 'local', 'national' and 'global' ourselves as shorthand for the different levels of authority and decision-making in which citizen action may attempt to intervene.

4 We shall not be able here to do justice to the richness of these debates. For good summaries and reviews see Falk (1994), Heater (2002) and Schattle (2008). Also, for a good annotated bibliography of literature on global governance and global citizenship, see Benequista and Levine (2009).

5 We agree with Schattle (2008: 4): 'While scholars in recent years

and debated various ... bal citizenship, we ... ratively little about ... s of global citizenship ... oint of view of individuals arou... e world who now think of themselves as global citizens, as organizations that have linked the idea of global citizenship to their activities, programs and strategies.'

6 Scholte (2008: 323) puts the question this way: 'A citizen's concern is no longer so much "what has my state done about this problem?" as it is "how has the relevant polycentric governance network affected me and my community?"'

7 De Sousa Santos and Rodriguez-Garavito (2005) challenge the notion of law as top-down and elitist and argue that law evolves through social mobilization and resistance. They further argue that the value of international or global legal processes is how they affect the global and how they protect the local from the negative forces of globalization.

8 Over the course of this project, case study authors met several times to review and discuss their findings. These cross-cutting factors emerged from these discussions.

9 Referring to McAdam, Tarrow and Tilly (2001: 33), Tarrow defines scale shift as 'a change in the number and level of coordinated contentious actions to a different focal point, involving a new range of actors, different objects and broadened claims' (2005: 121).

10 There is a large literature on the challenges of building legitimacy in international civil society, and accountability, and on the challenge of disconnections between global and local actors in transnational campaigns (see, for instance, Batliwala 2002).

References

Adler, E. and S. Bernstein (2005) 'Knowledge in power: the epistemic construction of global governance', in M. Barnett and R. Duvall, *Power in Global Governance*, Cambridge: Cambridge University Press, pp. 294–340.

Appadurai, A. (2000) 'Grassroots globalization and the research imagination', *Public Culture*, 12(1): 1–19.

Archibugi, D. (2008) *The Global Commonwealth of Citizens: Toward Cosmopolitan Democracy*, Princeton, NJ: Princeton University Press.

Batliwala, S. (2002) 'Grassroots movements as transnational actors: implications for global civil society', *Voluntas: International Journal of Voluntary and Nonprofit Organizations*, 13(4): 393–409.

Benequista, N. and T. Levine (2009) 'Literature review on local-global citizen engagement', Prepared for the Development Research Centre on Citizenship, Participation and Accountability in 2006, updated by Greg Barrett in 2009, www.drc-citizenship.org/publications/Local_Global_Literature_Review.pdf.

De Sousa Santos, B. and C. A. Rodriguez-Garavito (2005) *Law and Globalization from Below: Towards a Cosmopolitan Legality*, Cambridge: Cambridge University Press.

Della Porta, D. and S. Tarrow (2005) *Transnational Protests and Global Activism*, Lanham, MD: Rowman and Littlefield.

Ebrahim, A. and E. Weisband (2007) *Global Accountabilities: Participation, Pluralism and Public Ethics*, Oxford: Oxford University Press.

Edwards, M. (2008) *Just Another Emperor: The Myths and Realities of Philanthrocapitalism*, New York/London: Demos/Young Foundation.

Edwards, M. and J. Gaventa (2001) *Citizen Global Action*, Boulder, CO: Lynne Rienner.

Ellison, N. (1997) 'Towards a new social politics: citizenship and reflexivity in late modernity', *Sociology*, 31(4): 697–717.

Eyben, R. and S. Ladbury (2006) 'Building effective states: taking a citizen's perspective', Development Research Centre on Citizenship, Participation and Accountability, Institute of Development Studies, Brighton.

Falk, R. (1993) 'The making of global citizenship', in J. Breder, J. B. Childs and J. Cutter (eds), *Global Visions: Beyond the New World Order*, London: Black Rose Books.

— (1994) 'The making of global citizenship', in B. van Steenbergen (ed.), *The Condition of Citizenship*, London: Sage, pp. 127–40.

Florini, A. (2000) *The Third Force: The Rise of Transnational Civil Society*, Washington, DC: Carnegie Endowment for International Peace.

Fox, J. (2001) 'Vertically integrated policy monitoring: a tool for civil society policy advocacy', *Nonprofit and Voluntary Sector Quarterly*, 30(3): 616–27.

— (2005) 'Unpacking "transnational citizenship"', *Annual Review of Political Science*, 8: 171–201.

Heater, D. (2002) *World Citizenship: Cosmopolitan Thinking and Its Opponents*, London: Continuum.

Held, D. (1995) *Democracy and the Global Order: From the Modern State to Cosmopolitan Governance*, Cambridge: Polity Press.

Held, D. and A. McGrew (eds) (2002) *Governing Globalization: Power, Authority and Global Governance*, Cambridge: Polity Press.

Hoffman, J. (2004) *Citizenship beyond the State*, London: Sage.

Jasanoff, S. and M. L. Martello (2004) 'Introduction: globalization and environmental governance', in S. Jasanoff and M. L. Martello (eds), *Earthly Politics: Local and Global in Environmental Governance*, Cambridge, MA: MIT Press, pp. 1–29.

Kabeer, N. (2005) *Inclusive Citizenship: Meaning and Expressions*, London: Zed Books.

Keck, M. and K. Sikkink (1998) *Activists beyond Borders: Advocacy Networks in International Politics*, Ithaca, NY: Cornell University Press.

Leach, M. and I. Scoones (2006) 'Mobilizing citizens: social movements and the politics of knowledge', IDS Working Paper no. 276, Institute of Development Studies, Brighton.

Lukes, S. (2007) 'Power and the battle for hearts and minds: on the bluntness of soft power', in F. Berenskoetter and M. J. Williams (eds), *Power in World Politics*, London: Routledge.

McAdam, D., S. Tarrow and C. Tilley (2001) *Dynamics of Contention*, Cambridge: Cambridge University Press.

MacKenzie, H. (2009) *Democratizing Global Governance: 10 Years of Case Studies and Reflections by Civil Society Activists*, New Delhi: Mosaic Books.

McKeon, N. (2009) *The United Nations and Civil Society*, London: Zed Books.

Marston, S., J. Jones and K. Woodward (2005) 'Human geography without scale', *Transactions of the Institute of British Geographers*, 30(4): 416–32.

Miller, C. A. (2007) 'Democratization, international knowledge institutions and global governance', *Governance*, 20(2): 325–57.

Mohanty, R. and R. Tandon (2006) *Participatory Citizenship: Identity, Exclusion, Inclusion*, New Delhi: Sage.

Nyamu-Musembi, C. (2005) 'Towards an actor-oriented perspective on human rights', in N. Kabeer (ed.), *Inclusive Citizenship: Meaning and Expressions*, London: Zed Books.

Nye, J. (2004) *Soft Power: The Means to Success in World Politics*, New York: Public Affairs.

Rosenau, J. (2002) 'Governance in the twenty-first century', in R. Wilkinson (ed.), *The Global Governance Reader*, London: Routledge, pp. 45–67.

Schattle, H. (2008) *The Practices of Global Citizenship*, Lanham, MD: Rowman and Littlefield.

Scholte, J. A. (2002) 'Civil society and democracy in global governance', in R. Wilkinson (ed.), *The Global Governance Reader*, London: Routledge, pp. 322–40.

— (2005) *Globalization: A Critical Introduction*, Basingstoke: Palgrave Macmillan.

— (2008) 'Reconstructing contemporary democracy', *Indiana Journal of Global Legal Studies*, 15(1): 305–50.

Stammers, N. (2009) *Human Rights and Social Movements*, London: Pluto Press.

Tandon, R. (1981) 'Participatory research and the empowerment of people', *Convergence: An International Journal of Adult Education*, 14(3): 20–49.

Tarrow, S. (2005) *The New Transnational Activism*, Cambridge: Cambridge University Press.

Van Steenbergen, B. (1994) 'Towards a global ecological citizen', in B. van Steenbergen (ed.), *The Condition of Citizenship*, London: Sage, pp. 141–52.

Yashar, D. (2005) *Contesting Citizenship in Latin America: The Rise of Indigenous Movements and the Post-Liberal Challenge*, Cambridge: Cambridge University Press.

PART TWO

From global to local: the impact of global governance on everyday citizenship

2 · Mediated health citizenships: living with HIV and engaging with the Global Fund in the Gambia

REBECCA CASSIDY AND MELISSA LEACH

Introduction

The early twenty-first century is witnessing a new era of globalism in public health. The last decade has seen an array of new international initiatives and funding mechanisms, driven both by moral concerns with poverty and disease in poorer countries of the global South, and by Northern self-interest and mutual concern in an interdependent world in which not just money and finance, but also people and microbes, are highly mobile. Associated with new patterns of authority and institutional arrangements, these signal emerging dimensions of governance which challenge the pre-eminence of nation-states, yet connect with government institutions in new ways.

This chapter focuses on how such changing patterns of power and governance are unfolding in relation to HIV and AIDS, and how they have been manifested in the small West African country of the Gambia.[1] It explores how this changing landscape affected the meanings, practices and expressions of citizenship open to and performed by Gambians living with HIV, and the processes of inclusion and exclusion – of people and perspectives – that ensued. The chapter thus offers a particular lens on local–global citizen engagement. We understand this phrase to refer both to the intersection of globalized and localized expectations and practices around rights, knowledge and behaviour; and to how and how far people in local settings can exert claims and priorities in relation to global institutions and arenas. As we argue, these processes are linked, and the politics of mediation are central to both.

HIV provides an apt focus for considering such changing local–global engagements in the health field. What was, in the 1980s, seen as an emergency epidemic is now widely understood to have transformed into a 'long-wave event' with prevention and treatment opportunities and challenges more akin to a chronic disease. The global community has established three new funding mechanisms which are shaping programmes around the world: the Global Fund to Fight AIDS, Tuberculosis and Malaria (GFATM); the US President's Emergency Plan for AIDS Relief (PEPFAR); and the World Bank's Multi-Country AIDS Programme (MAP). In the early twenty-first century, these three funders have been providing the majority (57 per cent in 2004) of all donor resources to combat HIV and AIDS (Bernstein and Sessions 2007). By 2007 the GFATM alone had committed US$7.7 billion in 136 countries.[2] As Robins (this volume) emphasizes, the 'antiretroviral revolution' and HIV prevention programmes enabled by such funding have dramatically extended the reach of global biomedicine across African countries.

One of these countries was the Gambia, and it is the operations of the Global Fund (GFATM) there which are our particular focus. In a context of high national dependence on global funding, the engagement of the GFATM between 2000 and 2006 unleashed a new political economy of resource allocation, a new set of institutional arrangements and opportunities for mediation by state and non-governmental structures, and a new politics of knowledge around the meaning of disease. These have engaged with a particular disease context – in which, with HIV infection rates currently below 5 per cent,[3] living with HIV is still a socially unusual experience – and a particular political-economic context. Notable features of the latter include President Jammeh's democratically elected yet authoritarian regime,[4] a long history of international donor and NGO involvement in developmental affairs, and two decades of intensifying neoliberal policies which have prioritized private business entrepreneurs and the coastal tourist industry, leaving the majority of Gambians in deep poverty and a grinding everyday struggle for livelihoods.

Emerging forms and practices of local–global citizen engagement around HIV and AIDS very much reflect this context. For people living with HIV in the Gambia, treatment support groups linked to the GFATM offer to some extent new axes of identity as 'global therapeutic citizens'. In this vein, Robins (this volume) emphasizes the potential of health-related activism, strong illness identities and the scarcity of treatment to shape new subjectivities and types of health/biological citizenship, albeit in non-linear and mediated ways. In analysing HIV activism in Burkina Faso, Nguyen describes a 'biopolitical citizenship' that he calls 'therapeutic citizenship', encompassing 'claims made on a global social order on the basis of a therapeutic predicament' (2005: 126). Nguyen's emphasis on the broader industry that has arisen around HIV issues, the heterogeneous conglomeration of different actors and the activation of global networks suggests the emergence of forms of civil society mobilization whose alliances transcend national boundaries and connect local groups to key global players and knowledge. He argues that HIV has been able to bring together a range of different phenomena – from condom demonstrations and CD4 counts[5] to sexual empowerment and an ethic of individual sexual responsibility and compliance with drug regimes – into a stable, worldwide formation. These new global networks have helped to produce a form of therapeutic citizenship based on being HIV positive (biological), together with (political) claims to rights such as access to treatment, and (ethical) ways of integrating being HIV positive into a moral order. Yet in the Gambian context, amid poverty and the particular character of NGO and state mediation, what we see is less an image of active, treatment-rights-claiming, therapeutic citizens. Rather, a close examination of the meanings of support group membership from the perspectives of people living with HIV reveals instead a less empowered conformity to global discourses and procedures as a route to particular sorts of 'getting by'.

This chapter has three main sections. Initially we trace key elements of the changing landscape of power and governance linked to the GFATM, first in brief general terms and then as manifested in the Gambia. We then shift focus to 'see like a citizen', examining the meanings of this configuration from the perspectives of people living with HIV. People's engagement with and experiences of mediating structures (treatment support groups and NGOs) and the politics of knowledge (notions of disease and treatment) are considered in particular depth. In this context, the chapter concludes by reflecting on the axes of inclusion and exclusion emerging in this case, and their implications for current discourses around global therapeutic/health citizenship.

The Global Fund and shifting health governance structures

The GFATM is part of a new generation of global philanthropy, and a new era of global governance in health. International health has always relied to some extent on non-statist forms of authority. International organizations such as the World Health Organization (WHO) and Centres for Disease Control have long, in practice, overridden national sovereignty in the name of claimed universal goals of disease eradication and prevention (e.g. White 2005). Yet what is emerging today appears different in several important respects. First, the sheer size, scope and resources of the health programmes concerned. Second, the predominance of private, philanthropic and hybrid public–private arrangements, rather than international ones accountable to member states. And third, the moral authority that global health programmes can now exert in a globalized world of mobile people and microbes, where fears of epidemic spread and ideas of global health security abound (Dry 2008).

In material terms, these new global health initiatives aim primarily to channel funds, but in so doing contribute to the building of political-economic and authority structures geared to doing this 'efficiently' and 'appropriately' – as defined by the neoliberal and business-oriented models of this genre of 'philanthrocapitalist' development aid (Edwards 2008; Okie 2006). Initiatives such as the GFATM also have an epistemic influence: framed by particular perspectives and forms of knowledge concerning the nature of the problem, and hence the required solution, they also help to put such framings into broader play. Yet such power–knowledge relationships are always dynamic and negotiated to some degree, and shaped by the structures and mediation practices of global and local forms. The GFATM is interesting in this respect because it explicitly presents itself not as a top-down global mechanism, but as 'uniquely' locally responsive. Yet in practice, the extent to which citizens have been able to stake effective claims on the GFATM has been highly variable.

Since 2004, the GFATM, PEPFAR and MAP have been providing large volumes of new money for HIV programmes, representing a huge increase in funds at the country level in many African settings. In Uganda and Ethiopia, for instance, the money flowing from these three funders exceeded by 2005 the governments' 2003 budgets for the entire health sector (Bernstein and Sessions 2007). The scale of resources, and their dispersal through vertical, disease-focused programmes, has given rise to heated debate about the extent to which the globally structured 'AIDS industry' may be undermining national and local health systems and their broader priorities.

The funding and operating structures of global HIV initiatives, both in principle and in practice, shape how these global–national–local relationships play out. The GFATM's founding principles state that 'the Fund is a financial instrument, not an implementing entity' (Global Fund 2002), and it has no in-country presence or technical assistance expertise, instead aiming to operate within a broader network of partners, including national governments and civil society organizations (CSOs), through setting up a distinct set of structures in each country. In this model, money contributed to the GFATM (by governments, philanthropists, donor agencies, the private sector and public donations) is held in trust in an interest-bearing account at the World Bank, until the GFATM requests funds to make a grant at the country level. The preferred mechanism is for a single Coordinated Country Proposal (CCP) to come from the national level, through a Country Coordinating Mechanism (CCM), which becomes the focus for programme accountability. The CCM is the key, novel organizational model at the heart of the GFATM's framework, including its claims for civil society involvement. As the GFATM Framework Document states, the CCM 'should include broad representation from governments, NGOs, civil society, multilateral and bilateral agencies and the private sector [...] It should preferably be an already existing body. If no appropriate co-ordinating body exists, a new mechanism will need to be established' (ibid.: 5). In principle, this mandates civil society representation and 'ownership' as a condition for programme funding – and demands establishment of a structure to ensure this where none may have existed before. The framework document also allows the possibility – in political contexts where governments are illegitimate, in conflict or oppression of civil society activity – of forging funding partnerships directly with civil society.

The other key structure in the GFATM's funding framework is the Principal Recipient (PR) of a country grant. This is the organization to which funds are channelled, and which carries out disbursement to sub-recipients (SRs) as identified in the CCP. PRs are typically a government ministry such as the Ministry of Health, or a government agency such as a National AIDS Council. In some cases, a PR may be an NGO or a UN agency. When sub-grants are made, the PR remains responsible for reporting to the GFATM on the use of funding.

In theory, these principles give unprecedented scope for civil society groupings both to lever funds for their own activities and to shape country strategies for dealing with HIV and AIDS. Government representatives have sometimes critiqued the CCM model for this very reason (Brugha et al. 2005). In practice, however, experience has been more varied. For instance, Senegal was an early model for the GFATM's mechanisms in 2002, but as the country attempted to scale up its response to HIV, significant concerns arose about the lack of a coordinated national strategy and, especially, the marginalization of civil society – to the extent that the GFATM in 2005 threatened to withdraw funding. In the Senegalese case, the situation was shifted by a coordinated response from NGOs, which created a 'watchdog' organization which helped to push for a designated civil society part to the country's 2005 GFATM proposal, and for an NGO to become PR (International HIV/AIDS Alliance 2007). These struggles and tensions around the meaning of partnership in GFATM processes reveal deeper questions concerning the legitimacy and role of government in a world of globalized networks and partnerships involving CSOs (Brugha et al. 2005).

Birdsall and Kelly (2007: 12) draw attention to how 'centralised vertical programmes and channels [...] are criss-crossed at all levels by a flurry of smaller-scale activity that may or may not be linked to the official response framework'. Insightfully, they suggest that those activities that do become linked tend to be grouped around a relatively standard, ordered set of interventions. Many national plans – and proposals to international bodies such as the GFATM – contain such standard elements, despite widely varying epidemiological and socio-political contexts. Put another way, the global AIDS funding industry is helping to put into play an epistemological standardization – a standard set of solutions, responding to a standardized set of framings of the problem that link biomedical notions to what have become globalized received wisdoms about HIV and AIDS. These globalized framings do, of course, contain minor variations and contestations, responding to the diverse positions, histories and ideologies of different agencies. Nevertheless, these are largely variations within a broad, dominant contemporary framing of AIDS as an exceptional disease requiring exceptional responses which emphasize biomedical solutions and individual rights (Edstrom 2008).

Brugha et al. (2005) point out a competitive dynamic within countries' engagements with the GFATM process that perpetuates such globalized constructions. Thus in many cases CCMs have become focused on trying to identify what the GFATM was likely to fund, rather than what internal discussion suggested their countries might need. In the case of Uganda, for instance, the CCM focused on proposals that directly tackled disease – such as antiretroviral therapy (ART) – reflecting perceptions that the GFATM would be more likely to respond, and could expect impact indicators of the kind it prefers. Such proposals suit the mantra regularly repeated by the GFATM's executive director: that the GFATM's mission is to 'raise it, spend it, prove it'.

Structures of funding access can thus be seen to interplay with an epistemological standardization of problem and solution interpretation around HIV. The influence of such global framing often comes to extend beyond those organizations actually receiving funding. A wider global epistemic community (Haas 1992) or culture (Knorr-Cetina 1999) is emerging around HIV through the array of global networks and forms of knowledge exchange that these programmes are part of. As Nguyen (2005) argues, this has come to include citizens' networks and enwraps forms of therapeutic citizenship constructed around particular, globalized ideas of what it means to be HIV positive. While specific struggles may be taking place over who receives or fails to receive funding, and over precise programme priorities, much of this debate and struggle is now taking place only as minor bit-parts within the broader epistemological play that is AIDS globalism.

As we go on to explore, many of these general patterns of power and governance, albeit nuanced in context, have been evident in the Gambia's engagement with the GFATM.

Global AIDS funding in the Gambia

The first case of HIV in the Gambia was identified in May 1986. In 1987 the government established the National AIDS Control Programme (NACP) and approved the foundation of an advisory committee, the National AIDS Committee (NAC). The response at this time was strongly led by medical and public health perspectives and predominantly focused on information, education and communication activities, with funding from the WHO's Global AIDS Programme. Following the coup in 1994 when President Jammeh took power, in 1995 a first attempt was made to embark on a more integrated, multi-sectoral response to HIV – again funded by the United Nations Development Programme (UNDP) and the WHO. As in many other countries at this time, it was realized that 'a more targeted and intensified response is required to create awareness, provide treatment, care and support as well as mitigate the impact of the disease on individuals, families, communities and the nation as a whole'.[6] Many elements of what were becoming standardized global packages began to be put in place.

An application for MAP funding was approved in 2000, a landmark for HIV programming in the Gambia, making it one of the first countries to access funding from the HIV/AIDS Rapid Response Project (HARRP). The programme – providing US$15 million – came into effect on 31 July 2001. HARRP funding allowed an HIV treatment programme to begin, among other programme streams on institutional capacity; other health sector initiatives such as Voluntary Counselling and Testing (VCT) and prevention of parent-to-child transmission (PPTCT); and community and civil society initiatives.

Although there were problems with implementation, these funds enabled the setting of a broad agenda for HIV work in the country, and allowed support groups for people living with HIV to come together for the first time:

> HARRP put HIV at the forefront of the development movement, it was a wake up call at all levels [...] resources were made available to organisations that would've never had access before, and would never have worked on HIV. Santa Yalla [support society] came up, as they had resources, and also others had resources to do things with Santa Yalla.[7]

HARRP funding allowed the first strategic plan for the Gambia to be written, enabling the country to access GFATM financing. The GFATM grant, of US$14 million, successfully applied for in Round Three,[8] came into effect in 2004, and took over ARV treatment provision as planned. HARRP prevention programmes ran until the end of the life of the loan, 21 December 2006.[9] Applications to both Rounds Five and Six have failed, with some strong criticism from the GFATM of the way in which the applications were structured, and so with much internal criticism in the Gambia for those involved. Under the original GFATM grant, however, HIV programmes in the Gambia have continued to grow, with six ARV treatment centres operating around the country by 2006, as well as twenty-four VCT centres, and seventeen PPTCT sites.

The political authority and financial flows associated with HARRP and the GFATM have not bypassed the Gambian state, but have intersected with its structures, giving rise to new institutional arrangements and tensions. Thus prior to the arrival of massive international funding for HIV activities, the NACP within the Ministry of Health had run all prevention and PPTCT activities – albeit on a smaller scale, focused largely on education and sensitization activities. Once it became clear that large volumes of money for HIV programmes would be arriving in the Gambia, the National AIDS Secretariat (NAS) was set up to take charge. NAS was never formally constituted, however, and was funded not as a government department, but with HAARP money. While the NACP works under the Ministry of Health, and so under the authority of the Secretary of State for Health, NAS was created in the Office of the President.

In theory, as PR, NAS should have been an administrative body for global AIDS resources, while NACP should have been an implementing partner – one of many SRs to whom funds were released. In practice these boundaries blurred as NAS implemented its own projects. Resentment and jealousy from NACP and the Ministry of Health arose towards NAS, with the perception that NAS had usurped NACP's position once the cash arrived. NAS had its own internal problems, with what many characterize as weak leadership and staffing problems, and was still recruiting, finding offices and procuring basic equipment until the end of 2003. Many people also complained that NAS was disorganized and inefficient, failing to release funds on time. At the divisional and local levels NAS funds were also divisive, as they led to some staff within the health system receiving salary supplements and motorbikes, while others did not. Staff perceptions of who was and who was not receiving extra money were often wildly inaccurate, but the extent of the rumours indicates the divisiveness of these payments.

With the arrival of the HARRP money, NAS became extremely rich, as did many other people and organizations. Indeed, spending the HARRP money became a persistent problem. At one point an international consultant was contracted to advise on how to spend it faster. Across the Gambia a situation emerged in which more or less anyone – youth groups, women's *kafoo*,[10] or any kind of local organization – could apply to access funds. This appeared, for a short while, to represent genuine 'grassroots' civil society access to global AIDS funding. Yet many new organizations formed at this time, only to be disbanded shortly afterwards. The majority of the projects were one-off 'sensitizations', some of which were well organized and well attended: football matches, fun-runs and dramas, with T-shirts, slogans and speeches. Others seemingly did not exist at all. Millions of dalasi were spent in this way, and a predominant view took root that there is money in AIDS. For those who knew who and where to ask, and how, this was certainly the case. People were paid per diems to take part in events and discussions, in order to get the money out of the door. And expectations rose around how, and how much, HIV-related income could be made. The final report for the HARRP admits these shortcomings, and lists under 'lessons learnt':

> The passion for the fight against HIV/AIDS was mixed. A number of partners saw the HARRP as a money making enterprise hence the submission of substandard proposals. This invariably means that the screening and review process of proposals take [sic] a much longer time than necessary. In some instances, the rejection of proposals led to dissent by some of applicants.

After this initial period, some attempts were made to control what kind of programmes received funds. Although the Round Five proposal to the GFATM included forty-five partner organizations, running a variety of projects, it still included a number of one-off sensitizations. The GFATM rejected this proposal, citing a lack of coherence and vision. Those involved were not greatly surprised. The NAS office was frequently visited by people from assorted organizations clutching budgets with massive provision for various items, all costed and set out to the maximum extent possible. The expectations of an HIV gravy train were entrenched, and the feeling that you only had to ask widespread. Those putting together the GFATM proposal included everyone so as not to disappoint – but at the cost of the proposal being turned down.

With the end of HARRP in sight, the planning meetings for the GFATM Round Six proposal in 2006 were much more fraught, with organizations and individuals conscious that HIV might not be the guaranteed payout they anticipated. In the end this proposal failed as well, and the head of NAS was removed. As the life of the HARRP loan came to an end, in December 2006, it became clear that its money could not be spent and NAS offices closed around the country. The main office, as PR of the GFATM grant, continued to operate, although still not officially constituted as part of the government. The CCM met to discuss what came next; by late 2006 most people at all levels spoke frankly about the mistakes that had been made. It was decided that more time was needed to take stock and prepare an evidence base for Round Eight; Round Seven, seen to be too soon, passed without the Gambia submitting an application.

The recent history of the GFATM in the Gambia has thus involved shifting patterns of power and governance in health with several dimensions. In the context of the enormous funding flows available, the material and political economy dimensions have been crucial. First, the political and economic power of the GFATM has precipitated a re-shuffling of national political and institutional arrangements around HIV and AIDS, and tensions over which parts of the state – nationally and within the local health systems – are being supported and which not. Second, GFATM structures and expectations have promoted the multiplication and reinforced power of 'intermediary' organizations in the health and HIV field; both new (e.g. treatment support groups and new HIV-related community-based organizations – CBOs – and NGOs) and old (e.g. where established NGOs and CBOs acquire funding and position through AIDS-related opportunities). And third, GFATM presence has reinforced a certain globalized, biomedical framing of what an appropriate HIV and AIDS response should look like; many different interpretations may exist in the Gambia as organizations jostle, often ineffectively as we have seen, to gain funding, but these are largely variations within a common global-knowledge theme.

We now go on to consider how this emergent landscape of political economy, institutions and knowledge around HIV shaped – and perhaps was shaped by – meanings, experiences and practices of citizenship in the Gambia. We approach this from the perspective of people living with HIV, and the ways they engaged with treatment support groups. The latter constitute both the central space for organized citizenship identity and local–global engagement around treatment issues and a key mediator of individual relationships with national and global AIDS institutions.

Treatment support groups and citizen engagement with the Global Fund

It was in the context of global AIDS funding that the HIV support groups in the Gambia first began to appear. New support groups emerged throughout 2006, as well as two national networks, one specifically for women with HIV. In line with the original set-up of the groups, the majority of members agreed to visit after referral by their doctor or counsellor, to the group affiliated with the clinic they attend. This link remained strong, and new groups were set up linked to new ARV treatment centres upcountry.

To what extent are these groups vehicles for local–global citizen engagement, in the sense of people's exertion of effective claims and priorities in relation to global institutions and arenas? What does group membership mean to people in practice, and does it add up to a new form of therapeutic citizenship? In this section, we explore what group membership meant to those who joined (or chose not to). Second, we briefly consider the politics of knowledge involved in group membership – and the patterns of knowledge inclusion and exclusion that it implied during this period. Third, we address issues of mediation – how the interaction between support groups and other NGO and state organizations shapes both how groups operated, and the ways in which members could voice priorities and make claims in relation to the GFATM.

Meanings of support group membership The meanings of the groups from members' own perspectives have been strongly shaped by the daily realities of Gambia's grinding poverty, as well as a social and gender context which tends to promote conformism and hierarchical interactions, responsibilities and obligations. This social context presents an immediate contrast with the assumptions of individual rights-claiming which underlie the image of 'therapeutic citizens' in contemporary AIDS globalism.

The groups are formed of a wide variety of people, so that there sometimes seems to be little that ties them together – only a virus and its treatment. Yet such viral or therapeutic identity often seems, in practice, to be trumped for members by more immediate social and material meanings of group membership. At least in the urban and peri-urban areas, most of those who chose to join did so because they felt the need for an alternative social support network additional to their families, peer groups and neighbourhoods. Strong social bonds formed within groups, and for some, especially female members who spend days together in the centres with their children, they became a second home. Strong relationships have formed between members, and there has been one marriage. Among those who join are a disproportionate number of immigrants to the Gambia from neighbouring countries, recent migrants to urban areas, and others who for a variety of reasons feel they receive little support in their home environment – whether or not they have disclosed their HIV status. Those who attend regularly also know that if they don't attend, someone will call, and also provide transport to the clinic if they fall ill. This provides a reassuring link, especially for those who live alone in rented accommodation.

Membership is predominantly from poorer sections of the population. Those who join and spend regular time with the groups value both the social and economic support they provide. The latter includes nutritional support packages, school fees and other benefits. Indeed, the provision of food is a priority for many members. The original groups all provided a meal every day and so nutritional support for people who often cannot afford to eat. Members also lend each other small amounts of money and give gifts that help people to keep each other going, or help to cope with the added financial burden of unexpected family ceremonies and so on that arise in Gambian everyday life. Group members stress these factors as central in their motivation for joining and remaining in support groups – as well as the fact that they can share information and learn about their condition both in official meetings and more importantly from each other. The groups, in these ways, provide a sense of community. Not surprisingly, there are also tensions and arguments within them – notably when personalities clash or when some are seen to be gaining more advantages than others.

For many people living with HIV, however, the support groups impact only minimally on their lives. Some attend meetings once a month and drop into the centre when they are passing, or on the days when they have appointments, or collect their drugs from the clinic. Others join initially and then do not continue their involvement. For people who do not join or attend, there seems to be 'no need' – they see their time better spent attending to usual household duties, or working within their existing social networks. Moreover, access to the benefits of group membership has to be balanced against the real, or perceived, risks of disclosure of HIV status that membership of a public group can involve.

In the Gambia, many of those who have tested positive – often during pregnancy – are HIV-2+, often meaning that they have never been, or are very rarely, ill. For many of these people, the lived experience of being HIV positive is very different from what might be expected. Disclosure of status to immediate family has generally been a condition of access to ART in the Gambia, and this has been a source of contention and controversy. Many people are terrified of disclosure, given the high levels of stigma attached to the disease in a low-prevalence epidemiological context, and thus the potentially devastating consequences for social relationships. This is sometimes a reason for avoiding group membership. Thus in Gambian contexts, public expressions of therapeutic citizenship and solidarity are difficult and socially sensitive – and this has limited both the extent to which people join support groups, and the extent to which they experience and value them as sites to express their HIV-related identity.

Group membership and the politics of knowledge Alongside these crucial material dimensions to HIV support group membership are also epistemic ones. Being part of a group, to some extent, involved subscribing to dominant globalized framings of the nature of disease. Thus the GFATM and associated institutions constructed HIV in biomedical terms and as amenable to drug treatment through ARVs, rolled out in clinic settings. The strong links between the individual clinics and the support groups, and the referral of people to groups in the context of treatment interactions, emphasized such views of disease and treatment.

Yet this is in a broader Gambian context in which understandings of illness and therapy have long been highly pluralistic (Leach and Fairhead 2007). As they deal with ailments in everyday life and through their own cultural logics, people commonly appeal to a range of different disease aetiologies that range from viruses ('disease seeds') to witchcraft, sorcery and Allah. Accordingly, therapies may range across biomedical drugs and vaccines, herbs and amulets, each implying interaction with particular health providers and institutions. For some illnesses, people understand different therapies as complementary. Other diseases are seen as exclusively amenable to one kind of therapy or the other. Such pluralistic possibilities for interpreting and seeking therapy apply, in principle, to HIV as much as to other diseases in the Gambia.

Yet it appears that being part of an ART regime and associated support group membership went along – at least until the end of 2006 – with a reinforcement of globalized, biomedical perspectives as the predominant frame in which HIV could legitimately be discussed and treatment sought. In interviews through 2006, group members would sometimes speak about traditional medicine, but all were very careful to stress, at least in the public context of the support groups, that they no longer sought this kind of treatment and that they were 'with the clinic now'. Counselling at all the clinics involved a strong message that mixing local treatments with ART was unacceptable. Although many people said that 'other people' did this, no one wanted to discuss their own transgressions. The shared experience of being in a support group in turn reinforced the message of ART as the only and best way to deal with HIV, as people witnessed their friends' experiences. Especially for those who were HIV-2+, who had never been sick, seeing people become progressively sicker and then recover their health provided experiential evidence not only of the power of ARVs, but also to some extent of the existence of HIV. Thus global–local engagement through people's experience of ART and treatment support groups contributed to a particular politics of knowledge, in which globalized, biomedical understandings of HIV, AIDS and treatment options were privileged over those couched in other frames. Nonetheless, that more pluralized understandings resurfaced in public discourse from 2007, when a powerful traditional healing programme emerged in the Gambia, serves to emphasize how fragile and context-specific this privileging of biomedical perspectives actually was.

Mediation, expectations and entitlements Interacting with these significant day-to-day social, material and knowledge-related meanings of the treatment support groups for members was undoubtedly a sense of entitlement to global AIDS treatment and resources. Most people living with HIV and AIDS were well aware, at least in a general sense, that AIDS-related funds and programmes flow into the Gambia from international and 'foreign' sources and that support group membership offers a route to access and make claims on these. Yet the channels and forms such claims might take, as well as how groups were expected and able to operate as vehicles to make such claims, were highly mediated by the nexus of governmental and non-governmental institutions involved in GFATM funding and AIDS treatment in the Gambia. Such mediation led to tensions and constraints both in how support groups were able to operate, and in the ability of people living with HIV and AIDS to express their perspectives and priorities about how global funds should be spent.

Groups have been strongly criticized by partners in government, clinics and NGOs for failing to meet expectations. The stress on food provision, so important as a reason for members to attend, had, for instance, by late 2006 become a sign to outsiders of the groups' dysfunctionality – 'all they do is sit and eat'.[11] NGOs and government staff who interacted with the support groups claimed that they lacked a spirit of voluntarism. Many saw the support group members, and specifically those who held offices within the groups, as self-interested; looking for free meals, per diems and an easy life and not acting for the common good. Equally, the groups were not seen to act in line with a conception of how HIV-positive people *should* mobilize, based on international understandings and examples of activism. They did not easily conform, in this sense, to the image of active 'therapeutic citizenship' in which HIV-positive identity, treatment access claims and an ethical/moral order coalesce, nor can they easily be seen as part of the stable, worldwide formation of such therapeutic citizenship that global commentary is coming increasingly to identify. It is an intriguing sign of the globalization of such expectations of therapeutic citizenship that institutions working in the Gambia should expect groups to act in this way.

For members, being part of a group meant being drawn, to some extent, into such globalized expectations and practices. The political-economic spiral of global funding requires support groups to be included in many structures and committees; this is mandatory to signal the legitimacy of these processes to funders within the GFATM framework. Equally, while the 'sick role' associated with HIV once comprised being wasted and weak, or behaving badly and 'playing around', there is now a second role to which people feel pressure to conform after diagnosis: to work tirelessly as an advocate and project manager, or at least to take part in meetings and income-generating activities, such as making soap and tie-dye materials. Over time, and through interacting with partners and attending meetings, group members – particularly the leaders and those with official positions in the groups – learnt what the international community and the GFATM expects of a committee, its leaders and members. They learnt the expected procedural expertise, and to enact this effectively. The values involved are sometimes quite alien to prevailing social norms, for instance in their expectations about women representatives, gender and decision-making. They involve talk that people can find alienating, irrelevant or frustrating: for example 'yes, I went there [to a meeting] but it was just "stigma and discrimination", "stigma and discrimination" [...] talking about nothing'.[12] Yet people became well aware that speaking the language of funders and intermediary NGOs is the key to having productive engagements with them. This was also, therefore, the key to the material benefits that for many were a principal reason for joining the groups. For many people, the per diems, lunches and so on associated with group meetings became their major source of income.

Tensions have also arisen around 'ownership' by intermediary organizations. Certain NGOs and organizations, as SRs of the GFATM grant or otherwise, take prominent roles in establishing groups by funding their activities and core functions such as rent and utility bills. There are relatively few groups, however, leading to competition between organizations and staff to work with them, and resentment when they see others as interfering with 'their' support group. Rather than facilitating group members' ability to negotiate and press for their own priorities, this competitive situation has become a minefield in which group managers have been cast as 'dishonest' in not disclosing to one organization what another was funding, and taking advantage of overlapping programmes – such as two organizations providing the same training. For instance, one group member showed all the certificates he had for management training. Spreading them out on the floor, he said, 'They're all the same. But what's the point – I can never use what they tell me.'[13] The main function and benefit of these repeated trainings, to this man, was the food provided on the day and the per diem.

In the increasingly constrained funding environment of late 2006, competition for scarce resources arose within and between the groups – again shaped by mediating organizations. As meetings or workshops came up, so decisions as to who represents the groups, and how many delegates from which groups, often caused tensions. When the National Network of People Living with HIV was set up in 2006, power plays arose between different members, given that representation implies a more secure livelihood. Tensions over the use of English or local languages, and the ability to read and take notes, meant that the majority of members – illiterate women – were seen as ill equipped to represent themselves or the groups. Within these groups, those members who were more 'active' – attending regularly – and more 'educated' tended to hold a monopoly on workshop attendance and therefore this income stream – despite the intervention of group members and intermediary organizations with ideals of participation and gender equity, who tried to spread the benefits.

Tensions over money and salaries also arose between members of support groups and intermediary organizations. Group members see their salaries as a necessary part of what should be funded, although in the majority of cases these are not forthcoming. They would look at the government, NGO and other agency staff who attend the same workshops and meetings on full salary and receive the same per diems, arriving in air-conditioned cars, not on public transport, and ask 'why should we work for free?'. Such disparity confirmed, to many members, a sense that GFATM money was not going to those who really needed it. Indeed, by 2006 many group members felt that a great deal of the global funding that they knew had arrived in the country 'for us' had been wasted, rather than given to those directly affected by HIV. There was a feeling that many government and NGO staff had benefited from getting involved in HIV work in a very superficial and self-interested way, seen in the big cars and offices that some had gained, and that nothing lasting had been done: this was often expressed as 'they just ate the money'. Moreover, by late 2006 many support group members were aware that there was over a million dollars still remaining, which would be sent back when the project ended. Many expressed – at least in private – bitterness and resentment, knowing how they could use the money and yet being told it could not be justified according to the original HARRP proposal aims and objectives. When the second GFATM proposal was refused with significant HARRP funds left unspent, feelings ran high as people living with HIV, and in poverty, were acutely aware of what was happening yet felt powerless to influence these massive flows of money. As one support group member put it: 'how can they ask for more money with one hand, when they are giving it back unspent with the other? They know [...] they talk to each other, the World Bank and the Global Fund.'[14] Thus a transnational, and stateless, sense of entitlement to funding was widespread, with the World Bank (through HARRP) and the GFATM presenting themselves as duty-bearers from whom these HIV-positive citizens in the Gambia could claim rights. These rights were not played out or fulfilled as expected, however, and people living with HIV were quick to attribute the failures to those agents within the Gambia through which these funders operate. These were exacerbated in the Gambian context by the relatively small population and tightly linked community. Gambians often say that 'we are all family'. Whereas in most countries the staff of an NAS or governmental organization would not be personally known to support group members, here individual people as well as their organizations were seen as responsible for misuse of 'our' money. The project cars or improvements made to their homes by some staff were seen as illegitimate and highlighted as evidence of the failures in how the 'AIDS industry' was functioning.

The planning meetings for the GFATM Round Six proposal in the second half of 2006 were particularly fraught. People from the support groups were invited, and were set the specific task of looking at care and support programmes. This consultation process was used to inform the writing of the proposal by consultants, but how much this participation was a tokenistic and cosmetic process, rather than a real opportunity to affect the final document, is open to conjecture. Many support group members, who already felt that 'NAS treats us like children', felt left out. Those who did attend were included, although all discussion was in English, and some felt ill and left halfway through. In some 'corridor talk' among national staff, this was assessed as inability to take part due to people's poor education levels, and they interpreted illness as faked to disguise laziness and ignorance. Tokenism is suggested by the fact that some organizations were invited to the first round of meetings, but not the second. Equally, submission deadlines for comments sometimes failed to tally with meeting times, implying that there was no intention of including them.

Arguably then – and certainly in the view of many people living with HIV – the structures put in place by the GFATM to enhance participation and inclusion of 'civil society' in the Gambian context functioned to the benefit of NGOs and more established bodies. These organizations, able to act as SRs, take on the role of intermediaries for the beneficiaries of GFATM programmes – people living with HIV. Some intermediaries can be said to coordinate and fund projects that could not have been organized by the support groups themselves, and in this fill a knowledge and experience gap between the capabilities of groups and the requirements of funders in terms of reporting and justification. Yet in other instances, it seems that these intermediary bodies simply increased the distance and difficulty for those at the sharp end seeking to make claims on global resources to meet their perspectives and priorities.

Conclusions

While people living with HIV in the Gambia in this period sometimes took on board and used biomedical and NGO discourses around individualized rights and democracy, these were also rejected in favour of more comfortable family and kinship ties. These primarily local meanings have been cast as problematic by actors in the globalized policy processes around funding and treatment, who expect people living with HIV to conform to particular views of global therapeutic citizenship. Yet at the same time, group members (as a necessary route to access material benefits) became caught up in such dominant spirals of globalized citizenship and power knowledge: enactors of their procedures, and bearers and performers of their notions of disease and therapy.

We have argued that, at one level, the GFATM treatment programme constructed notions and possibilities for citizenship: defined in terms of an HIV-positive identity, and individualized rights claims with respect to biomedical treatments. This is a notion of citizenship constructed in accordance with a particular, dominant, globalized narrative about AIDS response (Edstrom 2008). Yet in 'seeing like a citizen', examining the experiences, perspectives and practices of people living with HIV and their support groups, we have seen that people's priorities lie in the immediate social and livelihood benefits that come with associating with local–global regimes. Treatment support groups in the Gambia have, for their members, been primarily experienced as routes to seeking vital economic and social support in local conditions of extreme poverty and deprivation. For some, they also provided an important community – while others have been excluded because of worries about stigma and disclosure in their particular social circumstances. To access these benefits, people living with HIV have been prepared to 'play the game'; to assimilate the globally expected and highly mediated procedures, practices and discourses that have become part and parcel of expected support group operations. For people so extremely poor and vulnerable, in these power effects such global initiatives sweep them up into a vortex of discourse and procedure that may look like local–global citizen engagement but are perhaps better cast as subjection to (global) governmentality.

This is not to suggest a lack of agency or reflection among Gambian citizens. As Robins (this volume) cautions and illustrates, the apparently disempowering effects of the global biomedical industry are tempered by diverse forms of agency, active appropriation and contestation by its 'target groups'. In the Gambian case, some people living with HIV have certainly come to reflect on and speak actively about treatment rights and claims. Arguably the support groups created a space for active engagement and rights-claiming in the GFATM context, limited as this sometimes was by the GFATM's structures of mediation and implementation as they played out in the Gambia. Furthermore, as our exploration of people's engagement with the support societies begins to reveal, there are many other meanings and expressions of rights and citizenship in the Gambian context that may be more significant to people in their daily lives. These include membership of family, neighbourhood or community, and the informal economic and social rights that come with this, as well as notions of what it is to be Gambian or a foreigner. These, and other, meanings of citizenship find some expression and reinforcement in the ways that people, in practice, make use of support groups and live with HIV. Such expressions of citizenship are marginalized, however – and sometimes the subject of outright disapproval – in relation to notions of what individualized therapeutic citizens ought to be like according to dominant global AIDS narratives.

Recognizing and enabling alternative forms of AIDS-related citizenship, in the Gambian context as elsewhere, is thus a compelling task for future research and advocacy (MacGregor and Edstrom 2008). This suggests, among other things, the need for greater openness on the part of NGOs and other local mediating agencies to the priorities and understandings of people living with HIV. It suggests the need to acknowledge, respect and enable alternative forms of organization and procedure which follow local cultural and political logics – whether based around kinship and patronage networks, for instance, or emergent alliances of experience among particular groups of women or men. National institutional arrangements, in this light, need to provide real channels through which local citizenship priorities can be expressed, suggesting attention to the actual practices, as well as avowed claims, of institutions such as National AIDS Secretariats and GFATM Country Coordinating Mechanisms. And global policy and funding arrangements, it could be argued, may need to open up to – and become accountable to – claims from countries and groups that do not conform so neatly to dominant globalized ideas and procedures. Overall, this suggests a shift in the balance so that perspectives and priorities flow more smoothly from local to global (as well as vice versa), and a shift in the emphasis of mediation to enable such upward flow (rather than closing it down).

This chapter has also, however, highlighted the intense politics and contestation – around authority, resources, knowledge – that pervade AIDS-related policy processes in the Gambia, as elsewhere. It thus highlights, as does Robins (this volume), that neither the imposition of global regimes, nor, it follows, suggested changes to them, could ever proceed in a linear fashion. Rather, the assemblages and practices of global biomedicine land in real political and historical settings and will interlock with processes there to produce particular patterns of embedding, reinterpretation and contestation, often with unpredictable effects. In the Gambia, for instance, negotiations and tensions described in this chapter interlocked with state and health knowledge politics to produce an entirely unpredicted shift in the AIDS treatment landscape by 2007, when the president introduced his own 'traditional' treatment regime. The fall-out of these events, which we describe elsewhere (Cassidy and Leach 2009b), interlocking with further dimensions of institutional politics, raises questions for the future and form of global AIDS funding in the Gambia.

Such uncertainties are an inevitable result of the interplay of global technical practices and regimes with political and social processes in dynamic local and national settings. Those who attempt to understand and intervene in global health therefore need, we suggest, to appreciate and work with these realities. Equally, understandings of contemporary citizen engagements in a globalized world will have to contend with the grounded economic, social and political realities that shape how people frame and prioritize their rights claims; and with the power dynamics through which expressions and practices of citizen agency are negotiated. In settings where all of this is in play, local–global citizen engagement – whether in relation to health or other issues – may come to look different indeed from the forms that capture the imaginations of analysts and activists alike.

Notes

1 This chapter looks at the period up to the end of 2006 and should be read as an account of a particular moment in the interactions between different actors in the HIV and AIDS arena. Events since January 2007 show quite a different picture and are not represented here. The researchers interviewed approximately thirty people working in HIV research and programming, including government officials, NGO workers, representatives of international agencies and clinic staff; and engaged with four support groups in urban and peri-urban areas. A longer version of this chapter appeared as an IDS Working Paper (Cassidy and Leach 2009a).

2 See www.theglobalfund.org/en/, accessed July 2007.

3 Sentinel Surveillance data for 2007, which was not published – in fact suppressed – gave prevalence rates of 2.8 per cent for HIV-1, and 1.1 for HIV-2. This is a rise from the previous survey, which showed a reduction in both to below 2 per cent, but is probably a more realistic estimate given that it tallies with 4 per cent in Senegal. The sensitivities around HIV in the Gambia from 2007 relate to the politics surrounding the president's 'cure' for HIV; see Cassidy and Leach (2009b).

4 President Yahya Jammeh took control of the country in a bloodless military coup in July 1994, and was elected as president two years later in September 1996.

5 A CD4 count is a blood test measuring immune response, used to evaluate and track the progression of HIV.

6 Interview, HIV worker, 2008.

7 Interview, HIV worker, January 2008.

8 The GFATM has at least one yearly 'round' of funding, currently totalling nine. A call is made with a deadline to submit proposals. The Gambia's HIV programme was funded through Round Three, and a Round Eight proposal has been accepted.

9 HARRP had been due to finish in July 2005, but was extended until December of the following year.

10 Peer group organizations, often age- or gender-based, that play central roles in Gambian communities.

11 Several interview respondents used this and other similar phrases to express a general disparagement of the work ethic of support groups.

12 Informal discussion, support group member, 2007.

13 Informal discussion, support group member, 2007.

14 Informal discussion, support group member, December 2006.

References

Bernstein, M. and M. Sessions (2007) *Trickle or a Flood: Commitments and Disbursement from the Global Fund, PEPFAR, and the World Bank's Multi-Country AIDS Program*, Washington, DC: Center for Global Development.

Birdsall, K. and K. Kelly (2007) *Pioneers, Partners, Providers: Dynamics of Civil Society and AIDS Funding in Southern Africa*, Johannesburg: Centre for AIDS Development, Research and Evaluation.

Brugha, R. with M. Donoghue, M. Starling, G. Wallt, J. Cliff, B. Fernandes, I. Nhatave, F. Ssengooba, G. Pariyo and P. Ndubani (2005) 'Global Fund tracking study: a cross-country comparative analysis', Report of the Global HIV/AIDS Initiatives Network, www.ghin.lshtm.ac.uk/downloads/publications/Brugha_et_al_cross_country_analysis_2005.pdf, accessed 23 July 2007.

Cassidy, R, and M. Leach (2009a) 'AIDS, citizenship and global funding: a Gambian case study', IDS Working Paper no. 325, Institute of Development Studies, Brighton, www.drc-citizenship.org/publications/Wp325%20web.pdf, accessed 28 August 2009.

— (2009b) 'Science, politics and the presidential AIDS "cure"', *African Affairs*.

Dry, S. (2008) 'Epidemics for all? Governing health in a global age', STEPS Working Paper no. 9, Social, Technological and Environmental Pathways to Sustainability Centre, Brighton.

Edstrom, J. (2008) 'Constructing AIDS: contesting perspectives on an evolving epidemic', Paper presented at a workshop on 'Epidemics', STEPS Centre, Brighton, 8/9 December 2008.

Edwards, M. (2008) *Just Another Emperor? The Myths and Realities of Philanthrocapitalism*, New York/London: Demos/Young Foundation.

Global Fund (2002) 'The Framework Document for the Global Fund to Fight AIDS, Tuberculosis and Malaria', www.theglobalfund.org/en/files/publicdoc/Framework_uk.pdf, accessed 23 July 2007.

Haas, P. (1992) 'Introduction: epistemic communities and international policy coordination', *International Organization*, 46.

International HIV/AIDS Alliance (2007) 'L'Observatoire: la transformation de la réponse au VIH/SIDA au Sénégal grâce à l'engagement de la société civile', Policy Briefing, International HIV/AIDS Alliance, www.aidsalliance.org/custom_asp/publications/view.asp?publication_id=265, accessed 23 July 2007.

Knorr-Cetina, K. (1999) *Epistemic Cultures: How the Sciences Make Knowledge*, Cambridge, MA, and London: Harvard University Press.

Leach, M. and J. Fairhead (2007) *Vaccine Anxieties: Global Science, Child Health and Society*, London: Earthscan.

MacGregor, H. and J. Edstrom (2008) 'Health-related identities and citizen claims beyond the "therapeutic": interactions of public health responses with diverse new claims for representation and recognition', Paper presented at the CRESC conference on 'Culture and Citizenship', Oxford, 5/6 September 2008.

Nguyen, V.-K. (2005) 'Antiretroviral

globalism, biopolitics, and therapeutic citizenship', in A. Ong and S. Collier (eds), *Global Assemblages: Technology, Politics and Ethics as Anthropological Problems*, London: Blackwell.

Okie, S. (2006) 'Global health: the Gates-Buffet effect', *New England Medical Journal*, 355.

White, L. (2005) 'The needle and the state: immunization and inoculation in Africa, or the practice of un-national sovereignty', Paper presented at the conference on 'Locating the Field: The ethnography of biomedical research in Africa', Kilifi, Kenya, 4–9 December 2005.

3 · Mobilizing and mediating global medicine and health citizenship: the politics of AIDS knowledge production in rural South Africa[1]

STEVEN ROBINS

Introduction

In recent years a number of observers have written about the dramatic expansion of antiretroviral therapy (ART) in Africa and elsewhere in the global South. Nguyen (2005), for example, describes 'antiretroviral globalisation' in Africa as an intervention on a scale similar to that of colonialism. Global biomedical interventions in the time of AIDS have extended their reach on a dramatic scale. Similarly, AIDS activists in South Africa and Brazil have become part of a global health movement that has introduced new ideas about rights to healthcare as well as new forms of health citizenship (Robins 2004).

This chapter is concerned with how these global biomedical interventions are mediated by a group of AIDS activists in the rural villages of Lusikisiki District in the Eastern Cape Province, South Africa. It focuses on how AIDS activists, as 'true believers' in AIDS science and medicine, seek to 'convert' rural villagers into acceptance of the fundamentals of AIDS science through recourse to rhetorical strategies that are not that dissimilar to those deployed by Christian missionaries (Niezen 1997; Turner 1992). Similar to the missionaries before them, AIDS activists, and health professionals, have had to resort to persuasive arguments, rhetoric and translations that resonate with or challenge local idioms and discourses on illness and healing.

Although the global expansion of biomedicine in the developing South has been taking place for decades, the 'antiretroviral (ARV) revolution' and HIV/AIDS prevention programmes have dramatically extended their reach. This has been facilitated through the massive injections of resources from international agencies such as the Global Fund, the President's Emergency Plan for AIDS Relief (PEPFAR), the Gates and Clinton Foundations, the World Health Organization (WHO), the World Bank, the Joint United Nations Programme on HIV/AIDS (UNAIDS) and many others. In addition to the infusion of these global health resources, there has been a dramatic expansion of NGOs, CBOs and globally connected health social movements, such as South Africa's Treatment Action Campaign (TAC). These social movements, together with NGO allies such as Médecins Sans Frontières (MSF, Doctors without Borders), mediate these new biomedical technologies and forms of health citizenship in ways that can, under certain conditions, contribute towards the promotion of innovative forms of agency, citizenship and solidarity (Robins 2004, 2006). But this is clearly not a seamless narrative of scientific and biomedical progress and citizen empowerment. The case study discussed in this chapter suggests that activist mediators of AIDS knowledge regularly encounter small acts of resistance in their daily attempts to disseminate scientific facts and medical solutions. The study highlights the forms of friction encountered when global processes land in local spaces.

The 'conversion' of people living with AIDS into activists and 'true believers' of modern science and medicine is often understood as evidence of the empowering and redemptive consequences of access to biomedical knowledge, technologies and resources. Alongside this heroic and emancipatory narrative of the progress of biomedicine and science in Africa, there is of course considerable evidence of colonial legacies of distrust and scepticism of scientific expertise (Robins 2004; Steinberg 2008; Cassidy and Leach, this volume). There is also the phenomenon of contemporary forms of globalized technocratization and medicalization that are generating their own resistances as part of emergent regional modernities and nationalist politics (Cassidy and Leach, this volume). These responses include nationalist assertions of post-colonial sovereignty in the face of the expanding reach of transnational health programmes, donors and NGOs. Such a response was evident in South Africa, where former President Mbeki and his health minister sought to contest AIDS science orthodoxy and promote 'African solutions' to HIV. It has also been evident in the Zimbabwean and Sudanese governments' harassment and expulsion of Western NGOs involved in medical and humanitarian aid. This diversity of reactions to modern medicine has been very evident in responses to HIV programmes throughout the global South. Rather than focusing on governmental responses, however, this chapter is particularly concerned with the responses of AIDS activists, citizens and 'targets' of these global health programmes.

The chapter is divided into two sections. The first provides background on the global and national dimensions of AIDS politics and programmes in South Africa. The second provides an ethnographic perspective on the everyday experiences, interactions and rhetorical strategies of community-based AIDS activists involved in treatment literacy and HIV prevention programmes in a rural village in the Eastern Cape Province. This case study suggests that global health programmes, and their local NGO and activist mediators, often encounter considerable contestation from national state actors, who may view such donor-driven programmes as challenges to national sovereignty, as well as from village-level actors, who may subscribe to alternative conceptions of illness and healing. The chapter's conclusion draws attention to both the limits and possibilities of these grassroots activist mediations and translations of global health messages, practices and technologies.

Global health and AIDS activism in South Africa

In 2002, the Global Fund to Fight AIDS, Tuberculosis and Malaria (GFATM) was launched as a private–public partnership that aimed at financing treatment programmes to fight these three killer diseases. A year later, in October 2003, following almost five years of concerted AIDS activism, the South African government finally agreed to provide free ART to the five to six million people living with HIV who could require treatment within the public health system. By then there had been drastic reductions in ARV prices, again largely due to activist pressure. Responding to this shift in the government's AIDS treatment policy, the GFATM agreed to provide R430 million over five years to support the Western Cape Province's Department of Health in its ARV roll-out programme. The highly successful MSF–Western Cape Department of Health ART programme established in Khayelitsha in Cape Town in 2001 was one of the first recipients of this donor funding. By June 2006, over 20,000 people were receiving ART treatment in the Western Cape Province, and by 2008 over 350,000 people were on ARVs in South Africa's public health system.[2]

Although donors such as the GFATM contributed significantly towards funding the South African national ART programme, which is now one of the largest in the world, the Department of Health has never been reliant on this donor funding. Unlike the situation in many other African countries, there have been no signs of financial dependency in terms of the relationship between international donors and the South African state. If anything, donors have operated in South Africa under conditions determined largely by the South African government. The South African National AIDS Council (SANAC) was meant to regulate relationships between donors, civil society and the state. Owing to the ongoing tensions resulting from former president Mbeki's dissident position on AIDS, SANAC remained ineffectual and paralysed until quite recently. By 2009 the dissident position articulated by former president Mbeki had virtually vanished from political discourse, and South Africa had developed one of the biggest ART programmes in the world. President Zuma and his health minister adopted an orthodox view on AIDS science that was in line with the positions of AIDS activists and health professionals.

SANAC, as the Country Coordinating Mechanism (CCM) for GFATM grants, was meant to facilitate a culture of participatory governance, yet during the period of the Mbeki administration it found itself caught in the crossfire of highly conflictual AIDS politics. Notwithstanding these ongoing tensions, the South African government's HIV policies have been influenced by the strong emphasis of both activists and global health agencies on human rights and non-discrimination towards people living with AIDS (PWAs). For instance, the South African government did not seriously consider compulsory notification, and confidentiality and Voluntary Counselling and Testing (VCT) were prioritized in HIV policies, protocols and programmes. In other words, human rights concerns were at the centre of these public health interventions from the onset. This case study is concerned with the role and influence of global heath actors in mediating human rights discourses and biomedical ideas, practices and technologies. It is also concerned with the role of community-based health activists as grassroots mediators of global forms of citizenship and scientific knowledge about HIV and treatment.

Activist mediators of health citizenship In South Africa, the political landscape after apartheid created new opportunities for citizens and social movement activists who were capable of activating the country's 'cutting edge' democratic constitution. Nowhere was this more visible than in the assertions of health citizenship made by AIDS activists fighting for access to ARV drugs and better healthcare. Yet these political demands and rights claims were somewhat clouded by former president Mbeki's persistent denial of the scale of the pandemic. It became increasingly clear from the former president's speeches that he believed that AIDS discourses, including those of health professionals and AIDS activists, reproduced racist and colonial assumptions about disorderly and undisciplined African bodies and sexualities (Robins 2004). The former president's dissident position, and his reluctance to respond to calls for ART provision in the public health sector, also resonated with those black South Africans who had learnt to distrust colonial and 'Western' science and medicine (ibid.; Fassin 2007; Steinberg 2008). For the latter, AIDS, and the biomedical responses to it, were associated with the excesses of colonial domination and white minority rule. So, on the one side there were newly acquired rights to healthcare that TAC and MSF activists, health professionals and NGOs had won through tenacious global, national and community-based mobilization in the courts, on the streets and through the media. On the other side, there was a political response 'from above' that undermined the activists' campaigns for access to AIDS treatment.

What emerged in the course of this David and Goliath battle for AIDS treatment was a creative reinvention of anti-apartheid political traditions and strategies of mobilization. These included strategies of litigation, spearheaded by NGOs such as the Legal Resources Centre and the AIDS Law Project, alongside grassroots mobilization in churches, township streets, shebeens, universities, schools, trade unions, at funerals and so on. The TAC was also responsible for global mobilization in its struggles against the international pharmaceutical industry and the state's initial reluctance to provide treatment. Mobilization also involved international health and human rights agencies and NGOs and social movements that were sympathetic to the AIDS activists' cause. This transnational AIDS alliance, along with grassroots campaigns, contributed to the successes of the TAC, MSF and their allies.

TAC contributed towards politicizing healthcare in South Africa in ways that were unprecedented, and these democratic gains have diffused into the public health sector and influenced NGOs and CBOs involved in health matters. In the past few years, I have become increasingly interested in community-based offshoots from TAC. These include the community and nurse-driven MSF treatment programme in rural Lusikisiki in the Eastern Cape Province, as well as Khululeka, a support group for men living with HIV in Cape Town (Colvin and Robins 2009). Both of these initiatives draw attention to the shifting terrain of AIDS activism and health citizenship in South Africa. They also draw attention to the immense difficulties of translating and mediating global health messages in local spaces. They foreground the contentious politics of knowledge and competing ways in which health, illness and disease are framed by differentially situated actors. The Lusikisiki case study highlights how a global health programme was translated and mediated by MSF and TAC activists and health professionals in rural villages in which health resources and scientific knowledge about AIDS were very thin on the ground. The case study locates this translation process within the context of South Africa's national ART programme.

Global medicine in local places: the contentious politics of AIDS knowledge

HIV/AIDS has become a window on and a mirror to global inequalities between the North and the South (Benatar 2001, 2002; Farmer 2004; Schoepf 2001). Whereas from the late 1990s, HIV/AIDS increasingly became a manageable chronic illness in the North, it remains a harbinger of death and devastation in the South, where 90 per cent of PWAs live. At the start of the new millennium an estimated nineteen million people had died of AIDS, and more than thirty-six million were infected. Some 70 per cent of those infected, an estimated twenty-seven million people, were Africans (Schoepf 2001). With limited and uneven access to ARTs in Africa, notwithstanding recent international efforts to make ARVs available, it was estimated that the vast majority of PWAs alive in 2000 would have died by 2006. In other words, in the North people can live with AIDS, while those in the South die. These were the stark realities of global health inequalities at the beginning of the twenty-first century (Benatar 2001; Bastos 1999; Schoepf 2001), and it was in this context that international health and development agencies became involved in AIDS interventions in the South.

Like most forms of globalization, the processes of embedding and translating biomedical discourses in particular places are anything but straightforward or stable. Former president Mbeki's dissident position on the science of AIDS[3] suggests that the global hegemony of Western medicine and science is often vulnerable to challenges from political and religious leaders (Nattrass 2007; Fassin 2007; Epstein 2007). Similarly, it should not be surprising that the increasing involvement of international health agencies in health programmes in the South has periodically unleashed backlashes from governments claiming that these humanitarian interventions represent 'foreign interests' and constitute 'Western' threats to national sovereignty.

Mbeki's persistent questioning of the authority of mainstream biomedicine and scientific orthodoxy is a particularly striking example of such challenges to scientific expertise and global medical hegemony (Robins 2004; Fassin 2007; Nattrass 2007). This has tended to take the form of a knowledge politics in which senior officials, primarily the former president and his health minister, contested the findings of the scientific establishment. This included challenging statistics on AIDS mortality and morbidity, and questioning the efficacy and safety of ARVs. It has also taken the form of government support for the promotion of 'African solutions' for AIDS such as Virodine (an industrial solvent), 'traditional medicines' such as *ubejane* (a mixture of herbs), and an 'alternative diet' of garlic, lemons, African potatoes and olive oil advocated by the former health minister, Manto Tshabalala-Msimang. These challenges to scientific orthodoxy have at times taken on the form of anti-imperialist and anti-racist rhetoric, and arguments about the imposition of Western hegemony and the undermining of 'African culture' and the national sovereignty of African countries (Fassin 2007).

These national-level challenges to global biomedicine also often connect in complex ways with local expressions of distrust, scepticism and opposition to 'Western' medical interventions (Steinberg 2008). Such responses are often based on alternative indigenous understandings about the causes of illness, for instance African beliefs in witchcraft (Ashforth 2000, 2005; Rodlach 2006; Epstein 2007). They may also involve consumer preferences for alternative and complementary treatment such as traditional African medicine, New Age treatment or homoeopathy. The fear and shame associated with HIV may also trigger a refusal to test for or even accept the existence of the disease. This rejection of the scientific authority and claims of global biomedicine were also evident in the South African minister of health's support for Matthias Rath, an AIDS dissident and wealthy multivitamin manufacturer who claimed that ARVs were dangerously toxic and who promoted his own vitamin products as effective treatment for HIV-related illnesses.[4]

In South Africa there are many examples of government officials *and* ordinary citizens expressing deep suspicion of the motivations of practitioners and advocates of Western science and biomedicine (Robins 2004). South Africa is of course not unique in this regard. Similar responses elsewhere in Africa include conspiracy theories and popular myths about the dangers of modern medicine, ranging from resistance by Islamic clerics in West Africa to 'Western' immunization programmes to the promotion of 'alternative cures' for HIV by political leaders and healers in the Gambia. In South Africa, official challenges to the findings of the mainstream scientific establishment have also involved direct government interference in the institutional arrangements of key medical bodies. This has included government attempts to influence the composition and positions of the SANAC, the Medical Research Council and the Medical Controls Council. Some of the most visible clashes between government officials and AIDS activists have been in international fora such as AIDS conferences. These public conflicts have generally been between government officials, especially the health minister, and TAC and MSF activists. They also involved UNAIDS' outspoken representative Stephen Lewis and, to a lesser degree, officials from the GFATM and other international funding organizations. While much of the attention of the media and scholarly analysis has focused on AIDS politics at the national and international levels, less is understood about the local dimensions of global AIDS interventions in South Africa.

MSF's biomedical foot soldiers in Lusikisiki village

In 1971 a small group of French doctors and journalists established MSF in response to the perceived inadequacies of humanitarian responses to the Biafran war in Nigeria. This new humanitarian organization, unlike the International Committee of the Red Cross, strove to be fully independent of the conventions of state boundaries. By 2006, MSF had grown into a massive humanitarian organization that had field missions and advocacy positions in eighty-three countries and over 1,500 expatriate and 13,000 national staff.[5]

Typically MSF intervenes in contexts defined by the breakdown in state health and welfare services, often precipitated by war, famine, population displacement, disease, drought and natural disasters. Generally these interventions involve providing emergency health and welfare services to ensure physical survival rather than providing more long-term needs. This form of medical intervention is characterized by the 'humanitarian kit' – a mobile repository of medical logistics designed for rapid action in the field (Redfield 2007). Redfield also describes MSF's modus operandi as an evolving tradition of *temoignage* (witnessing) in which NGOs 'now play a central role in defining secular moral truth for an international audience' (2006: 3). This form of collective advocacy and 'motivated truth' aims to leverage resources and shame states and international agencies into action in settings demanding immediate humanitarian aid. Redfield argues that by integrating medical expertise and public advocacy, MSF participates in producing and mediating scientific and technical knowledge that can be used for ethical ends.

MSF's response to AIDS in South Africa fits in with the overall ideology of the organization. It aimed to ensure, through activist strategies of blaming and shaming the state, that the public health system benefited from the fruits of the 'ARV revolution'. This involved not only ensuring that state clinics were stocked with ARVs, but also promoting community-based treatment literacy programmes and scientific understandings about HIV among the general population. From the start, MSF's aim was to catalyse, and perhaps shame, the South African state into action by showing that it was indeed possible to provide ARVs to people living with AIDS in Africa. MSF's Lusikisiki project, like its partner project in Khayelitsha in Cape Town, was integrated into the country's public health system at the primary healthcare clinic level.

It was specifically designed as a short-term intervention that would be handed over to the Department of Health after three years. By establishing ARV programmes in South Africa, however, MSF ended up committing itself to more long-term involvement than its more typical short-term modes of humanitarian intervention.

In October 2003 the National Department of Health gave the green light for MSF to provide ARVs in Lusikisiki, and on 10 December 2003 the programme was officially launched by ex-president Nelson Mandela. By mid-2006, less than three years later, approximately 2,500 people had been started on ARVs, and 46,039 had been tested (MSF 2006: 4). The programme's treatment success rates were recorded in medical journals and celebrated at international AIDS conferences, and Lusikisiki received considerable positive attention in the national and international media. This extraordinarily successful community and nurse-driven AIDS programme involved VCT, condom distribution, prevention of mother-to-children transmission of HIV, HIV/TB integration, and ART. It included doctors, pharmacists, nurses, adherence counsellors, pharmacy assistants, community care givers, support groups, community clinic committees, activists and PWAs. The October 2006 MSF report on Lusikisiki describes the workings of this innovative decentralized ART programme and the various roles of the health staff:

> The traditional model of community care givers is to do community-based health promotion. In Lusikisiki they work in the clinics, taking on some of the nurses' workload (including VCT, opening of HIV folders with social history, transferring lab results into folders, conducting support groups). Given the nature and magnitude of the HIV epidemic, it is critical to educate service users to empower them to take responsibility for their own treatment, rather than relying on the community health worker going to the community to enforce directly observed therapy. Defaulter tracing is done by support group members who come from the same rural village as the person who missed their appointment. These support group members are appointed by the adherence counsellors and are given training on approaches to ARV adherence. (Ibid.: 11)

The MSF-driven Lusikisiki programme involved a close partnership with both TAC, a social movement, and the state's public health system. By working closely with both a social movement and the state, MSF was able to redefine its usual mode of operation, and it became increasingly involved in more long-term processes of policy engagement as well as programme implementation. MSF and the TAC were also able to leverage access to state health resources by legally challenging the pricing and patent protocols of the global pharmaceutical industry,[6] as well as by deploying the South African constitution to legally challenge the state for its initial refusal to provide ARVs in the public health sector. These forms of legal activism and social mobilization, which resonated with the 1980s political traditions of anti-apartheid activism of the United Democratic Front (Robins 2004), contributed to the emergence of new forms of health citizenship that have migrated beyond AIDS activism to include health mobilizations around cancer, mental health and disability. In addition, the culture of health activism promoted by TAC and MSF has also diffused into the broader South African society and the public health system.

From Brussels to Khayelitsha to Lusikisiki: bringing ARVs and hope to Pondoland In an interview a few years ago, Dr Eric Goemaere from MSF-Belgium told me about his first attempt in 1999 to persuade South African Department of Health (DoH) officials to establish a national ART programme. His meetings with DoH officials in Pretoria went nowhere. It became clear quite early on that there was no political commitment for establishing such a programme. Government's arguments against treatment included the high cost of ARV drugs, as well as assertions by some senior members of the political leadership that these drugs were toxic and ineffective. Given the lack of government interest in such an initiative, Dr Goemaere decided to visit Cape Town for a few days before returning to Belgium. It seemed to be a clear-cut case of 'mission unaccomplished'. In Cape Town, however, he met Zackie Achmat, a Cape Town-based AIDS activist and co-founder of TAC. In October 2003, many TAC media campaigns, demonstrations and court cases later, the South African government finally agreed to establish a national ARV programme.

The success story of South African AIDS activism provides insights into the workings of global health citizenship in the twenty-first century. Focusing on this extraordinarily heroic account of an epic struggle against the might of 'Big Pharma' and the South African government, however, can also obscure the more mundane aspects of the fight against the pandemic. The following account describes the story of how ARVs arrived in Pondoland.

When MSF doctors and nurses and TAC activists began their ARV treatment 'trial' in 2000 in the Xhosa-speaking working-class township of Khayelitsha in Cape Town, they were fully aware that they had their work cut out for them. Government and public health sceptics seemed to have concluded that the public health system would not be able to implement what was portrayed as an unaffordable, complicated and inappropriate 'First World' AIDS treatment regimen. By implementing an ARV programme in an urban African context, MSF doctors and nurses hoped to challenge this claim. As the findings of the studies of the efficacy of the Khayelitsha programme began to be released, it became clear that ARVs could work in Africa (Coetzee et al. 2004). Sceptics were still not satisfied. The next problem they posed was whether it would be possible to replicate an urban-based ARV programme in a rural site. Influential public health professionals and academics argued that a dysfunctional and under-resourced public health system, along with rural poverty, inadequate sanitation, poor nutrition and poor transport infrastructure in most rural areas, meant that the Khayelitsha ART programme could not be reproduced in most parts of the country. Whereas the health minister's prescriptions of alternatives to ARVs could be dismissed on strictly scientific grounds, the dire conditions in underdeveloped rural areas had to be taken seriously. It was with this in mind that MSF and TAC identified the Eastern Cape Province health district of Lusikisiki as their first rural ARV site.

MSF's first line of attack at Lusikisiki was opportunistic infections. Prior to the arrival of MSF, nurses knew extremely little about HIV/AIDS, and had no training in treating people with HIV with the drugs already in their clinics. Patients who presented typical HIV symptoms at the clinics were routinely sent back to their home villages and told to prepare themselves for death. With the arrival of MSF, clinic nurses were empowered with knowledge and drugs to treat thrush and a range of other opportunistic infections. Treatment of opportunistic infections dramatically altered popular perceptions about this dread disease. This created a new sense of confidence among nurses, volunteers, counsellors and ordinary villagers. Suddenly HIV/AIDS was no longer a death sentence. Even though ARVs were not yet available in the local hospitals and clinics, there was a palpable sense of hope among AIDS activists and health professionals. I was told that once nurses learnt that it was possible to treat HIV/AIDS, those diagnosed with HIV were no longer seen as the 'walking dead'. By the time national government announced its national ARV treatment programme in October 2003, Lusikisiki health workers were trained and ready.

The discussion below is based on fieldwork done during visits to the MSF programme in Lusikisiki. It focuses on the role of MSF and TAC lay counsellors (LCs) and treatment literacy practitioners (TLPs) who sought to mediate scientific discourses on HIV in the rural villages of Pondoland. These pedagogical and epistemological interventions hoped to produce 'scientific' ways of understanding the body, disease, sexuality and treatment. These forms of medical activism and knowledge politics, it will be argued, are revealing in terms of what they can tell us about the globalization and localization of these discourses on science, medicine and citizenship.

Mediators of global medicine and contested 'facts'

At a TAC congress in Cape Town a couple of years ago, a veteran AIDS activist told me that the fundamental goal of TAC was to convert members to 'a scientific worldview'. This would, he believed, shift people away from attributing illness and misfortune to witchcraft and the ancestors. The TLPs and LCs that I met in Lusikisiki appeared to share this absolute faith in science and modern medicine. They seemed unquestioning and unwavering in their belief in the importance of disseminating the 'scientific facts' about AIDS to 'the masses'. They themselves had acquired these 'facts' during the course of numerous TAC and MSF workshops on AIDS awareness, sex education and treatment literacy. In addition, a significant number of them had acquired their scientific and biomedical literacy as a result of being HIV positive and being on ARVs.

Notwithstanding their deep commitment to the 'scientific facts' about HIV and AIDS, activists encountered numerous obstacles and challenges during their daily attempts to implant these 'facts' in the hearts and minds of residents in the small towns and rural villages in which they worked. These obstacles included age and gender hierarchies and sexual taboos. For example, local teachers questioned the scientific knowledge and authority of these youthful AIDS activists, especially young women who spoke about sex, condoms, AIDS science and biology. Older people were particularly offended by 'sex talk' from young people. For instance, activist educators found it difficult to identify culturally appropriate words for genitalia and sexual intercourse. Other challenges came from members of the community who questioned the actual existence of HIV and AIDS, and who attributed illness and death to sorcery and *umthakati* (witchcraft). Some claimed that what activists and health workers referred to as HIV/AIDS' opportunistic infections were simply pneumonia, diabetes or TB, and that these were therefore 'not new diseases'. Similarly, certain opportunistic infections and HIV-related illnesses were identified as *twasa*, which was widely understood as being a sign that the ill person had been chosen by the ancestors to become a *sangoma* (diviner). The following section examines the experiences and rhetoric of conversion deployed by two TAC activists, Anna and

Sipho.[7] Although global health programmes can be seen as standardized global assemblages, the responses of the mediators and targets of these programmes can contest the truth claims of these biomedical discourses. Like the Christian missionaries before them, in the face of scepticism and alternative conceptions of illness and healing, activist mediators of these biomedical discourses strive to develop convincing scientifically based rhetorics of persuasion.

Latter-day Livingstones and the gospel of global medicine These accounts of village workshops, discussions and arguments about science, medicine, ancestors and witchcraft resonate with the well-known narrations of Dr Livingstone's attempts to convince African chiefs and rainmakers that it was God, rather than the ancestors, who delivered rain, well-being and health. In the cases below, AIDS activists deployed the authority of science and medicine, rather than God, to fight a pandemic widely attributed to ancestors, witchcraft and other 'non-scientific' causes. Activists like Anna fought these epistemic battles by drawing on the authority of science and medicine as well as their personal experiences and testimonies of illness, treatment and the harrowing passage from 'near death' to 'new life' (Robins 2006). As Anna told me, 'in my work as a treatment literacy practitioner I preach the gospel of AIDS prevention and treatment based on my own experiences'.

Contrary to the universalistic and decontextualized scientific language of mainstream public health discourses (e.g. family planning, and AIDS education manuals, curricula and guidelines), the specificities of gender, age and education influenced the encounters between AIDS activists and community members in Lusikisiki. For example, Anna, an HIV-positive Xhosa-speaking woman in her twenties, spoke of how, during the AIDS awareness workshops at schools, some teachers challenged her about her knowledge of science and biology: 'Sometimes they're kind of confusing you [...] They're happy when you don't understand more biology than them. They only want to prove the point that they know more about biology than you.' These age, gender and educational barriers were especially visible when it came to 'sex talk':

> We do have that challenge more especially when you go to the rural areas where you cannot teach old men how to use condoms because they will tell you 'You're not going to teach me how to have sex with [...] my wife. How can you teach me about sex because you're so young, it's really unacceptable.' [...] When I use penis in Xhosa I say *ipipi*. Then elders say 'No, you're not supposed to say that.'

My discussions with activists such as Anna revealed that they experienced concerted challenges 'from below' in the course of their treatment literacy and AIDS awareness workshops and discussions with villagers. There appeared to be myriad ways in which the power of science and medicine was contested in places like Pondoland. For instance, Anna spoke of how she attempts to convey the 'scientific facts', which include references to HIV transmission, viral loads, CD4 counts, the immune system, drug regimes and resistance. These 'facts' were mediated through accounts of her own experiences as an HIV-positive woman who uses ARVs. She conceded, however, that not everyone was persuaded by these 'facts'.

> They will tell that there are people who don't believe in HIV and AIDS. They will tell you that if you've got shingles it's because you've got stress, and that people who always get shingles are the same people who always have stress and that it's not AIDS [...] If you're losing weight, you've got shingles and you've got peripheral neuropathy and you don't want to wear shoes because your feet are always paining, people will always tend to think that you are *twasa*. We tell them if you've got these opportunistic infections then you can go and become a *sangoma* but at least go to the clinic and do HIV tests and see what the results are. Then if your results are positive it means you've got HIV, you're not a *sangoma* [laughs].

It was also quite common for people to refuse to believe that TAC and MSF activists and TLPs such as Anna were themselves HIV positive. It was often said that they looked too healthy to have AIDS and that they were being paid by NGOs to make false claims about their status. In addition, many discussions between these TLPs and villagers focused on claims that symptoms of opportunistic infections such as diarrhoea and physical wasting were in fact a result of witchcraft and the actions of jealous neighbours. Anna claimed, however, that with the increasing availability of AIDS treatment it was becoming easier to persuade ill people to go to the clinics for testing. Yet if clinics were overcrowded, understaffed and at some distance from people's homes, villagers would tend to seek help from *sangomas* instead.

> People [in Lusikisiki] were denying that there is this virus because they wanted to believe that they have been bewitched and they were saying it was from *ukudlisa*, which is like being poisoned. And they wanted to believe that because when you're being bewitched or poisoned, you're getting thin and you have got a running stomach and then it's really similar to the opportunistic infections of HIV. But now people are starting to go to the clinic to do VCT.

Sipho, a Xhosa-speaking man in his twenties, and a TAC activist in Lusikisiki, attributed this rejection of the 'scientific facts' to elders' beliefs in ancestors, witchcraft and the efficacy of *muti* (traditional medicines). According to Sipho, they were also extremely suspicious of doctors and modern medicines, and claimed that 'whites are the people trying to kill us coming here with their pills'. By contrast, the younger generation, according to Sipho, subscribed to modern science and medicine. Sipho recalled how he grew up with his grandparents' and neighbours' suspicion of modern medicine and 'modern diets'. The elders, he claimed, blamed these modern drugs and foods for making the younger generation weak and susceptible to illness.

> The grandmothers and grandfathers don't want any person to take the ARVs or any tablets from the hospital. When I was young I wasn't fed eggs and drinking milk, I was eating maize only. The old people told us that eggs and eating the nice food of the whites every day is why we're getting sick [...] They tell us that the HIV is coming here because we're eating eggs, eating cheese and everything, that's why we're getting sick. 'If you're getting sick, *umtwanam* [my child], I can't take you into hospital. The only thing I can do is go into the forest and dig for roots and make *muti*. This can make you strong, rather than using the tablets.'

Both Anna and Sipho concluded that rural villagers in Lusikisiki resorted to traditional healers and *sangomas* because they did not have easy access to clinics and medicines, or because the nurses were rude and disrespectful towards patients. This, they argued, increased the numbers of those who turn to traditional healers for help. Anna thought that better-resourced and more accessible clinic services would bring more patients to the clinics, and ultimately win them over to 'scientific medicine'. In other words, from Anna's perspective, it was not necessarily belief in treatment efficacy alone which determined whether someone went to a clinic or a traditional healer. Accessibility, she argued, was the key factor.

Sipho and Anna spoke also extensively about 'AIDS myths' that circulated in Lusikisiki.

> SIPHO: There are other bad stories about youth who think if you have sex with a virgin, if you're HIV positive, the HIV is going out [...] Some believe it but we tried to tell them that the virus is in the whole body, it's not in the penis. Because they think the HIV and AIDS is staying in the penis [and] not going anywhere else. Because they think that's why, if you have sex without a condom [...] the virus is not staying in the vagina and the penis, it can go out. But we convince them, no, man, if this thing

is living in the penis, why if you're going to test your blood, maybe the drop of blood is taken from your finger, then you test positive. If ever this thing was staying in your penis or in the vagina I think the blood test should be done in the vagina or the penis.

STEVEN ROBINS: So they have a very different understanding of the disease, where it is located and how it works [...] How do you explain what the virus is?

SIPHO: We try to tell the people, the virus is like a germ. Then we're living with a germ in the body.

Sipho was convinced that the major obstacle to scientific understanding in Lusikisiki was the 'backwardness' of the traditionalist elders, a theme that he repeated throughout our discussions. It is also quite plausible that Sipho's positing of a generational divide – between modern, scientifically literate youth and traditionalist elders – is also reflective of a sharp rural–urban divide in terms of access to health resources. Rural areas tend to be at a significant disadvantage when it comes to the availability of trained staff and access to medicines and equipment.[8] This may account for the widespread use of traditional healing in rural areas. Although TAC activists such as Anna and Sipho appear to subscribe to a totalizing scientific worldview that has no place for things traditional, it is not inconceivable that, were they to experience difficulties in accessing modern medicines, they too could be driven to seek the services of traditional healers. Given TAC's stridently scientific worldview, however, which could perhaps be described as a form of 'techno-fundamentalism', TAC activists may be reluctant to acknowledge in interviews or at TAC branch meetings that their beliefs and behaviours, like those of 'the elders', may not always conform to a strictly scientific rationality. These activists' mastery of the basics of AIDS science and treatment literacy allowed them to imagine themselves as modern subjects rather than docile objects or 'targets' of biomedicine. Yet this access to scientific and biomedical literacy and modern subjectivity did not necessarily preclude them from appropriating the same 'traditionalist' beliefs and practices that they attributed to 'the elders'. Yet, in the face of government lethargy in relation to supporting AIDS treatment, as well as AIDS dissident thinking within government and unsubstantiated claims by traditional healers that they could cure AIDS, many TAC and MSF activists seemed to be driven towards an intransigent techno-fundamentalist position in relation to AIDS science.

The political fall-out surrounding HIV/AIDS was a serious obstacle to the spread of the 'scientific facts' in Pondoland, as it was in other parts of South Africa. Anna and Sipho blamed former president Mbeki and his health minister, Manto Tshabalala-Msimang, for 'confusing people'. Anna mentioned that some people in Lusikisiki interpreted the health minister's nutritional anti-AIDS diet of African potatoes, garlic, lemon and olive oil as an alternative to 'dangerous ARVS'. Anna's mother, who was a nurse in Lusikisiki, was sympathetic to the health minister's 'African solutions'. As a result Anna was given this *muti* when she became seriously ill as a result of HIV. She was also sent conventional allopathic medicines by her uncle, who at the time was a senior official in the Department of Health. Anna eventually confronted her mother, and subsequently joined TAC and was selected for the MSF ART programme in Lusikisiki. Her own life experiences as a person living with AIDS infused her approach to AIDS awareness and treatment literacy programmes. The excerpt below draws attention to the highly personalized, and at times quite improvised, rhetorics of persuasion and evidence that are deployed by activists in their responses to scepticism towards medical science, ARV treatment and AIDS messages:

> ANNA: Yes, some people are saying that they don't believe in HIV and AIDS because it's the [former] president who's saying that [it doesn't exist]. What we always do is to educate them about HIV [...] But when they ask about the African potato and stuff, obviously I won't have good answers for that because I'm not sure. But the only thing I always say is, 'I'm sure what ARVs are doing because I'm using ARVs. So that's the only thing I can tell you about' [...] I cannot just say, 'go and use garlic because it's good'. It is not approved [so] I cannot promote that [...]
>
> STEVEN ROBINS: How do you deal with people who say nutrition is more important than ARVs?
>
> ANNA: Ja, I tell them that I agree that nutrition is important, but nutrition doesn't lower the viral load in the body. Nutrition can boost your immune system, but when we deal with the virus, then we deal with the viral load as well as the CD4 count. And that's when you need nutrition and you need treatment. And then, let's say you've got oesophageal thrush, it's not easy to eat because you are in pain. Then that's where you need treatment to treat oesophageal thrush so that you can be able to eat. That is why I strongly believe that they work hand in hand, they work together, you need nutrition and you need treatment, you see.

Sipho also spoke about the widespread scepticism, questioning, suspicion, rumours and open opposition that he encountered in response to his treatment literacy and 'safe sex' messages. He also spoke of popular beliefs that government condoms were contaminated with 'maggots'[9] and HIV, a topic that was widely discussed among clients at shebeens.[10]

> In my location there's a tavern where young girls are drinking beer and brandy and they get into love with older people who are maybe HIV positive [...] They often say that if you have sex with a condom you're wasting your time. Both the men and the women say they don't want condoms. They will say, 'No, I want flesh to flesh.' The other one's telling you 'You can't eat a sweet with the paper wrapping. I want flesh to flesh.' They will tell you it's nice to have sex without a condom. But I tell them the condom is protecting you not from the virus only, but even from pregnancy, because some of the girls are teenagers but they already have two children [...] People are also saying the free condoms from government have maggots [...] They say it's better to not use condoms because they are scared of these [government] condoms. My brother was telling me, it's better to use a plastic bag than to use a condom from the government [...] If you're HIV positive, you have the virus but you may not have AIDS. You are living with the virus. But most people think that if you are HIV positive you already have AIDS and you're going to die immediately.

Sipho's reflections on sexuality, including the widespread antipathy to the use of condoms, are supported by Steinberg's (2008) observations in Lusikisiki, which found that young men avoided testing because they felt that if they tested positive no women would want to marry them and risk having children with them, and they would thus lose their reproductive and sexual capacity. In other words, the virus and an HIV-positive status were perceived to be a direct assault on a man's virility and 'his capacity to have children who would bear his name and thus on his permanence beyond the grave' (ibid.: 9). It was this combination of social and cultural factors, which included profound fear and shame associated with a potentially fatal disease, which threatened to stymie AIDS interventions in Lusikisiki.

Sipho also identified the churches in Lusikisiki as a serious obstacle to AIDS activists' attempts to make people more aware of HIV and AIDS and treatment. He claimed that Christian religious ideas presented major barriers to HIV/AIDS and sex education efforts in Lusikisiki. Far from being part of a biomedical juggernaut, the attempts of activists such as Sipho to mediate these AIDS messages encountered constant questioning, evasion and resistance from villagers they encountered in Pondoland; religious beliefs, beliefs in witchcraft, *itwasa*, AIDS dissident science, conspiracy theories and myths all contributed towards this resistance to the dissemination of biomedical truth. As Sipho put it:

The churches here also don't understand [HIV and AIDS] easily [...] I was trying to educate the church elders about HIV and they told me, 'This is a church, don't talk like a sinner because here we are praying for each other each and every day. If you're getting sick come in front and pray, God can help you no matter what happens.' Last month the reverend died of AIDS. No one from the church wanted to attend the funeral because he died badly, from AIDS. AIDS is a big disgrace in this place [...] A big reverend [in Lusikisiki] told me 'If I attend this funeral God can punish me.' [...] So we need to destroy this discrimination in the churches.

Those who are not 'true believers' in medical science may be profoundly ambivalent, uncertain and sceptical, if not outright hostile, towards scientific explanations of HIV and ARV treatment. Even those who claim to have been 'converted', and who appear to accept the truth of biomedicine, may waver in the face of evidence of its failures and vulnerabilities. For instance, given that not all those who undergo ARV treatment survive, people in places such as rural Lusikisiki watch closely for signs of treatment success or failure. There appears to be an agnostic and experimental attitude towards both modern medicine's 'magical drugs' and the claims of traditional healers and diviners. In other words, people in places like Lusikisiki do not necessarily fully buy into either, and instead may demand concrete, observable evidence of their efficacy. For instance, if nurses are seen to be able to effectively treat shingles – commonly seen as the result of witchcraft – and another person with shingles goes to an *inyanga* (traditional healer) and is not cured or dies, then the popular interpretation could be that nurses and doctors have more powerful *muti* than the traditional healers and diviners.

People living in areas of high HIV prevalence often closely observe and follow the progress or regression of those who go on to ARVs. For example, when an HIV-positive person who is asymptomatic becomes visibly ill because of ARV side effects, this often leads to lay interpretations that the drugs brought there by 'the whites' are dangerous and toxic. Deaths and side effects that are seen to be associated with ARVs can of course seriously set treatment programmes back. Yet if a seriously ill person is seen to go through a Lazarus-like recovery as a result of ARVs, this can dramatically shift the balance of power in favour of modern medicine at the expense of traditional healing. Given the precarious and risky nature of AIDS treatment, the rhetorics of persuasion deployed by activists and health workers require the production of sound arguments and hard evidence. These mediators of global health are called upon to embed the 'scientific facts' within local conceptions of truth, power and evidence.

Conclusion

This case study from Lusikisiki has drawn attention to the agency of the targets of biomedicine. It has also shown how AIDS activists and treatment literacy practitioners engaged with both biological and biomedical concerns and the recruitment of new members into their epistemic communities. These social mobilization processes involved translating and mediating biomedical ideas and practices into vernacular forms that could be easily understood and acted upon by the 'targets' of these recruitment strategies. These processes of 'vernacularization' or localization of biomedical knowledge, however, occurred in contexts where even the most basic scientific understandings and framings of medicine could not be taken for granted. It was therefore not surprising that these brokers of biomedicine encountered resistance and contestation in their interactions with the targets of these biomedical interventions.

The chapter has argued that AIDS activists from MSF and TAC can be seen as part of a modernist vanguard of foot soldiers responsible for mediating global discourses on biomedicine, science, rights and responsibilities. They can also be seen as cultural translators and catalysts for the creation of globally connected epistemic communities and new forms of solidarity and social belonging among people living with AIDS (Robins 2004, 2006). Although the long-term outcomes of these activist interventions are far from predictable, this chapter has questioned assumptions by critics who bemoan the disempowering effects of an all-powerful and depoliticizing biomedical industry. Instead, the Lusikisiki case study suggests that the scientific authority of the activist foot soldiers of modern medicine and public health is often fragile and routinely contested. This contestation, it would seem, is particularly visible in places like Pondoland, situated as they are in the heartland of southern Africa's rural periphery.

These TAC and MSF AIDS activists are, of course, not the first wave of modernist reformers to embark upon sexual education in Pondoland. Monica Hunter's *Reaction to Conquest*, a path-breaking ethnography of Pondoland first published in 1936, describes the partial successes of attempts by Christian missionaries to outlaw premarital sexual practices of Mpondo teenagers (Hunter 1979). Family planning, AIDS prevention and sex education materials and interventions have become remarkably globalized and standardized since the colonial-era interventions of the Christian missionaries that Hunter writes about. Yet, like the first wave of Christian reformers, today's reproductive health and sex education HIV practitioners also have to take cognizance of the small acts of resistance to these conversion processes. Not surprisingly, the biomedical ideas and practices associated with the forms of health citizenship promoted by MSF and TAC continue to encounter resistance in the rural hinterlands of South Africa and beyond.

The case study also serves as a helpful antidote to studies that treat globalization as a juggernaut that simply sweeps aside all forms of local agency and cultural autonomy that it finds in its path. Instead, it suggests that there is no necessary and inevitable linear trajectory or teleology in relation to the outcomes of interventions by global health agencies. Nor can there be any predictability concerning the relationship between these globalizing and biomedicalizing governance initiatives and local citizen engagement. In other words, the scientific knowledge regimes, practices and technologies of global biomedicine can be contested, circumvented, accommodated or embraced depending on specific social and cultural settings and national and local political histories. So, in conclusion, global health initiatives, like other globalizing processes, seldom result in the seamless imposition of global epistemologies, assemblages and forms of therapeutic citizenship. Instead, these global health interventions, in which local health workers and activists routinely act as foot soldiers and mediators, often result in complex citizen responses and contested forms of knowledge politics.

Notes

1 I would like to thank Chris Colvin, Phumzile Nywagi, Akhona Nsuluba, Herman Reuter, Elizabeth Mills and Tobias Hecht for their insights and assistance. I would also like to thank John Gaventa and Rajesh Tandon for their helpful comments on the chapter. I am also particularly grateful to Melissa Leach for her ongoing engagement with my work on health citizenship and AIDS activism. Most of the interviews and observations for this study took place in Lusikisiki, Eastern Cape Province, between January and February 2004. A longer version of this chapter appeared as an IDS Working Paper (Robins 2009).

2 The estimated number of people needing treatment in South Africa was 764,000 by the middle of 2006, of which a total of 353,945 (46 per cent) were enrolled in the ART programme (www.tac.org.za/community/keystatistics, accessed July 2009).

3 For accounts of the politics surrounding President Mbeki's position on HIV see Fassin (2007), Nattrass (2007) and Robins (2004). It is important to bear in mind that most ANC leaders, including the ANC's trade union and Communist Party alliance partners, did not appear to share the president's controversial dissident views on AIDS.

4 The controversial Rath Foundation sought to establish 'trials' in Cape Town's African townships to show that whereas ARVs produced toxic side effects, Rath multivitamins were a safe and effective way to

treat AIDS. The TAC took the Rath Foundation to court on a number of occasions, claiming that the government was not monitoring Rath's 'trials' adequately, and that his unverified claims to contain and reverse the trajectory of HIV infection constituted a violation of existing medical regulations.

5 See Redfield (2005, 2006) for excellent accounts of the emergence of MSF and its evolving ideas and practices.

6 This particular legal challenge to the global pharmaceutical industry was launched together with the South African government.

7 These are not their real names.

8 Similar disparities in access to health resources exist between provinces, with the Western Cape Province being considerably better resourced than the Eastern Cape (Chris Colvin, personal correspondence).

9 During a visit with MSF and TAC activists to a Lusikisiki tavern to demonstrate the femi-condom, a number of inebriated clients told us that if you poured hot water into the condom you could see these 'maggots'. It appears that they were referring to the lubricant in condoms.

10 In September 2007, 20 million government condoms had to be recalled as a result of the nationwide distribution of 'reject condoms'. The government's decision followed allegations that quality control officials were bribed to pass these flawed contraceptives. This has no doubt heightened fears and suspicions about government condoms.

References

Ashforth, A. (2000) *Madumo: A Man Bewitched*, Cape Town: David Philip Publishers.

— (2005) *Witchcraft, Violence and Democracy in South Africa*, Chicago, IL: University of Chicago Press.

Bastos, C. (1999) *Global Responses to AIDS*, Bloomington: University of Indiana Press.

Benatar, S. (2001) 'South Africa's transition in a globalizing world: HIV/AIDS as a window and a mirror', *International Affairs*, 77(2).

— (2002) 'The HIV/AIDS pandemic: a sign of instability in a complex global system', *Journal of Medicine and Philosophy*, 27(2).

Coetzee, D., A. Boulle, K. Hildebrand, V. Asselman, G. van Cutsem and E. Goemaere (2004) 'Promoting adherence to antiretroviral therapy: the experience from a primary care setting in Khayelitsha, South Africa', *AIDS*, 18(S27–S31).

Colvin, C. and S. Robins (2009) 'Positive men in hard, neoliberal times: engendering health citizenship in South Africa', in J. Boesten (ed.), *Gender and AIDS in Africa*, Avebury: Ashgate.

Epstein, H. (2007) *The Invisible Cure: Africa, the West and the Fight against AIDS*, London: Viking.

Farmer, P. (2004) 'An anthropology of structural violence', *Current Anthropology*, 45(3).

Fassin, D. (2007) *When Bodies Remember: Experiences and Politics of AIDS in South Africa*, Berkeley, Los Angeles and London: University of California Press.

Hunter, M. (1979) *Reaction to Conquest: Effects of Contact with Europeans on the Pondo of South Africa*, abridged paperback edn of 1936 original, Cape Town: David Philip.

MSF (Médecins Sans Frontières-Belgium) (2006) *Annual Report*, Cape Town: MSF-Belgium.

Nattrass, N. (2007) *Mortal Combat: AIDS Denialism and the Struggle for Antiretrovirals in South Africa*, Scottsville: University of KwaZulu-Natal Press.

Nguyen, V.-K. (2005) 'Antiretroviral globalism: biopolitics and therapeutic citizenship', in A. Ong and S. Collier (eds), *Global Assemblages: Technology, Politics and Ethics as Anthropological Problems*, Oxford: Blackwell.

Niezen, R. (1997) 'Healing and conversion: medical evangelism in James Bay Cree society', *Ethnohistory*, 44(3).

Redfield, P. (2005) 'Doctors, borders, and life in crisis', *Cultural Anthropology*, 20(3).

— (2006) 'A less modest witness: collective advocacy and motivated truth in a medical humanitarian movement', *American Ethnologist*, 33(1).

— (2007) 'Vital mobility and the humanitarian kit', Unpublished paper for SSRC workshop 'The problem of biosecurity: approaches from the critical social sciences', 6/7 April.

Robins, S. (2004) '"Long live Zackie, long live": AIDS activism, science and citizenship after apartheid', *Journal of Southern African Studies*, 30(3).

— (2006) 'From rights to "ritual": AIDS activism and treatment testimonies in South Africa', *American Anthropologist*, 108(2).

— (2009) 'Mobilising and mediating global medicine and health citizenship: the politics of AIDS knowledge production in rural South Africa', IDS Working Paper no. 324, Institute of Development Studies, Brighton, www.drc-citizenship.org/publications/Wp324%20web.pdf, accessed 29 August 2009.

Rodlach, A. (2006) *Witches, Westerners and HIV: AIDS and Cultures of Blame in Africa*, Walnut Creek, CA: Left Coast Press Inc.

Schoepf, B. (2001) 'International AIDS research in anthropology: taking a critical perspective on the crisis', *Annual Review of Anthropology*, 30.

Steinberg, J. (2008) *Sizwe's Test: A Young Man's Journey through Africa's AIDS Epidemic*, Jeppestown, NY: Simon and Schuster.

Turner, B. S. (1992) *Regulating Bodies: Essays in Medical Sociology*, London: Routledge.

4 · Enhancing everyday citizenship practices: women's livelihoods and global markets

JULIE THEKKUDAN[1]

Introduction

The process of globalization has created interconnections across the world as never before – in economics, politics, technology and communications, even in cultural expressions. It has emphasized the heady power of the market and allowed the growth, often unregulated, of multinational corporations (MNCs) in neoliberal regimes. It has also brought into prominence the shifting nature of global authority in the economic sphere, affecting the political mandate of the state, illustrated by its withdrawal from functions and roles which hitherto had been its prerogative. Countering the shifting forces of the market, governance institutions, civil society and individuals have emerged as change agents, attempting to transform the landscape of governance, politics and the economy. Their efforts have aimed at the integration of those who have been excluded by the changing landscapes of globalization, by opening up new spaces and creating mechanisms to increase their interaction and participation in governance processes.

This chapter examines the dynamics of integrating thus far excluded sections of society within the global economic chain. The arguments are based on research into Project Shakti,[2] an initiative promoted by the Indian state in collaboration with Hindustan Unilever Limited (HUL), the Indian division of Unilever, a multinational corporation. The research was undertaken in 2006 in two poor districts in Andhra Pradesh, Nalgonda and Medak, where Project Shakti was implemented, supporting poor rural women to deal in Unilever goods, sometimes building on existing networks of self-help groups (SHGs). The research looked at the ways in which changing patterns of power and governance (in the form of actors, spaces and diffusion of authority delinked from territory) affect the meaning, experiences and practices of citizenship in a globalizing world. The chapter highlights the ways in which this attempt to include the previously excluded in the global economy may have made spaces for the active representation and participation of the various project stakeholders, the mobilization processes of these different actors, and their associated legitimacy and accountability. Governance processes in today's context are multilayered, and each actor – state or non-state – brings the potential to achieve meaningful and effective inputs into the 'governance wheel' of citizenship, participation and accountability (Tandon 2000).

Towards a more inclusive global governance

The most visible manifestation of globalization all along has been economic, with an integration of national economies through a free movement of goods, services and capital. Alongside this has been increased competition between firms in their search for new markets for both production and consumption. Globalization was seen by some as the means to greater economic participation by all people, leading to poverty reduction and improved indices of development. Greater economic participation has been most evident through the local production of goods for global companies, most commonly seen in the textile, garments and footwear industries. The less common mechanism of economic integration is the sale of global products within a particular region, achieved by previously excluded people becoming a part of the retail chain for large corporations.

In developing countries like India, poverty reduction through the promotion of livelihoods, especially within the rural context, has frequently been initiated through the medium of SHGs and micro-finance. Lack of access to credit has often been identified as a major source of constraint for women working in the informal sector (Mayoux 2003), and the SHG model of microcredit provided poor women with access to financial services and small amounts of credit to raise their income levels and improve living standards. With the growth of this model and its perceived benefits to many rural women, the concept of microcredit has been broadened to include a wider range of services such as linkages to the market, and strategies for all products developed by women's SHGs to be marketed more widely, thereby realizing better returns and enhancing incomes for women. Another route towards similar outcomes is seen as the marketing of branded goods and services by women's groups as opportunities to expand businesses and make additional incomes. Globalization of economic activities, and the subsequent entry of large MNCs seeking new markets, has broadened the scope of market linkages for SHGs.

Associated with this economic development, the SHG model also intended to enhance the practice of conventional citizenship rights and responsibilities. Women, who had been thus far excluded from the processes of development, would by their economic participation and the formation of collectives begin a process of self-empowerment. The economic worth of these women would improve their positions within the household and the larger community. It was assumed that they would begin actively participating in socio-political spheres of decision-making. They were viewed as the change agents for addressing existing social evils like domestic violence and dowry.

The current global economic meltdown, and the continuing collapse of free-market-based economies across the world, has led to a growing scepticism about this globalized economic model, even in former havens of free market capitalism. The spread effect of the meltdown has resulted in many states providing huge bailouts, credit access, direct subsidies and tax sops. The pinch of the meltdown is being felt by all, developed, developing, the mainstream and the excluded. Export-oriented markets seem to be the worst hit, affecting the employment of many across the globe. In such conditions, those who have gained a recent entry into the markets may be at the mercy of such global shifts without the ability to defend their interests.

Globalization has increased the strength of large corporations, which had successfully made inroads into the domestic markets of many countries, and led to them pushing for more freedom from state controls. In their bid to promote their reputation as an important stakeholder in development, while simultaneously reaching out to a larger share of the market, corporations have, since the beginning of the 1990s, adopted the notions of corporate social responsibility (CSR) and corporate governance. CSR is termed as the 'ethical behaviour of a company towards society' (Agarwal 2008: 12), and ideally involves engaging directly with local communities, identifying the needs of community people, and attempting to integrate these identified needs with the goals and strategies of the business. From the government's viewpoint, CSR becomes the company's contribution to the nation's sustainable development goals.

The accountability of corporations and the history of corporate governance can be traced to the Cadbury Committee 1991, the Organisation for Economic Co-operation and Development Principles of Corporate Governance, and the Sarbanes Oxley Act in the USA in 2002.[3] Global efforts like the United Nations Global Compact and the Global Reporting Initiative have not had a strong effect as there is no mandatory compliance either from the signatories or the governing authority. Over the years, various businesses have also developed their own codes of conduct and ethics, owing to an inherent fear among corporations of a 'fall from grace'.

In India, corporate governance was initiated in 1996 with a voluntary code that was framed by the Confederation of Indian Industries, adopted by over thirty large companies within the first three years of finalization. The notion of corporate governance was taken farther by the Securities and Exchange Board of India, the Kumara Mangalam Birla Committee (1999) and the Narayana Murthy Committee (2002) to raise the standards of transparency and ethical practices to international standards.[4] Yet, corporate governance in India has fallen grossly short, as is evident in the now infamous Satyam fraud.

The two models of globalized economic participation – producing goods for the global market and becoming a part of the retail chain for global corporations – have led to corporate campaigning and transnational solidarity networks to hold various large corporations accountable for their actions. Campaigns like the Babymilk Action Campaign (against Nestlé for the irresponsible marketing of baby milk in developing countries) and Behind the Label and the Clean Clothes Campaign (against clothing manufacturers for abuse of labour standards and human rights) have pricked the moral conscience of both the manufacturers and the consumers of global products (Clark 2003).

Debates on global markets and rural livelihoods in a developing country like India and their effect on the experience and practice of citizenship need to be empirically rooted. What do processes of global integration entail for citizenship identities rooted in a local context like Andhra Pradesh? How are meanings of 'globality' manifested in the daily practice of local citizens when they are part of a global economic enterprise? Or do they continue to understand their rights and obligations largely in the sub-national 'domestic' sense? And are citizens able to exercise their own agency in the face of such global shifts?

Project Shakti: a market-led solution for enhancing women's livelihoods

In 2001, Project Shakti was initiated by HUL with the aim of creating income-generating capabilities for underprivileged rural women, by providing a sustainable micro-enterprise opportunity, and improving rural living standards through health and hygiene awareness. It aimed at transforming underprivileged household women into entrepreneurs. HUL envisioned the creation of 100,000 *Shakti Amma* (Empowerment Mothers, as the women are called in Andhra Pradesh), covering 500,000 villages, and touching the lives of 600 million rural people by the year 2010.[5] For HUL, Project Shakti was started as a CSR endeavour.[6] According to HUL, Shakti is a pioneering effort in creating livelihoods for rural women and improving living standards in rural India, providing critically needed additional income to these women and their families, by equipping and training them to become an extended arm of the company's operation.[7] The sustainability of the project rests on the growth of the company's core business, which would be mutually beneficial to both the population for whom the project is intended and for the company.

Seeking to expand on its CSR activities, and motivated by the Grameen Bank model from Bangladesh, HUL approached the government of Andhra Pradesh (GoAP) for collaborations on sustainable rural development. The GoAP was on its own exploring options for transforming women from within the SHG movement into successful entrepreneurs in their own right. In December 2000, HUL entered into a public–private partnership with GoAP to initiate Project Shakti in fifty villages of Nalgonda District. The pilot was initiated in 2001, and from 2002 operations were scaled up to the states of Karnataka, Gujarat, Madhya Pradesh, Uttar Pradesh, Tamil Nadu, Chattisgarh and Orissa. By 2006, there were 3,077 *Shakti Amma* spread across twenty-two districts of Andhra Pradesh.[8]

State endorsement of the partnership was further evident in the support provided to HUL in the pre-feasibility market research. A livelihood and marketing support agency, Marketing and Rural Team (MART), in collaboration with the State Department for Rural Development's Andhra Pradesh Rural Livelihoods programme in Nalgonda District, proposed the idea of retailing HUL products. After detailed discussions with HUL representatives, details of the collaboration were worked out. State support was further evident in the fact that the GoAP, through the District Rural Development Agency (DRDA), was jointly involved with HUL and MART in the selection of the *Shakti Amma*. In some cases, DRDA staff and *mandal* (block, the second tier of Indian local government) officials have also been instrumental.

Implemented in villages with a population of approximately two thousand, the basis for Project Shakti was worked out by HUL, which conducted a survey on the feasibility of the project and expected sales. The market research revealed that rural households spent roughly Rs100 per month on products of daily use like soaps, detergent and cosmetics. It was assumed that a *Shakti Amma* would know almost everyone in the village, and that by enlisting neighbours and friends as prospective and dedicated clients, a *Shakti Amma* would be able to sell Rs100-worth of products to many households. Villages with less than two thousand population were to be treated as satellite villages that could be tapped by the nearest *Shakti Amma*.

As most of these *Shakti Amma* lived below the poverty line, an additional earning of Rs1,000 would be significant in helping them to overcome poverty. HUL also envisaged that, along with economic independence, there would be a marked change in the women's status within the household, with a much greater say in decision-making. HUL felt that this CSR model would be beneficial for both HUL and the consumers, some of whom would come to depend on the organization for their livelihood, which would build a self-sustaining cycle of growth for all.[9] To give a further push to Project Shakti, HUL also launched a health and hygiene programme, Shakti Vani (public voice), whereby women are trained to address the issue of health in the rural community.[10] An Internet-based rural information service, iShakti, was also developed in 2003, to provide information and services to meet rural needs in medical health and hygiene, agriculture, animal husbandry, education, vocational training and employment and women's empowerment.[11]

The modus operandi for Project Shakti implementation has differed across the country depending on the feasibility of the approach. In some states the collaboration is with the state government, in other areas through NGOs, financial institutions and even directly through individuals. In various districts of Andhra Pradesh, five NGOs partnered with HUL to implement the project. In two blocks (Anantpur and Srikakulam) Project Shakti was implemented through the government programmes of the District Poverty Initiatives Project and the Integrated Rural Development Services respectively, further evidence of state endorsement of the project. HUL approached NGOs already involved in promoting microcredit, which, impressed with the strategy of Project Shakti, were instrumental in promoting individual women entrepreneurs within their areas of intervention.[12]

Economic augmentation for rural women

On average, women entrepreneurs invested Rs10,000 in purchasing stocks from HUL, some provided by the NGOs, some given as loans by the SHGs they were members of, but mostly generated on their own. HUL expected Shakti entrepreneurs to make a profit of Rs1,000–3,000 per month on this investment, which required a sales turnover between Rs10,000 and Rs30,000 per month. According to HUL, a minimum of 8–9 per cent profit could be expected on the turnover. The average expected turnover from each *Shakti Amma* was approximately Rs10,000 per month.

For about half the *Shakti Amma*, the profits from their dealership doubled following the start-up phase. For a few, the increase in the profits was not significant, while for some, the profits were less than when they began. A few had stopped the dealership owing to a drop in sales and an increase in the number of retail outlets in the villages. Others were unable to state their profits.

HUL worked out different margins for the sale of the Shakti entrepreneurs' products to various clients – goods to the shopkeepers in the village at a margin of 3 per cent; to other SHG members at 6 per cent; and a 9 per cent margin if the *Shakti Amma* sold from a retail outfit. On the whole, Shakti Amma adhered to these margins, but a few innovated, giving products to other SHG members at 5 per cent margin and some at the market price. HUL admits that although the company advocates different margins for different consumers, they leave the final decision to the *Shakti Amma*.

Initial research on the *Shakti Amma* in 2004 indicated that in Nalgonda 231 Shakti entrepreneurs were promoted either by the government or the NGOs (APMAS 2006). Within the next two years a 5 per cent dropout was seen. With profits from the dealership largely depending on the sales of the HUL products in the village, women entrepreneurs have stated that they were unable to meet the expected targets since the time and effort invested in the dealership did not justify the profits. Only where the *Shakti Amma* is already a shopkeeper was the profitability of the initiative assured.

The initiative was time consuming, with the women devoting between two and eight hours to it daily. For most, the dealership was a collective effort of the entire household. Husbands or sons employed outside the village or having means of transport by which they could easily access other villages become primarily responsible for taking orders and delivery of goods to the nearby villages. The *Shakti Amma* relied on her children, in-laws or unmarried siblings to cater to customers in her absence. She also relied on women family members, especially daughters, to do more household chores to give her the time to take up the dealership more actively.

Enhanced formal citizenship but limited empowerment

Citizenship and the notion of identity – how people see themselves as citizens with their multiple identities of caste, sex and class – have an impact on their perception of rights, obligations and participation in public spheres (Jones and Gaventa 2002). Acquiring a sense of independent identity has become a starting point for changing this perception of the self as a citizen for some *Shakti Amma*. Prior to this initiative, many were housewives, teachers, working in their fields or in the family shop. After the initiative, they started earning money of their own and now contribute to the family expenses. The ability to do so within the confines of their homes has increased their self-confidence and their awareness and knowledge of their surroundings. Those who did not share this perspective had a variety of reasons – inexperience, increased costs and a drop in sales.

For a limited few, engaging in Project Shakti has given access to formal notions of citizenship. Socially, almost all *Shakti Amma* have stated that they have more respect and recognition within their villages. A few have claimed to establish good linkages with the teacher, *sarpanch* (village head) and other important members of the village community, as a result of becoming the *Shakti Amma*. Some expressed a sense of pride and satisfaction in recognition by their first names rather than their surname, which is indicative of caste affiliation. One even stated that the villagers may not know her as a *Shakti Amma*, but if anyone in the village asks for the person who sells soaps, they are quickly directed to her.

Though the economic benefits and social recognition may be evident, participation in the political sphere is rather limited. Only three of the women interviewed have contested elections to the local self-government institutions, while three more have formally supported election candidates. One stated that she would not be averse to contesting elections if she were given the chance but had not pursued it actively. Another stated that politically her role in the village is limited, as she is a 'daughter' of the village. Only the 'daughters-in-law' can contest local-body elections as daughters are expected to leave the village after their marriage. Yet another stated that contesting elections would affect the sale of products, as more time would be spent on the political campaign. During the previous elections, the reduced sales resulted in increased pressure from HUL to meet targets and, subsequently, she has not reconsidered contesting elections.

Empowerment – the freedom of choice and action to shape one's life along with control over resources and decisions – is not an evident result of the project. Though many dealerships are in the names of women, the actual running is undertaken by husbands. Women's limited mobility is often cited as a reason for the continuation of the existing gender relations within the community. The *Shakti Amma* is the Indian equivalent of the 'Avon lady' in Western countries, who moves from door to door selling the concept of feminine beauty through cosmetic products; similarly, the *Shakti Amma*, in their bid to become 'power mothers', have in reality become 'beauty agents'. Associated with the concept of health and hygiene, the crux of HUL products, are also the sense of modernity and a 'modern' notion of feminine beauty as epitomized by Fair and Lovely, a skin-whitening cream that is a very popular HUL brand. With globalization, even in the small towns of India, there exist more universal understandings of beauty (often Western notions) aided by the electronic boom and MNCs trying to acquire new markets (Bhattacharya 2004).

Opportunities for exposure to experiences outside the village in rural Andhra Pradesh are very limited, and when some villagers, particularly women, do move beyond the village, it is perceived to be an empowerment of sorts. Similarly, if from earnings of Rs1,000 the village women spend Rs300 on soaps and consumer items, this is construed as an empowering process. Marketing strategies offering products in small quantities for a lower price (for example, HUL's sachets of shampoo costing a single rupee) have brought within the capacity of young girls and women the aspiration to clean and perfumed hair and skin.

Though Project Shakti may have brought the *Shakti Amma* outside the ambit of their private spheres (their homes and, to a limited extent, their villages), it is doubtful whether the project has exposed them to anything beyond the village, the district or the state, let alone the global. At the most, *Shakti Amma* are aware of HUL as a producer of 'good-quality soaps and detergents'. Their awareness of processes beyond their immediate spaces is at best nascent. Engagements with HUL have not given women an understanding of the global processes it embodies.

With reference to a sense of global identity, ability to access and participate in trans-state institutions and decision-making fora, *Shakti Amma* do not come across as being 'globalized'. The existence of a sense of global citizenship among *Shakti Amma* is very weak. The terms of their engagements with global processes in production and consumption have been mediated and negotiated either by the state government or NGOs, with no direct involvement of the *Shakti Amma* themselves. Such engagements do not seem to have enriched the lived experiences of those directly involved.

Spaces for representation and its legitimacy

Although individual agency may be a central aspect of claiming rights and observing duties, collective struggles to redefine governance processes through claiming rights have sometimes been successful in institutional transformations leading to more inclusive practices of citizenship (Kabeer 2003). Project Shakti has led to a strengthening of individual identity for almost all, but an identity formation among *Shakti Amma* as a collective engagement with global economic processes, possessing some commonalities, has neither been promoted nor developed. This is largely due to the fact that the institutional space for such a collective was not created either by the company or by the state. The absence of any feedback mechanism to inform HUL's senior representatives about problems encountered by *Shakti Amma* on the ground, and of any attempt to consult the *Shakti Amma* about solving problems, was an important limitation on the project's success. HUL's lowest-level direct interaction with the *Amma* is through its Rural Sales Persons (RSPs), who are given vast territorial areas to cover, and hence have tremendous pressure to meet their targets. Only a few of the successful *Shakti Amma* have had the opportunity to meet the senior representatives in HUL, such as the district or regional managers at reward ceremonies held in Bangalore and Tirupati. Unofficial corroboration of this problem by senior representatives is indicative that the scope for the involvement of the women is something that HUL had not even thought about. This meant that no action was taken to ensure regular interaction among the *Shakti Amma* within a specific region to ascertain their opinions on the project and ways to improve its existing processes, as an enhancement of the business.

The absence of a collective for the *Shakti Amma* is also indicative of the many problems that they have faced in the project. The idea of credit was not encouraged by HUL either for the *Shakti Amma* or for their clients. The *Shakti Amma* felt that, given the rural situation, and their economic background, the idea of credit could have been explored. A few *Shakti Amma* have, on their own initiative, given credit to other SHG members to promote the initiative within the village. But this was the responsibility of the individual, as it entailed a lot of cajoling of SHG members to buy products from the *Shakti Amma* and following up on customers who had taken products on credit. Moreover, the entire process of retailing also threw up other related issues. For instance, the issue of storage of stock (either building a shed, an investment borne by the entrepreneur, or storing stock in the limited space available within a house); unsold stock (HUL had promised to take back unsold stock, but later declined); the appropriate quantities of products for sale (stock was often over-ordered, and comprised products that did not have a wide market in the rural areas); and the delivery of stock (often delayed and sometimes in instalments).

Probably the formation of a collective body of *Shakti Amma* and a legitimate space for their participation in decision-making processes (both among themselves and with other stakeholders) could have been instrumental in eliminating many of these problems, from understanding margins to keeping accounts at the start of the initiative. Government stakeholders seemed to be of the opinion that the mere act of engaging with the MNC and becoming economically solvent had empowered these *Shakti Amma* enough to take on the role of active citizens, and if need be challenge the might of the MNC. Assuming, however, that *Shakti Amma* would have an autonomous sense of agency to change the terms of such engagements in the absence of support is thrusting upon them a responsibility for which they are currently ill equipped.

Collaborating NGOs came to be caught in a dilemma, unable to decide upon an appropriate role for themselves. On the one hand, having collaborated in Project Shakti, they had in some senses agreed to the basic principles of such initiatives. On the other hand, problems in the actual implementation of the project raised doubts for NGOs about their own role, and how it was perceived as uncritically promoting the initiative. This could explain why four of the five NGOs involved have discontinued their promotion of the project. Critiquing it, they point out that Project Shakti is only an income-generating activity and not livelihood promotion in the more substantial sense of building assets for present and future generations. HUL has used the SHG model to build the entrepreneurial skills of women, which alone does not amount to a livelihood. There were no activities of production based on existing livelihood opportunities available in the area, which is mainly an agricultural context. Questions have also been raised regarding Project Shakti's sustainability. The failure of NGOs to come together and establish horizontal linkages around the issues on which they differed from HUL, or to support collective representation for participating women, was instrumental in the lack of a constituency to compel HUL to reform Project Shakti. This in turn led to the project's problems being replicated as it was implemented across the country.

Accountability of different actors

The rationale for state endorsement of this initiative was most likely the perceived percolation of the benefits – both economic and in terms of ideas – of the initiative from individuals to groups. GoAP's initial enthusiasm has waned over the years. It gradually withdrew from the role of facilitator in the second and third years of the project. Participating government officials felt that once the project was in place, both the Shakti Amma and HUL could manage it on their own. Although the government officials were very confident that women would approach them if they faced problems in the initiative, there was no proactive interaction with the *Shakti Amma* to ascertain the problems, if any, associated with the project. Problems individually communicated to the government officials at the lower levels may not have been considered as common to a sizeable proportion of the *Shakti Amma*. The government admits that monitoring of the project is totally absent, and that this may be laxness on their part.

As processes of globalization have proceeded, the state has drawn back from its former welfare role. As the recent economic situation has shown, the state cannot totally abdicate its responsibility towards its citizens, especially in a developing country like India. The stakeholders within initiatives like Project Shakti do not possess equal knowledge of processes or bargaining power. It is therefore the mandate of the state to ensure that the terms of such initiatives are not harming the less powerful actors. It seems that the state never questioned the objective of HUL in starting this initiative, but took the philanthropic objectives for granted.

Worldwide, Unilever, the parent company of HUL, has attempted to transform itself by minimizing the negative impacts of its business, and become part of the solutions to crises across the globe. Through an analysis of its 'economic footprints' in Indonesia and South Africa, the company is striving to understand its economic, social and environmental impacts on the countries where it does business (Kapstein 2008).[13] In India, HUL has endeavoured to be a good 'citizen' through its CSR approach to '[integrating] our social, economic and environmental agenda with our brands, our people and the way we conduct our business'.[14] Yet HUL has not really been forced into a position of accountability to any stakeholder, whether the GoAP, with whom they had negotiations regarding Project Shakti, the NGOs that were the implementing agencies or the *Shakti Amma*.

Though the *Shakti Amma* – identified and selected by the government and NGOs, before being 'developed' by HUL – saw HUL as the duty-bearer, they were quite unsure whom to approach for resolution of problems in their dealerships. They were uncertain whether HUL would be able to resolve the existing problems. Those promoted by NGOs looked to them to mediate with HUL on their behalf. For most, there seemed to be an implicit trust in the state that whatever it promoted would be in the interest of its citizens; the *Shakti Amma* stated that they looked to the government to give women more employment and livelihood opportunities for their social and economic development. They wanted the government to give subsidies or loans to underprivileged women, to provide them with training to start their own small industries, and most importantly to help in the marketing of such initiatives. NGOs should, according to them, focus on vocational training, especially in the preparation of household products, which might be useful for the villagers to enhance their livelihoods. But in Project Shakti, the *Shakti Amma* may have become the stakeholder with the least say in the initiative. In the absence of state or NGO mediation, these women were very much on their own in trying to achieve socio-economic empowerment in its total sense.

Inclusion and exclusion

The idea of implementing Project Shakti through the SHG Federation was explored during the pilot phase, since it afforded a bigger scale of operations.[15] Yet practical difficulties were encountered. The federation was unwilling to bear all the expenses that would be incurred by the process, which would have included infrastructure costs for a retailing unit. Federation members were also unwilling to remunerate members who would manage the business. It was decided to encourage individual members to take up this initiative on their own (APMAS 2006). The position of SHGs and the power and agency of the collective were to a certain extent undermined by this process. SHGs were not actively involved in the project, and there were no efforts at poverty reduction through group savings and credit, one of the aims of forming a SHG. Limited as they may have been, there were traces of jealousy between group members over the economic gains from the project, which diluted the social cohesion that might have existed within the group in its savings and credit form.

Although it is not a direct player in this initiative, such engagements with global processes also affect the family. The sphere of the family has always marked the distinction between the public and the private realms. The public realm has been one dominated by the male members of the household, while most women remain restricted to the private realm, highlighting their reproductive role rather than their productive abilities. Project Shakti has to a certain extent promoted this understanding of the distinction between the private and public realms – even though its goal may have been just the opposite. The project looked at the husbands of potential *Shakti Amma* with the assumption that, as men, they would be more capable of undertaking the initiative. And as has been stated above, in many cases it was the husband or other male member of the family who assumed the mantle of running the dealership.

Communities are also indirect stakeholders in the project, despite the fact that it had no space for active engagements on the part of community members. In fact, Project Shakti initially raised opposition from the other traditional village shopkeepers, and some other men in the community. The shopkeepers were opposed to *Shakti Amma* as unequal competitors in their traditional occupation. The men opposed the initiative being targeted only at women. There was limited scope in the project to bring about greater social and economic cohesion or integration within the community. There were no sustainable livelihood opportunities, in the form of asset building or resource sharing generated by the project that would lead to the overall development of the community as a whole. During the groundwork for the start of the project, there were opportunities for incorporating the community as a whole within the process of production and not merely consumption, but no attempt was made to do so. Suggestions about sourcing castor oil from this region to boost local incomes and the manufacture of low-cost detergents locally were not taken up.[16]

Project Shakti has undeniably been an opportunity for HUL to build its brand in hitherto untapped and unsaturated markets, improving its traditional distribution system, which was unable to reach out to nearly 87 per cent of India's villages with a population of 2,000 or less.[17] Now, with the *Shakti Amma*, the company has achieved enhanced popularity and increased sales for more of its products. Although HUL representatives claim that Project Shakti has not generated an income equivalent to the investment in the project, in 2006 the size of the business in terms of turnover was a little over Rs1,000 million, and it was targeted to be Rs10,000 million by the end of 2007.[18] At this rate of growth, it has the potential to become as large as the current size of HUL in a decade.

Conclusion

Changing landscapes of power and governance in the global arena have significant implications for all actors, state and non-state. Globalization has provided different actors with varied opportunities. For rural women of Project Shakti, income generation opportunities as marketing agents for an MNC may have helped some of them to actualize their formal conception of citizenship. But this opportunity may not be emancipatory enough in creating the 'power mothers' that the *Shakti Amma* were intended to be. Rather, the result was the making of 'vulnerable salesgirls' unable to empower themselves in the absence of state mediation and support from civil society. In the absence of spaces and mechanisms that would enable their true participation, *Shakti Amma* had little role in shaping this part of their livelihoods, or, even indirectly, the policies that affect them. These promoters of cleanliness and the modern and popular notions of feminine beauty in the rural villages may in reality have undermined the strength of the collective, the SHG that was intended to provide the mechanism for a transformation of the existing relations in society.

The case of Project Shakti also calls into question the accountability of large corporations in promoting livelihood opportunities for women. By failing to incorporate the active participation of *Shakti Amma* in the project, from its inception to its implementation, HUL may have lost out on an opportunity to become yet again a pioneer in its CSR activities and in its goal of being a responsible citizen. This opportunity could also have been utilized to make the business of the project as viable as the core business of the MNC.

In the current economic meltdown, it has become very clear that the power of the state is far from diminished. The core guarantor of common goals of social and economic justice, genuine citizenship through the participation at the national and sub-national levels, the state has an important role in advocating and negotiating on the common public good at the sub-national, national and global levels. For the state, then, endorsement of such market-led initiatives is a significant responsibility. In future, it should be more rigorous in checking the implications of such initiatives before lending its support. Moreover, it may not be sufficient to merely support such initiatives, but equally important to constantly monitor and regulate their impact on citizens and the formulation of the common public good.

Civil society actors such as NGOs have an important role to play in initiatives that span the spectrum from local to global. As intermediary between the state, the market and its citizens, NGO support of such initiatives may run the risk of becoming the midwife of market penetration. NGOs may have to become more discerning in the partnerships they forge within global processes, and in some cases they may have to be prepared to be the catalyst that takes local struggles to more public arenas of debate and discussion. The capacity of some NGOs may give them the agency needed to bring together both vertical and horizontal mobilizations in the national and the global spheres.

Notes

1 I acknowledge the contribution of K. Rakesh in data collection, Shri Nimmaiah, director of People's Action for Creative Education (PEACE), for facilitating meetings with *Shakti Amma*, and Pavan Kare and Santoshi R. for their support and help in the study. I also thank Dr Rajesh Tandon and Dr John Gaventa for their valuable comments, which have brought out some dimensions of this chapter more strongly.

A longer version of this chapter appeared as an IDS Working Paper (Thekkudan and Tandon 2009). The research was carried out in 2006 in Nalgonda and Medak in Andhra Pradesh. Researchers interviewed HUL personnel, government officials from state and district levels, and heads of NGOs collaborating with HUL. A questionnaire was administered to forty *Shakti Amma*, half from each district.

2 *Shakti* means strength, but also implies empowerment.

3 The UN launched negotiations for a Corporate Code of Conduct for transnational corporations in the 1970s, owing to demands by developing nations that their sovereignty be protected, but it died a slow death in the 1980s owing to dramatic changes in the world economy and ideological and policy shifts.

4 Unilever has a code of business principles, which describes the operational standards that everyone at Unilever follows, wherever they are in the world. It also supports its approach to governance and corporate responsibility and covers all stakeholders. http://www.unilever.com/ourvalues/purposeandprinciples/ourprinciples/default.asp (accessed September 2006). HUL's Code of Conduct is based on the principles of fairness, transparency and accountability as the cornerstones for good governance. http://hul.co.in/investor/corporate_governance.asp (accessed September 2006).

5 www.hllshakti.com/sbcms/temp1.asp?pid=46802171, accessed June 2006.

6 HUL has successfully integrated business benefits with CSR initiatives in the past. Lifebuoy *Swasthya Chetna* (health awakening) is an HUL initiative in rural health and hygiene, launched in 2002, which has covered more than 17,000 villages across the country. The basic message concerned the hygienic habits of hand-washing. In 2003/04, the sales of Lifebuoy soap increased by 20 per cent. The company has termed the programme 'a marketing programme with social benefits'. The company goes on to state in a report, 'We recognise that the health of our business is totally interconnected with the health of the communities we serve and if we are to grow sales of our brand we have to increase the number of people who use soap' (Agarwal 2008: 185–6).

7 www.hll.com/citizen_lever/project_shakti.asp, accessed June 2006.

8 Ibid.

9 Ibid.

10 Ibid.

11 Ibid.

12 Interview with regional manager, Project Shakti, HUL, 23 November 2006.

13 One of the important findings in Indonesia was that 'participation in value chains such as Unilever Indonesia's does not automatically guarantee improvements in the lives of people living in poverty. For supply and distribution chains to benefit poor people even more, there need to be other social institutions and resources in place such as credit and saving schemes, marketing associations, and insurance schemes as well as diversification of income streams to reduce dependency on any single company or market'; www.unilever.com/ourvalues/environment-society/case-studies/economic-development/indonesia-exploring-links-between-wealth-creation-poverty-reduction.asp, accessed December 2008.

14 As well as Shakti, HUL has

on its website, under the heading of 'Citizen Lever', programmes like Greening Barrens (water conservation and harvesting), Lifebuoy *Swasthya Chetna* (health and hygiene education), Fair and Lovely Foundation (economic empowerment of women) and Happy Homes (special education and rehabilitation of children); hul.co.in/citizen_lever/index.asp, accessed June 2006.

15 Interview with regional manager, Project Shakti, HUL, 23 November 2006.

16 Interview with director, PEACE, 19 November 2006, www.itcportal.com/newsroom/press_25apr_05.htm, accessed June 2006.

17 In 1999, HUL invited its employees to provide suggestions on its future growth opportunities. One of the suggestions that came up was loosely termed 'rural', while the other was the idea of alternative channels, like the Grameen Bank of Bangladesh. The growing SHG movement in the country provided the impetus for trying something hitherto untried; www.itcportal.com/newsroom/press_25apr_05.htm, accessed June 2006.

18 www.itcportal.com/newsroom/press_25apr_05.htm, accessed June 2006.

References

Agarwal, S.K. (2008) *Corporate Social Responsibility in India*, New Delhi: Response Books.

APMAS (2006) *Shakthi: A Case Study of SHGs as Retailers*, Unpublished.

Bhattacharya, M. (2004) 'The travelling woman and the trails of modernity', in M. Bhattacharya (ed.), *Globalisation: Perspectives in Women's Studies*, New Delhi: Tulika Books.

Clark, J. (2003) *Worlds Apart: Civil Society and the Battle for Ethical Globalization*, London: Earthscan.

Jones, E. and J. Gaventa (2002) 'Concepts of citizenship: a review', *IDS Development Bibliography*, 19, Institute of Development Studies, Brighton.

Kabeer, N. (2003) 'Making rights work for the poor: Nijera Kori and the construction of "collective capabilities" in rural Bangladesh', IDS Working Paper no. 200, Institute of Development Studies, Brighton.

Kapstein, E. B. (2008) 'Measuring Unilever's economic footprints: the case of South Africa', www.vcr.csrwire.com/node/6018, accessed July 2009.

Mayoux, L. (ed.) (2003) *Sustainable Learning for Women's Empowerment: Ways Forward in Micro-Finance*, New Delhi: Pradhan.

Tandon, R. (2000) *Citizenship, Participation and Accountability*, Concept note for Development Research Centre on Citizenship, Participation and Accountability planning meeting.

Thekkudan, J. and R. Tandon (2009) 'Women's livelihoods, global markets and citizenship', IDS Working Paper 2009-9, Institute of Development Studies, Brighton.

5 · The politics of global assessments: the case of the IAASTD[1]

IAN SCOONES

Introduction

Global assessments have become all the rage. The International Assessment of Agricultural Knowledge, Science and Technology for Development (IAASTD) is one of many, coming on the back of the Intergovernmental Panel on Climate Change (IPCC), the Millennium Ecosystem Assessment (MA) and the Millennium Project's Millennium Development Goal (MDG) task forces, among others. The IPCC even won the Nobel Peace Prize in 2007, the first assessment to do so.[2] All of these attempt to combine 'expert assessment' with processes of 'stakeholder consultation' in what are presented as global, participatory assessments on key issues of major international importance. Such assessments contribute to a new landscape of governance in the international arena, offering the potential for links between the local and the global, and present ways of articulating citizen engagement with global processes of decision-making and policy. In many respects such assessments respond to the critiques of the top-down, Northern-dominated, expert assessments of the past and make attempts to be both more inclusive and participatory in their design and process, offering new opportunities for mobilization and the articulation of alternative knowledges in the global policy domain. But how far do they meet these objectives? Do they genuinely allow alternative voices to be heard? Do they create a new mode of engagement in global arenas? How do local and global processes articulate? And what are the power relations involved, creating what processes of mediation, inclusion and exclusion?

Taking the case of the IAASTD, this chapter explores these issues through a focus on the underlying knowledge politics of a global process. Four intersecting questions, central to the concerns of this book (Gaventa and Tandon, this volume) and at the heart of contemporary democratic theory and practice, are posed: how do processes of knowledge framing occur; how do different practices and methodologies get deployed in cross-cultural, global processes; how is 'representation' constructed and legitimized; and how, as a result, do collective understandings of global issues emerge? Drawing on a detailed analysis of the IAASTD process between 2003 and 2008, the chapter argues that in such assessments the politics of knowledge needs to be made more explicit, and that negotiations around politics and values must be put centre-stage. The black-boxing of uncertainty, or the eclipsing of more fundamental clashes over interpretation and meaning, must be avoided in order for processes of participation and engagement in global assessment processes to become more meaningful, democratic and accountable. Following Mouffe (2005), the paper offers a critique of simplistic forms of deliberative democratic practice, and argues that there is a need to 'bring politics back in'.

The International Assessment of Agricultural Knowledge, Science and Technology (IAASTD)

The overall purpose of the IAASTD, which concluded with a final plenary session in Johannesburg in April 2008, was 'to assess agricultural knowledge, science and technology in order to use it more effectively to reduce hunger and poverty, improve rural livelihoods, and facilitate equitable, environmentally, socially and economically sustainable development'.[3] No one could argue with that, of course. But how was this ambitious aim to be realized?

The IAASTD was announced during 2002, and was initiated on five continents in early 2003 with a series of consultation meetings. Since then five regional reports and one global report (IAASTD 2009) have been produced, all contributing to a synthesis and summaries for decision-makers for each continental and the global report. A total of 400 authors were recruited to write the reports, and an overall framework was hammered out in a series of meetings,[4] a process overseen by a complex governance structure (Scoones 2008).

The IAASTD had very substantial financial backing from a wide range of bilateral donors, UN organizations and the World Bank, with a total budget of over US$15 million.[5] With agriculture and technology rising up the development agenda again, many agencies saw this as an excellent opportunity to map out a way forward. A combination of a multi-stakeholder and an intergovernmental UN process appealed, as this offered the combination of inclusion and dialogue, including civil society and private business actors, as well as formal decision-making and buy-in by nation-states. Was this perhaps the model for the future – picking the best of the IPCC and the MA and combining them in an approach to global decision-making that was at once scientifically sound, politically legitimate and participatory?

A number of unique attributes are highlighted by the director, Robert Watson, including: an advisory structure which encompasses governmental representatives as well as civil society; the 'inclusion of hundreds of experts from all relevant stakeholder groups'; an 'intellectually consistent framework'; a global, multi-scale and long-term approach, resulting in 'plausible scenarios' to 2050; the 'integration of local and institutional knowledge'; and a multi-thematic approach, encompassing nutrition, livelihoods and human health, linking science and technology issues to policies and institutions.[6] As a multi-stakeholder process involving everyone from grassroots groups to scientists and representatives of large corporations, with the final product being signed by national governments, there has to date been no parallel. As such the IAASTD provides fascinating insights into processes of participation and global engagement, and the implications these have for the contestation of global knowledge and the construction of global citizenship.

Globalization and civil society: the place of international assessments

The IAASTD, like the other global assessments, is seen by its proponents as a brave attempt at engaging a diverse group of stakeholders on a key topic with major global ramifications. In this regard it is a major departure from previous models of global expert decision-making, where attempts at dialogue and debate were largely absent and processes were open only to an exclusive expert elite.

In this way, the IAASTD chimes with a central theme of the more optimistic strands of the literature on globalization and civil society. These suggest that, with the opening up of opportunities for engagement at the global level, and the increasing connections between local-level actors and issues and those in global arenas, the opportunities for participation and influence increase through a 'global civil society' (Edwards and Gaventa 2001; Keane 2003; Archibugi 2008). With this opening up, processes become more complex and require increasingly sophisticated forms of mobilization by activists and movements in order to engage (Tarrow 1994). But the net result is a pluralization of knowledges, claims and inputs into cosmopolitan global contexts, resulting, it is argued, ultimately in a more democratic and accountable system of governance and policy-making (Held and McGrew 2002; Heater 2002).

The IAASTD could be seen as one avenue for such new styles of engagement, knowledge production and claim-making; and indeed, the rhetoric associated with it suggests that this is in part the wider aim. A vision of cosmopolitan diversity and democratic decision-making is portrayed, governed by rules and procedures allowing rational decisions and objective science to prevail.

A closer look at the processes and practices of the IAASTD, however, reveals some major limits to such a vision. In particular it highlights, following Fischer (2000), the important contemporary tensions between professional expertise and democratic governance, and, as Jasanoff and Martello argue, with the reassertion of local knowledge claims in global environmental processes, 'the construction of both the local and the global crucially depends on the production of knowledge and its interactions with power' (2004: 5). Tracing these knowledge–power interactions is thus central to any understanding of local–global engagements. The aim has been to go beyond the well-rehearsed rhetoric of participation, inclusion and citizen engagement and ask: what has been the practice, experience and underlying politics of the IAASTD? The next section looks at the particular interaction between diverse sources of expertise, and the way this politics of knowledge constructs notions of citizenship.

Experts and citizens

The assessment process has seen diverse forms of expertise becoming engaged. What has this revealed about the relationships between experts and citizens, and how have diverse forms of citizenship been practised in such local-to-global engagements? NGO activists engaging with the IAASTD have laid out some of the challenges. Marcia Ishii-Eiteman of the Pesticide Action Network (PAN) of North America (PANNA) reflects:

> Key to the success of the Assessment, from a civil society viewpoint, will be the extent to which it accurately reflects the voices, experiences and priorities of small farmers around the world, and provides an analysis of corporate industrial agriculture's failings as a strategy to reduce hunger and improve rural livelihoods. This in turn depends upon our abilities as sustainable agriculture and social justice movements to put forward authors who will critically assess the impacts of powerful public institutions such as the World Bank and the World Trade Organization as well as the private sector on the generation, access and use of knowledge, science and technology. To the extent that the Assessment reflects the knowledge and concerns of small farmers, it will provide civil society organizations (CSOs) with an important advocacy tool for specific campaigns as well as for the long-term movement towards social justice and equitable and sustainable development.[7]

At the same time, as Romeo Quijano, PAN Philippines representative on the Assessment's Advisory Bureau, argues:

We must always be acutely conscious of the fact that the balance of forces are stacked largely in favour of the dominant corporate model of agriculture. The discussions on hunger and poverty hardly go into the realm of power relations and the underlying socio-political and economic forces that are major determinants of what kinds of agricultural knowledge, science and technology are generated, distributed, used and accessed and who are the main beneficiaries. [...] A major challenge is how to correctly inject and project the grassroots perspective in the Assessment, given the fact that most progressive farmer and peasant organizations are not participating in this exercise. We should aim for maximum articulation and public dissemination of the core issues being discussed, and carry out a broad and intensive public awareness campaign on the issues being debated. The civil society organizations that are participating formally in the Assessment – as authors and members of the Bureau and design teams – must continuously reach out to peasant groups who are left out of the process and strive to reflect their perspectives on the key issues. (Quoted by Ishii-Eiteman 2005)

Here an explicit perspective is laid out about how to link local and global processes through the intermediation of civil society representatives. The talk is of 'injecting grassroots perspectives' and 'reaching out to peasant groups', while at the same time quite clearly specifying in advance an agenda about what progressive views should be – regarding industrial agriculture, trade regimes and so on. This, as NGO players involved in the assessment admit, is a highly positioned mediation role, one that potentially carries much power and influence, and, with it, responsibility. In interviews, such individuals argue pragmatically: if we don't do it, no one will. They argue that the choice to engage was strategic, with the aim, as explained above, to use the assessment as a mobilization tool in the future; to help push forward positions that they hold dear. The sense that they were entering an open, deliberative space where rational negotiation of consensus would emerge was often far from their conception. This was a highly political setting, dominated by powerful groups, deploying powerful methods (such as scenario models) which can act to undermine alternatives, and they needed to mobilize to deploy some form of countervailing power.

Getting involved, and nominated as an author or reviewer, was critical. The nomination process which took place during 2004 was somewhat opaque, but, according to the guidelines, nominations from all key stakeholders – from government to industry to NGOs – were possible. With the first call for authors, PANNA in particular organized a wide appeal for people to get involved during mid-2004, both through list-serves and direct approaches, arguing that the assessment offered an important opportunity for civil society engagement and awareness-raising around issues of corporate control and agribusiness interests, as well as highlighting the potentials for more sustainable forms of agriculture. The review of the drafts was seen as another key juncture for a wider civil society engagement. The Greenpeace Bureau member sent out a request to a wide network in September 2006. In a widely circulated email, he comments:[8]

> The production of this first draft was, not surprisingly, a highly contentious endeavour, and in some cases chapter authors have not yet agreed on the contents or analyses put forth by co-authors. Thus you will find at this stage a mix of viewpoints, perspectives, arguments, assumptions and types of evidence put forth, as well as some contradictory findings, and a massive tension between the more conventional econometric, technocratic and production-oriented analyses, and those emphasizing environmental, social and political issues such as governance, equity, rights, ecosystem integrity and 'services', local and indigenous knowledge and rights, and the multi-functionality of agriculture.
>
> The primary objective of the first review is to identify main gaps, flaws and contradictions in analysis, lack of referral to key bodies of literature, and to critique the presentation of controversial issues (e.g. impacts of conventional agriculture; the role of transgenic biotechnology in achieving 'sustainability and equitable development' goals; the 'scientific' basis of policy formation (whose science, whose technology); the relevance of LEISA (low external input agriculture), organic and alternative agriculture; IPR (intellectual property rights), trade, investments, etc. We hope that reviewers will not hesitate to point out flaws in the draft (as well as any strengths), as this will be immensely helpful to those of us on the inside.

The issues around which there was an expectation that civil society groups would comment was clear – rights, governance, ecosystems, indigenous knowledge, organic/alternative agriculture, intellectual property, trade and so on. Through the Ag Assessment Watch site, PANNA, in a call for 'real reviewers', have provided a guide to how to respond, offering editorial suggestions as well as requests to provide more input on particular themes.[9]

In international assessment processes of this sort much of the hard work comes in the review and editing process. Here the minutiae of textual differences are discussed, and a particular wording and pitch are required. A (perhaps) apocryphal story suggested that the US government had employed a thousand people in the US Department of Agriculture and USAID to go through the final documents with a fine-tooth comb, picking up sections, paragraphs, even words which their negotiators would dispute in the final sessions before any text was agreed. Certainly US government employees were heavily involved in the external review process, often reflecting particular knowledge and interests. As for UN treaties and conventions, the diplomatic process of square-bracketed disagreement and free text agreement was followed.[10] Engagement at this level of detail was new for some of the NGO and activist participants, usually excluded from formal governmental negotiations, so they had to learn the tricks of the trade, and become involved in the fine detail. As one informant put it: 'Our work is unrecognisable in the final version. The odd bit here and there, but often not the meaning.'[11] Another countered: 'this is part of the reshuffling of understanding that is the positive outcome of multi-stakeholder dialogues and efforts to create something new together'.[12] The internal dynamics of author groups was critical, along with the capacity for effective, inclusive facilitation.

But to what degree does this sort of process allow for the 'injecting' of alternative, grassroots perspectives from farmers themselves? How does 'the local' get represented in 'the global'? And what kinds of knowledge politics emerge? In discussions with a variety of participants in the assessment, a number of themes were raised.[13] Everyone recognized that, because of the way the IAASTD was organized, 'real' farmers and their organizations did not really get a look in – whether at the early consultation stages in the regions (see Scoones 2008 for discussion of the Africa case) or subsequently. Some regarded this as a fundamental design flaw of the whole process, undermining the legitimacy of the effort as a whole; others saw it as a probably necessary consequence of convening such a process, but one which allowed space for representation by NGOs and other CSOs. For some this mediation role was not a problem: these were people who worked on the ground in different locations and so could reflect the concerns of farmers on the ground. Others saw the processes of intermediation and translation as problematic, as well as the claims made by NGOs to 'represent' others. Some industry and government participants, for example, claimed that GM crops were a concern to (Northern) NGOs, but not farmers from the global South.[14]

Participants also reflected on their own positionality – both as experts and citizens from particular places – and how their origins, ethnicity, gender and experience were intimately bound up with their contributions as experts. As one African author, a middle-class university lecturer in Zimbabwe, trained in the UK, but originally from a rural home in a farming area, observed: 'Yes, I am an economist, but I am also from Africa, and I am a woman. I have lived in these places, and experienced the life of farming in a dryland setting.'[15]

This explicit reflection on positioning was notably more evident among those I interviewed from Africa. They were after all involved in a regionally specific contribution which was by definition located. Others associated more with the global assessment and often Northern researchers from international organizations emphasized their contributions as experts with credentials – as an expert on crop, pests, forestry or soil and water conservation, for example. As one participant put it:

> Each of the authors are members of diverse networks, often reaching deep into truly 'local' communities, through previous field work experiences, and these were in my experience often mobilised to review particular paragraphs of draft text, clarify the key points of concern, highlight very local experiences and generally to raise within the process the issues of evidence, legitimacy and accountability. So do not underestimate the multiple flows of communication and representation at work![16]

Thus everyone acknowledges that their background and life experiences affect their contribution as an expert in such a process. Although often professing the importance of generalized, universal, global knowledge (say, of the impacts of climate change), no one I interviewed was very keen to accept the idea that they, as participants in the IAASTD, were a global citizen – certainly part of a globally linked epistemic community, a network based on a focus on shared expertise and contribution to a particular debate, but not strictly talked about in terms of citizenship.[17]

Thus in people's own experiences of the IAASTD there is a multiplication of identities, types of affiliation and forms of solidarity. A fragmented and contingent notion of citizenship is realized through such experiences – and the wider political action that this implies (see Leach and Scoones 2006). As Ellison argues, by dissolving the more conventional boundaries between the public and private, the political and social, and directing action to more diverse and dispersed sites and spaces, beyond the nation-state:

> 'citizenship' no longer conveys a universalist sense of inclusion or participation in a stable political community; neither does it suggest the possibility of developing claims organised around a relatively stable set of differences; nor, for that matter, can the term be made to conform easily

to the living out of a series of socially constructed identity positions on the decentred social subjects. Instead, we are left with a restless desire for social engagement, citizenship becoming a form of social and political practice born of the need to establish new solidarities across a range of putative 'communities' as a defence against social changes which continually threaten to frustrate such ambitions. (1997: 217)

Citizenship is thus redefined in more actor-oriented and performative terms, in effect as practised engagement through emergent social solidarities (Leach and Scoones 2005, 2006), ones that are offered opportunities to develop and form through engagement in an assessment process.

Many participants, of course, are quintessentially 'global', not easily located in one particular place and comfortable and accomplished across several spaces, even if they do not self-identify as 'global citizens'. For example, one of the co-chairs is an African, female scientist, educated in the USA, head of an African research/policy institute and highly well connected internationally (indeed, I have discussed this work three times with her – once in London, once in Falmer and once in Lewes). She is deeply committed to giving the perspectives of Africa a voice in the process, yet would never claim to be the legitimate voice of peasant Africa. Yet can such people, part of the international research and policy elite, from their acquired positions of power and authority offered through their qualifications and expertise, provide this, and how, in turn, is their input legitimized?

There is, of course, much politically correct talk associated with the IAASTD about Southern perspectives and involvement, but in practice the Southerners who get a look in are sometimes as elite – in their lifestyles, outlooks and influences – as many of their Northern counterparts. Does living behind razor wire in a smart suburb of Harare or Nairobi provide special access and insights? Or is this just another of many different 'lived citizenships' that are rather selectively added to the mix?

The aim was to involve a more diverse group of expertise than would be usual in a conventional approach, with a very conscious effort to be inclusive, but in the end it was deliberation on the basis of scientific evidence which would be the key. Interestingly, this is the view held both by 'mainstream' scientists and NGO representatives. For the former, 'good science' requires rigorous methodologies and systematic processes of international peer review, and the Assessment's design is very much in line with this thinking.

There was a strong commitment to the rigorous testing of evidence, and, following Habermas (1994), to the importance of building consensus through multi-stakeholder dialogue. Yet this is not to say that politics, values and moral positions were not discussed, often intensively, during author group meetings. Evidence had to be assessed in context, asking 'what type of expertise and evidence, having what voice?' This was an inevitably partial, political and value-laden exercise. Positionality and subjectivity are thus central to the assessment process, and with this come politics, values and judgements that go way beyond simple rational science and expertise, as discussed in Chapter 2 of the global report (IAASTD 2009).

Thus, in the discussion of the IAASTD, there is an interesting contradiction in the simultaneous talk of engagement and involvement of diverse, multi-stakeholder perspectives and its confrontation with the ideal of consensus and an appeal to a universalized objectivity of science and expertise: the ultimate global vision. This tension was often not addressed and resulted in some underlying challenges of knowledge politics and power relations not being confronted, and some major fudges resulting. Yet, in a more pragmatic tone, one participant commented:

> Perhaps for the first time, different constituencies had to wrestle with the evidence and experiences that inform a point of view. These could no longer be dismissed as simply differing ideologies or power gradients. We *all* had to put our trust in the IAASTD principles. The hard part was getting all contributors to be accountable to them.[18]

The politics of knowledge in global assessments

So, what does the IAASTD experience suggest for the wider debates about democracy and participation – and the wider themes of this book – in global arenas?

The IAASTD reports, as we have seen, like many others of a similar ilk, present the bringing together of diverse knowledges as largely unproblematic. The emphasis is on neutrality and objectivity. For example, the guidelines state, 'assessment reports should be neutral with respect to policy, and deal objectively with scientific, technical and socio-economic factors' (IAASTD 2003: Annex III, p. 7). But these assumptions are difficult to uphold under closer scrutiny. Further questions inevitably arise: whose expertise counts? How are cultural and institutional commitments brought into supposedly neutral expert statements and review processes? What overt and tacit routines legitimize and validate collective knowledge? What happens to other forms of knowledge and expertise – with different epistemological and ontological bases? These processes played out in different ways in different parts and at different moments in the assessment. Sometimes the knowledge encounters were productive and fruitful, challenging participants to reflect on assumptions and to include otherwise neglected perspectives. At other times, such engagements were less productive, being dominated by particular perspectives and interests.

While the explicit, formal design of the Assessment was rather blind to the questions of knowledge politics, in practice, in the author groups, the review process and the wider discussion around the Assessment, there was intense reflection on knowledge, its validity and the nature of expertise. As the examples discussed above have shown, contests over knowledge claims, and the framing of issues, have been very important. The end result allowed a plural set of perspectives to emerge, despite attempts to constrain the debates. This shows, at one level, a sensitivity of the process to such issues. But this was not explicitly part of the formal design, and a key lesson has been that such issues of knowledge framing need to be more centrally and explicitly considered from the start.

A key feature of such assessments is that they are in some way 'representative', investing as they do in large-scale – and very expensive – consultations. The IAASTD website makes great play of the diversity of actors involved, and the Secretariat includes a number of Southern researchers, activists and others. Clearly, simple forms of representation – direct or indirect – are impossible at a global level. But how do global processes of this sort gain legitimacy for what they do, and how are representatives and representation constructed, by the organization itself, its sponsors and the actors involved?

The formal process allows for representation by different groups according to strict quotas, with non-government and government, NGO and business all careful numerically balanced on the IAASTD Bureau, for example. As it is an intergovernmental process, representation is also via states, with 110 countries involved and thirty government representatives from all regions on the Bureau. And in the public review process, the web commentary facility allows anyone with access to the Internet to have their say. This means representation, and routes to influence the process, can happen via multiple routes. The NGO/civil society grouping, for example, has been very active in mobilizing participants, engaging in debate and tracking the process through a dedicated website. Equally, the US government invested substantial resources in the review process, persistently trying to get its view across and objecting to alternative framings.

The NGO/civil society grouping is seen by the conveners of the Assessment as a key route through which voices of poorer farmers across the global South can have a say, thus bringing wider legitimacy to the process and its outcomes. But this is an awkward intermediary, bridging position. Some NGO groups argue that, despite the fact that they have no formal mandate to represent 'poor farmers', this is a legitimate role, one based on solid experience and dialogue with people in the field. Yet this position clearly comes with much baggage. It is far from neutral. Indeed, there is a clear line on many issues, linked to some high-profile, strategic campaigning, something that critics see as more reflective of a middle-class, left-leaning, European/North American position than the legitimate voice of the masses. In the context of the IAASTD, whether on issues around GM crops or industrial agriculture, the position of some NGO groupings has been voluble and consistent, something not necessarily reflecting the diverse and often conflicting views of poorer farmers across the world.

In debates about the role of 'civil society' in political processes, this is of course a long-running, and probably irresolvable, discussion. As many commentators point out, in addition to questions about representation, there remain important tasks in encouraging transparency and carrying out monitoring and review of formal processes to generate systems of accountability in governance arrangements, particularly at the global level.

What does this mean for ideas of citizenship, and particularly global citizenship? In terms of the forms of engagement with the process, we can see at least three different forms of 'emergent solidarity' which might be termed 'citizenship' (cf. Ellison 1997; Leach and Scoones 2005). First, participants in the process have identified with their particular groupings. The NGO/civil society 'group' represents one set of transnational actors, operating across diverse networks. In this sense, they could be described as being part of a 'global civil society', and so perhaps global citizens. But this is not all. Often the same actors have engaged in other ways: as citizens more traditionally defined in relation to the nation-state; as experts, part of wider 'epistemic communities' and associations (Haas 1992); and as cyber-citizens, engaging as individuals or groups in Internet discussions and consultations. Are all these engagements the practices of 'global citizens', reflective of an emergent phenomenon of 'global citizenship'?

Informants were almost universally dismissive of such an idea. The vision of global cosmopolitanism was far from their perspective. They self-defined in different ways, sometimes in relation to their expertise, sometimes their ethnic origin (although often beyond a country level, to the level of a continent, at least for Africa) and sometimes as part of a movement or campaign (for sustainable agriculture, against GM crops and so on). Very often, of course, people identified across these categories, reflecting on how they would 'put different hats on' for different purposes. While recognizing the importance of engaging in global processes and the important influence they have on today's world, identities remained much more restricted, and very often hybrid and complex, rather than the apparently simple 'global' assignation (Schattle 2008).

A key challenge for democratic theory in an era of globalization is how collective perspectives, values and outcomes are negotiated across diverse cultural and institutional settings at an international level. Global assessments, such as the IAASTD, claim to do this through a process of expert assessment supported by stakeholder consultations. But how collective is the 'collective vision' that is exemplified in the final report? What have been the processes of exclusion, dissent and controversy that lie behind an expert-approved 'consensus'? What are the unwritten codes and practice that shape formal choices and decisions reflected in the final report? How have perspectives from particular places, including those drawing on more experiential knowledges, interacted with global ones, situated in particular centres of power?

As we have seen, the final global report, as well as the summary for decision-makers, has been at pains to include a diversity of views (IAASTD 2009). For some this is a 'lowest common denominator consensus – a twenty-four-hour wonder';[19] for others it is the result of effective inclusion, where controversies have been dealt with and compromise sought. Three styles of knowledge politics were ongoing simultaneously in the IAASTD (see Jasanoff 2005): 'the view from nowhere', dominated by 'objective', universalized facts and statistics, competed with 'the view from somewhere', based on particular, located experiences and case studies, and was mediated in turn by 'the view from everywhere', which tried to incorporate, combine and generate consensus through a complex representative stakeholder process, defined by governance structure and the writing and review procedures. Each of these styles of knowledge politics acts to include and exclude, creating winners and losers in the process. Those able to move between such approaches – arguing their case on the basis of formalized data at the same time as drawing legitimacy from particular settings and experiences – were those most able to make the case that theirs was the consensual 'view from everywhere'.

The complexity and intensity of the process added to the processes of exclusion too. Only those with the time and resources – and endless patience and attention to detail – were able to engage effectively to the end. While there were opportunities for linking those in expert mediating roles with broader communities, this was often in practice limited. As one African author explained: 'There is no money to do consultations. We are based here and try to reflect the situation, but we cannot go out and have discussions with farmers. We must look at the literature and find our way.'[20]

Indeed, it was often the practical difficulties of communicating and discussing under intensive deadlines which were the major constraint. As the African author put it: 'The time is too tight. The chapter draft comes, we have to revise it, and then we must go to the next meeting. My email was down for weeks here at the university so we are very behind on our chapter.'[21]

The elaborate governance structure and procedural arrangements for the preparation of the reports created a particular style of knowledge-making. This was centred on the principles of inclusion and deliberation, but within severely circumscribed limits. Again, such formality excluded some. A set of institutionalized routines allowed for the involvement of different interest groups or 'stakeholders'; each had particular representation on the decision-making body of the Bureau and each was supposed to have equivalent input into the expert-led report production and review process, garnering a procedural accountability and so, it was hoped, trust and confidence in the authority and legitimacy of the process. This structured form of representation thus aimed at global coverage, covering all bases and creating a comprehensive, all-encompassing approach to knowledge-making on the global scale.

But these formal arrangements were, of course, also complemented by more informal interactions and processes of alliance-building and lobbying. As discussed in relation to the NGO/civil society grouping (and no doubt replicated among governments and private sector 'interest groups'), there was much manoeuvring to gain access and influence. Peer-to-peer relationships within the Africa writing group too allowed more personal connections to be made, and informal networks to arise through the process, which often transcended the 'interest group' categorization of the governance structure to create forms of association around the regional, African position vis-à-vis the 'global' perspective.

This vision of multiple voices being heard in an open deliberative forum at the global level is certainly the ideal that many aspire to. In this sense, the IAASTD is seen as a potential for the realization of a global deliberative democratic institution that numerous theorists and commentators have argued for (Dryzek 2002). A key argument of the IAASTD is that, through engaging multiple stakeholders in an open debate about the future, an institutional form will develop, resulting in more robust frameworks for policy decision-making. This is an argument put forward by many involved in debates about institutional transformation, particularly when dealing with scientific debate and public controversy (Miller 2007).

The ideal is a 'reflexive institution' which is inclusive and deliberative and allows multiple, culturally embedded versions to be discussed, and a collective vision to be produced. It allows contrasting framings to be debated, and different political and value positions to be acknowledged. It also does not bury uncertainty, controversy or dissent, but makes these explicit in interrogating alternative options (Voss and Kemp 2006). This is a tough call, especially for disciplinary and professional orientations built on particular forms of certainty and expertise, and where ambiguity is threatening and admitting ignorance is unheard of.

Beyond the conceptual discussion of principles, discussion of what a 'reflexive institution' actually looks like is often vague, and certainly so at a global level. In many respects the IAASTD is seen by its proponents as an attempt at creating a reflexive institution, although not using this language. Many of the key design principles are there – inclusivity, openness, plurality of knowledges, and a commitment to democratic processes. But there have been notable limitations. These centre on two issues. First are the challenges of confronting uncertainty and controversy, and the expectation that these will be resolved by rational, objective, scientific debate among expert peers. Second – and related – is the obscuring of very real struggles over knowledge, politics and values in an attempt to construct the 'view from everywhere' by seeing this primarily in terms of representation of different interest groups. These two gaps, I would argue, have at times created a lack of reflexivity in the process; a lack of ability to reflect on positions, framings and politics, and so sometimes resulting in an inability to deal with the really tough issues and choices confronting the future of science and technology.

Conclusion

So what should be done? How can the politics of knowledge be made more explicit, and negotiations around politics and values be put centre-stage? How can we avoid black-boxing issues of uncertainty or more fundamental clashes over interpretation and meaning? And how can processes of participation and engagement become more meaningful, democratic and accountable?

These are, of course, big questions at the centre of debates about democratic theory, and at the core of the concerns of this book. As Chantal Mouffe (2005) argues in a critique of the recent arguments for deliberative forms of democratic practice, there is a need to 'bring politics back in'. In a withering attack on those who believe 'partisan conflicts are a thing of the past and consensus can now be obtained through dialogue' and the assumption that 'thanks to globalization and the universalization of liberal democracy, we can expect a cosmopolitan future', Mouffe challenges this 'post-political' position:

> Such an approach is profoundly mistaken and, instead of contributing to the 'democratization of democracy', it is at the origin of many of the problems that democratic institutions are currently facing. Notions such as 'partisan-free democracy', 'good governance', 'global civil society', 'cosmopolitan sovereignty', 'absolute democracy' – to quote only a few of the currently fashionable notions – all partake of a common anti-political vision which refuses to acknowledge the antagonistic dimension constitutive of 'the political'. Their aim is the establishment of a world 'beyond left and right', 'beyond hegemony', 'beyond sovereignty' and 'beyond antagonism'. Such a longing reveals a complete lack of understanding of what is at stake in democratic politics and of the dynamics of constitution of political identities and, as we shall see, it contributes to exacerbating the antagonistic potential existing in society. (Ibid.: 1–2)

It is this absence of an explicit attention to the political which has been perhaps the Achilles heel of the IAASTD. The formal assessment process did not confront controversy head on, even if the micro-processes in author groups and review interactions certainly did. No procedures or mechanisms appeared to exist to either expose or deal with such debates and divergent views. A lack of recognition of antagonistic politics – over knowledge, identity and the construction of futures – means that the cosmopolitan, deliberative ideal that the IAASTD presents as its model suppresses, diverts and bottles up such tensions; or at least relegates them to off-the-record debates within text-writing and reviewing groups rather than making such issues central and explicit. How can this be addressed?

On a practical level, a key lesson for the IAASTD – and similar assessment processes – is the urgent need to inject some systematic reflexivity into the process, involving all parties. This is an explicit way of meeting the challenge of Mouffe and others of ensuring that politics are central. As she argues:

> [...] the belief in the possibility of a universal, rational consensus has put democratic thinking on the wrong track. Instead of trying to design the institutions which, through supposedly 'impartial' procedures would reconcile conflicting interests and values, the task for democratic theorists and politicians should be to envisage the creation of a vibrant 'agonistic' public sphere of contestation where different hegemonic political projects can be confronted. (Ibid.: 3)

In focusing on the concept of 'reflexive institutions' and the governance processes they require, this chapter highlights the challenge of finding ways in which design elements can be introduced into the procedures and practices of assessments like the IAASTD so as to allow this type of explicit confrontation of politics, perspectives, values and interests. While the design of the process, its governance and institutional form, can be criticized for lack of reflexivity, the behind-the-scenes negotiations over framings, values and politics have, as we have seen, been heated and continuous. A key starting point, however, is to make the framing assumptions around diverse positions and knowledge claims more explicit: front of stage, not just backstage. This, of course, does not mean that the examination of scientific issues should not take place; instead such reflexivity hopefully results in increased rigour, avoiding the dangers of false, fudged 'consensus'. I would argue that opening up both the inputs and the outputs of the assessment process, including an acceptance that consensus and agreement may not be appropriate or desirable, can result in more effective, rigorous and more widely accepted outcomes. The IAASTD has been an ambitious attempt to create a forum for cross-stakeholder dialogue of a critical issue at the global level. It has inevitably been fraught and flawed, but there have been some important lessons learned, some of which have been highlighted by this chapter. The challenge for the future – as new, different issues emerge which require similar global responses – will be to develop new designs and processes that allow for even more effective, inclusive reflexive governance which builds firmly on these lessons.

Notes

1 Longer versions of this chapter appeared as Scoones 2008 and 2009. The chapter has been produced as part of the ongoing work of the Citizenship, Participation and Accountability Development Research Centre based at the Institute of Development Studies, University of Sussex. I would like to thank colleagues in the 'local–global' working group, together with Jan Aart Scholte, for feedback on earlier versions of this chapter, and Stephen Biggs, John Gaventa, Marcia Ishii-Eiteman,

Janice Jiggins, Beverly McIntyre, Erik Millstone, Marcelo Saguier and Rajesh Tandon, who provided detailed comments on different drafts. I would also particularly like to thank the many people who were involved in the IAASTD process in different capacities with whom I have held discussions over the last few years.

2 nobelprize.org/nobel_prizes/peace/laureates/2007/index.html, accessed July 2009.

3 www.agassessment-watch.org/docs/IAASTD_on_three_pages.pdf, accessed July 2009.

4 Global authors' meetings were held in Turkey (November 2005), Bangkok (May 2006), Costa Rica (November 2006) and Cape Town (June 2007). Africa report meetings were held in Nairobi (January 2006), Dakar (June 2006), Addis Ababa (November 2006) and Cape Town (June 2007).

5 The formal hosts are the Food and Agriculture Organization, GEF (Global Environment Facility), United Nations Development Programme, United Nations Environment Programme, United Nations Educational Scientific and Cultural Organization, the World Bank and the World Health Organization. The UK Department for International Development is a significant backer of the assessment.

6 See www.agassessment.org, accessed July 2009.

7 www.panna.org/resources/gpc/gpc_200508.15.2.13.dv.html, accessed July 2009.

8 Call to review major UN assessment of agriculture (IAASTD). From: 'Benedikt Haerlin', haerlin zs-l.de. To: review agassessment-watch.org.

9 See also Pesticide Action Network North America (2006), 'A road map for reviewers: a detailed outline of selected chapters of the first draft of the Global Report of the IAASTD, with commentary and unofficial notes provided in italics by Emily Adams and Medha Chandra', San Francisco; and IAASTD-Watch, 'Why and how to review the draft Assessment. Call for real experts: some advice on why and how to review the 2nd draft of the IAASTD. Why do reviews matter? What will happen to comments that are submitted?', www.agassessment-watch.org/review.html?Page=Bureau&ItemID=7, accessed 20 July 2009.

10 In UN negotiations, for example, square brackets enclose text which is still being negotiated.

11 Interview, Zimbabwe, 2007.

12 Personal communication, August 2008.

13 See the thoughtful commentary on the fraught knowledge politics at play by IAASTD insider Janice Jiggins (Jiggins 2008).

14 In making such claims, of course, these commentators were offering an unreflective, alternative intermediary position, suggesting that their views were 'better' representations of developing-world farmers than those of NGOs.

15 Interview, Zimbabwe, 2006.

16 Personal communication, August 2008.

17 Although some commented that such an 'emergent solidarity' was increasingly evident among a subset of IAASTD participants by the time of the final plenary in Johannesburg.

18 Personal communication, August 2008.

19 Interview, Austria, April 2008.

20 Interview, university researcher, Zimbabwe, 2007.

21 Ibid.

References

Archibugi, D. (2008) *The Global Commonwealth of Citizens: Toward Cosmopolitan Democracy*, Princeton, NJ: Princeton University Press.

Dryzek, J. (2002) *Deliberative Democracy and Beyond: Deliberative Democracy*, Oxford: Oxford University Press.

Edwards, M. and J. Gaventa (eds) (2001) *Global Citizen Action*, Boulder, CO: Lynne Rienner.

Ellison, N. (1997) 'Towards a new social politics: citizenship and reflexivity in late modernity', *Sociology*, 31(4): 697–717.

Fischer, F. (2000) *Citizens, Experts and the Environment: The Politics of Local Knowledge*, Durham, NC: Duke University Press.

Haas, P. (1992) 'Epistemic communities and international policy coordination: introduction', *International Organization*, 46.

Habermas, J. (1994) *The Theory of Communicative Action: Reason and the Rationalization of Society*, Boston, MA: Beacon Press.

Heater, D. (2002) *World Citizenship: Cosmopolitan Thinking and Its Opponents*, London: Continuum.

Held, D. and A. McGrew (eds) (2002) *Governing Globalization: Power, Authority and Global Governance*, Cambridge: Polity Press.

IAASTD (2003) 'An assessment of agricultural science and technology for development. The final report of the steering committee for the Consultative Process on Agricultural Science and Technology', www.farmingsolutions.org/pdfdb/annexI-III.pdf, accessed 20 July 2009.

— (2009) *Agriculture at a Crossroads. The Global Report International Assessment of Agricultural Knowledge, Science, and Technology*, Washington, DC: Island Press.

Ishii-Eiteman, M. (2005) *The IAASTD: Advances and Challenges for Civil Society*, www.panna.org/resources/gpc/gpc_200508.15.2.13.dv.html, accessed 20 July 2009.

Jasanoff, S. (2005) *Designs on Nature. Science and Democracy in Europe and the US*, Princeton, NJ: Princeton University Press.

Jasanoff, S. and M. Martello (2004) 'Introduction: globalization and environmental politics', in S. Jasanoff and M. Martello (eds), *Earthly Politics: Local and Global in Environmental Governance*, Cambridge, MA: MIT Press.

Jiggins, J. (2008) 'Bridging gulfs to feed the world', New Scientist, 5 April, www.panna.org/files/Comment_%20Bridging%20gulfs%20to%20feed%20the%20world%20-%20opinion%20-%2005%20April%202008%20-%20Print%20Article%20-%20New%20Scientist.pdf, accessed July 2009.

Keane, J. (2003) *Global Civil Society?*, Cambridge: Cambridge University Press.

Leach, M. and I. Scoones (2005) 'Science and citizenship in a global context', in M. Leach, I. Scoones and B. Wynne (eds), *Science and Citizens: Globalization and the Challenge of Engagement*, London: Zed Books.

— (2006) 'Mobilising citizens: social movements and the politics of knowledge', IDS Working Paper no. 276, Institute of Development Studies, Brighton.

Miller, C. (2007) 'Democratization, international knowledge institutions and global governance', *Governance*, 20(2): 325–57.

Mouffe, C. (2005) *On the Political*, London: Routledge.

Schattle, H. (2008) *The Practices of Global Citizenship*, Lanham, MD: Rowman and Littlefield.

Scoones, I. (2008) 'Global engagements with global assessments: the case of the International Assessment of Agricultural Knowledge, Science and Technology for Development (IAASTD)', IDS Working Paper no. 313, Institute of Development Studies, Brighton.

— (2009) 'The politics of global assessments: the case of the International Assessment of Agricultural Knowledge, Science and Technology for Development', *Journal of Peasant Studies*, 36(3): 547–57 (http://dx.doi.org/10.1080/03066150903155008)

Tarrow, S. (1994) *Power in Movement*, Cambridge: Cambridge University Press.

Voss, J. and R. Kemp (eds) (2006) *Sustainability and Reflexive Governance*, Cheltenham: Edward Elgar.

PART THREE

From local to global: the dynamics of transnational citizen action

6 · Campaigns for land and citizenship rights: the dynamics of transnational agrarian movements[1]

SATURNINO M. BORRAS AND
JENNIFER C. FRANCO

Introduction

During the past two decades nation-states in the South have been greatly transformed by a triple squeeze, namely: 'from above' through globalization, with some regulatory powers being ceded to international regulatory institutions; 'from below', through the partial decentralization of political, fiscal and administrative powers to local counterparts; and 'from the sides', through the privatization of some functions (Fox 2001). Central states remain important, albeit transformed, players in local, national and international politics and economics (Keohane and Nye 2000).

The changing international, national and local institutions that structure the rules under which poor people assimilate into or resist the corporate-controlled global politics and economics have presented both threats and opportunities to the world's rural population. This has encouraged and provoked national rural social movements to further localize (in response to state decentralization), and at the same time to internationalize (in response to globalization) their movements, advocacy and lobbying work, and collective actions, while holding on to their national characters. One result of this adjustment is the emergence of more horizontal, 'polycentric' rural social movements that at the same time struggle to construct coherent structures for greater vertical integration. The seemingly contradictory political directions of globalization and decentralization are thus also transforming the political-organizational processes of rural social movements.

Meanwhile, the nature of land rights and the location, power and authority of the institutions governing them have altered during the past decades. Since the Mexican Revolution ushered in the modern era of redistributive land reform in 1910, subsequent land reforms have followed many trajectories. But two broad paths were dominant: capitalist-oriented, with small family farming as an important component, and socialist-oriented, with collective and state farms as a key feature. The Cold War era led to a sharp divide between these two models, eventually drawing bilateral and multilateral development agencies to the land issue. The United States Agency for International Development (USAID), partly through the Alliance for Progress, was perhaps the most prominent of all agencies promoting a pre-emptive type of land reform across the world, aimed at containing the spread of communism. By the late 1970s USAID had started to carry out the earliest relatively coherent experiments in what would later become known as 'market-led agrarian reform'. This period also witnessed an aggressive role by the World Bank on the same pre-emptive land reforms, but also in private land titling programmes.

Amid talk about the demise of land reform, and with peasant-based national liberation movements still active in many parts of the world, the UN's Food and Agriculture Organization (FAO) convened the World Conference on Agrarian Reform and Rural Development (WCARRD) in 1979, hoping to widen the agenda. Conventional redistributive land reform, to be achieved through central government policy and emphasizing the significant role of small family farms, was among the key elements of the WCARRD Declaration, but this turned out to mark the beginning of the end of redistributive land reform. Aside from a handful of scattered land reform initiatives, the 1980s witnessed the fading out of land reform from global and national development policies.

The failure of structural adjustment programmes forced mainstream economists to think again about the productive assets of the rural poor, and land was resurrected in development discourses in the 1990s. Advocacy during this decade and onwards was marked by calls for privatization of collective and state farms in ex-socialist countries, promotion of decentralized non-state management of (forest) land resources, and the invention and subsequent promotion of market-led agrarian reform, based on the principle of land market dynamics and a 'willing seller–willing buyer' formula. Bilateral and multilateral development agencies also started to pay serious attention to land policies.

From 2003 to 2008, all bilateral and multilateral development agencies formulated their own distinct policies on land, gravitating around market-oriented frameworks inspired by new institutional economics. Meanwhile, from the mid-1990s onwards, scattered but dramatic land struggles have also occurred. These struggles were subsequently internalized by transnational agrarian movements, such as Vía Campesina, which later, in the 1990s, would emerge to become important global political actors. These 'initiatives from above' by international agencies and 'actions from below' by agrarian movements were largely responsible for the FAO convening a second global conference, the International Conference on Agrarian Reform and Rural Development (ICARRD), held in 2006 in Brazil. During the latter part of this period, while agrarian movements were actively mobilizing on the local and national scenes, they also frequently started to systematically extend their actions into the global terrain. Multilateral and bilateral agencies have taken a wide and coherent interest in land policies, and have intervened in them, pushing for non-state, market-driven and decentralized approaches to land reform. These contradictory currents have brought various actors together at different levels of the policy arena, resulting in both clashes and alliances.

It remains to be seen whether or not ICARRD will, like WCARRD, turn out to signal the end of another period of land policy reformism. But the post-2006 terrain seems to be less favourable to redistributive land policies. The promotion of market-oriented land policies and the recent food and fuel crisis may prove to be an explosive combination, possibly resulting in massive dispossession of the rural poor worldwide. National governments and transnational companies are currently hunting for land in the South that can be 'captured' to produce food and biofuel for export. Whether or not such efforts are successful will depend, in part, on existing land policies. Settings that have witnessed significant promotion of market-oriented land policies are likely to be where such far-reaching changes in land use and property control will happen. But political contestations around the global land grab have occurred, and will occur, at the local, national and transnational levels.

Understanding the dynamics of transnational agrarian movements (TAMs) and their struggles for land and citizenship rights requires an interrelated analysis of several actors, factors and dimensions in transnational politics. The rest of this chapter is organized around these issues, with a particular focus on one TAM, Vía Campesina, and analysis of its global campaign against neoliberal land reform.

The emergence of transnational agrarian movements (TAMs)

Transnational networks and social movements are not new. Several transnational agrarian movements, organizations, networks or coalitions, of varying size, sectoral focus, ideological provenance and political orientation, have existed in the past. Among the oldest remaining groups is the International Federation of Agricultural Producers (IFAP), founded in 1946 by farmers' associations mainly from developed countries. IFAP has become the mainstream agricultural organization, claiming and making official representations to (inter)governmental agencies and on agribusiness circuits. While not an economically homogeneous network, its politics do tend to be dominated by its economically and financially powerful members (Edelman 2003). On most, but not all, occasions it has thus seen neoliberalism as an opportunity, and so essentially supports such policies, while advocating some operational and administrative revisions (Desmarais 2007).

By contrast, Vía Campesina, an international movement of poor peasants and small farmers from the global South and North, was formally established in 1993 as a critical response to neoliberal globalization, which was perceived by many rural groups as a grave threat to their livelihoods. Today, this movement unites close to two hundred national and sub-national organizations from Latin America, North America, Asia, the Caribbean, Africa and Europe, advocating pro-poor, sustainable, rights-based and democratic rural development. An ideologically autonomous and pluralist coalition, it is both an actor and an arena of action (Borras 2004). Claiming popular global representation, Vía Campesina has lately emerged as a major actor in popular transnational struggles against neoliberalism, demanding accountability from (inter)governmental agencies, rejecting neoliberal land policies, and resisting and opposing corporate control over natural resources and technology. Vía Campesina's main agenda is to defeat the forces of neoliberalism and to develop an alternative. It adopts a confrontational stance towards international financial institutions, aiming to delegitimize them and decrease their influence, and refusing to engage in dialogue or consultative processes with them. Vía Campesina has thus emerged as an important alternative voice of poor peasants and small farmers, largely but not yet completely eroding the traditional hegemonic claim of IFAP.

At the same time, Vía Campesina has emerged as an important arena of action, debate and exchange between different national and sub-national peasant and farmers' groups. Put differently, it is an institutional space itself. It is this dual character – as both a single actor and an arena of action – which has made Vía Campesina an important institution of and for national and local peasant movements, and a complex entity for other transnational social movements, NGO networks and international agencies to comprehend and deal with.

As (inter)governmental institutions have been increasingly involved in actually framing, funding and pursuing land policy frameworks, agendas and strategies that have direct influence on national and local land policies, these agencies in turn become targets for transnational campaigns by poor peasants in the global South. As 'rights holders' (poor peasants) have tried to hold the 'duty bearers' (national governments) accountable for land policies, the dynamics of citizenship have necessarily been extended to a global terrain.

Vía Campesina's global campaign for agrarian reform has contributed to the creation of a new 'citizenship space', defining 'space' as an institutional process, venue or arena. Agrarian movements affiliated with Vía Campesina have created and occupied a distinct space for poor peasants and small farmers, within and through which Vía Campesina processes and aggregates the various perspectives and positions of its members, which it represents as it engages with other non-state actors working around global land issues, and interacts with (inter)governmental institutions linked to international land policy-making dynamics.[2] This is a 'citizenship space' because when using such a venue, Vía Campesina activists are politically conscious of their 'rights' as citizens, they use this arena to hold accountable institutions they perceive to be 'duty bearers'. What existed prior to this new citizenship space were institutional spaces used by NGOs and relatively well-off farmers – often claiming they were acting on behalf of poor peasants. Vía Campesina's new citizen space is distinct: created, occupied and used by and for poor peasants, different and separate from previous spaces. This distinct space and the assertion of its autonomy were completely unthinkable until the mid-1990s, yet now that autonomy is generally respected by a wide range of state and non-state global actors.

Aspiring to neither 'sink' nor 'float', the campaign opposing neoliberal market-led approaches in the land policies promoted by (inter)governmental institutions involves verticalizing action (Fox 2001; Edwards and Gaventa 2001) by connecting local, national and international groups. It uses a combination of strategies: 'exposing and opposing' neoliberal land policies and the institutions that promote them (principally the World Bank) and using strategic 'tactical alliances', with friendly institutions or groups within these institutions.[3] The venues are international conferences, workshops and meetings as well as electronic discussions, and the campaign platform is a combination of demands to drop neoliberal land policies, and to adopt an alternative vision. The main forms of action in the campaign include protests in international venues, participation in some official conferences, and non-participation in others, combined with continuing land-related actions 'from below' in national and local settings.

Vía Campesina's transnational land reform campaign has become an important political process through which various groups representing rural citizens from different local and national settings in the world have tried to resist neoliberal land policies imposed on them, demanded accountability in (inter)governmental land policy-making processes, defined and accorded their own interpretation of the meaning of land and land reform, and begun forging an alternative vision. For this reason, the campaign deserves closer examination. We now turn to doing just this. Our analysis revolves around four broadly distinct but interrelated areas of enquiry, namely the nature of the state, the politics of mobilization, the politics of intermediation, and knowledge politics. A view from the Philippines on every theme discussed below will be made in order to give a concrete illustration of the vertical alignment of movements involved in this campaign.

The nature of the state

The kind of land policy favoured in mainstream development today is different from the concept of redistributive land reform. This can be seen in at least three ways. First, numerous and diverse international development institutions are directly involved in land policy-making today, and other activities they support, such as 'access to justice' reforms, have an indirect impact on the land question (Franco 2008a). Despite the fantastic diversity of reasons and motivations behind the recent land policy revival, the dominant thinking within the mainstream institutions has revolved around the continuing search for the most economically efficient use and allocation of land resources. Thus, land property rights formalization projects, land registration and titling, land administration, and market-led land reforms clearly predominate.

Second, a complementary advocacy by these institutions involves the push for localized and decentralized approaches to land policy-making. This bias is based on the assumption that land policies tied to national governments are bound to fail owing to the inherently corrupt and distant character of the latter.

Third, the push by international institutions to 'go local' is linked to their advocacy of non-state, privatized transactions around land resources. The key policies here include eliminating restrictions on dynamic private sales and rental transactions in land (such as land size ceiling laws), promoting share tenancy arrangements, and 'willing seller–willing buyer' land sales transactions. Civil society groups are encouraged to take part in these privatized transactions by becoming private service providers, together with commercial banks, to local peasant groups involved in the process.

The Philippine experience fits perfectly the classic case of transformation of a nation-state in the era of neoliberal globalization. Recent years have seen the promotion of market-friendly land transfer schemes, formalization of land property rights, localized land titling and administration, and 'territorial restructuring' amid intensified promotion of extractive industries, especially mining, and preparations for large-scale cultivation of fuel and food crops, mainly for export to China. These policies are matched by pressures to eliminate legal prohibitions in land sales and rental activities, and the existing land size ceiling law, which is the spirit of the Comprehensive Agrarian Reform Programme, on which a large-scale redistribution of land was based between 1992 and 2001 (Franco 2008b). Such developments reveal the strong orientation of global institutions to eschew any engagement with the central state, except on the particular policy processes that attempt to limit it, while pushing localized actions and more privatized transactions. In the Philippines, neoliberal advocacy for downsizing central government means the promotion of land policies that privatize and decentralize the land policy process, the passage of laws geared towards substantially limiting the role of the central state, and the non-passage of laws that promote the central state's role in redistributive public policies (Borras et al. 2007). Despite this advocacy, the central Philippine state still remains a key actor in land policies. Meanwhile, the institutional spaces available for landless and land-poor rural citizens' engagement in inter-civil society and civil society–state interactions, as well as those interactions themselves, have become much more complex as a result of this changing context and terrain around land issues.

Fox's (2001: 2) explanation using the metaphor of squeezing a balloon is very useful in describing the situation:

> When one criticizes a state government agency, it is very easy for them to pass the buck, by blaming the federal government above, or the municipal governments below them [...] So who's got the ball here? This dilemma for civil society organizations is deepened by the lack of transparency at *all* levels of 'public' decision-making and policy implementation.

Civil society campaigns that are more vertically integrated have become a necessity. Yet connecting with other campaigners outside one's own local community has always been difficult for rural citizens for a combination of reasons, including geographic isolation, high costs of communication and transportation, lack of alternative information, and so on. One can imagine how these factors become even more problematic when crossing national borders. With globalization, however, the challenges in this regard have lessened dramatically for most people and groups, including those in the rural areas. In many instances, previously inaccessible and inhospitable 'spaces' have been opening up, enabling interested groups to undertake vertical networking and advocacy. Such changes have contributed to the emergence of new collective identities (e.g. 'global/land') among rural citizens, in addition to existing ones ('national/land'). Rural citizens have increasingly begun to invoke perceived citizenship rights at multiple levels. The process of claiming and exercising citizenship in this changed multilevel terrain, and the emergence of new identities and channels of solidarity, can be seen from a number of broadly distinct but interrelated perspectives – namely, the politics of mobilization, the politics of intermediation, and knowledge politics.

The politics of mobilization

Earlier discussions about nation-state actors and trends in global policy-making processes are key aspects of changing political opportunity structure (Tarrow 1994, 2005). Moreover, such political opportunities do not exist in isolation from the existing social relations in which claim-makers are embedded. Therefore, while it is critical to look at the (re)alignments of various relevant actors in examining the politics of mobilization, it is also relevant to look at their location in social relations. In this section, we will focus our discussion on some dimensions of political opportunity structure, through looking at Vía Campesina's internal politics and its external relationships with both rival and fraternal networks and organizations.

Vía Campesina and rival networks As mentioned earlier, institutional space for rural citizen engagement at the global level was previously dominated by IFAP, rooted in developed countries. Many of IFAP's members in developing countries are organizations that, while perhaps claiming to represent 'poor farmers', in reality are based mainly among middle-income and rich farmers and led by middle-class and agribusiness-minded entrepreneurs. It is perhaps for this reason that IFAP never really advocated for land reform despite its claim to represent the interest of the world's 'rural poor'. Owing to its dominant class base, IFAP's politics has tended to be relatively conservative.

In the Philippines, historically, two organizations held membership in IFAP – namely, Sanduguan and the Federation of Free Farmers (FFF). Sanduguan, a national coalition of larger farmers based in the rice sector, was founded by well-off middle-class professionals and agribusiness and rural banking executives. Its main agenda has been to gain more state support services for production and trading activities, to push the state into providing a better playing field in the rice trade, and to lobby the national government to enable its direct participation in import and export transactions. FFF, founded by a lawyer from a wealthy landowning family, emerged in the 1950s out of a national campaign for a liberal redistributive land reform, aimed partly at preventing a more radical reform (Putzel 1992). But while it began as a conservative organization, FFF split in the early 1970s, with a radicalized section leaving. What remained were politically conservative leaders and pockets of community organizations with concerns similar to those of Sanduguan. Perhaps for historical reasons, though, FFF leadership at times still pays lip-service to land reform issues.

During the 1990s, perhaps in response to Vía Campesina's growing strength at the international level, IFAP started to actively seek more members in developing countries, in the Philippines recruiting a moderate farmers' association, Pambansang Katipunan ng mga Samahang Magsasaka (PAKISAMA, National Council of Farmers' Associations). Coming from a broad social- and Christian-democratic tradition, PAKISAMA was founded in the mid-1980s to engage the government on the land reform issue using moderate forms of action. After a major land reform campaign in 1996, PAKISAMA shifted its focus to lobbying on agricultural productivity issues, and eventually formalized its membership in IFAP. PAKISAMA's land reform campaign was taken up by a new group, Task Force Mapalad, which employs relatively more radical forms of action, but has a limited geographic base.[4]

During the same period, IFAP started to at least formally and nominally get involved in land reform and land policy issues. This coincided with the start of a separate global initiative around land policy advocacy, the International Land Coalition (ILC). ILC is a global alliance of international financial institutions – e.g. the International Fund for Agricultural Development (IFAD) and the World Bank – intergovernmental institutions – the European Union, the FAO – and several NGOs. It is led by middle-class professionals based in a global secretariat housed at and partly funded by the IFAD in Rome. The ILC's politics has been erratic, ranging from voicing support for the World Bank's 2003 land policy (in contrast to Vía Campesina's strident criticism), to more recently starting to become an open venue for policy discussion by various groups. It does not represent any significant movements of landless peasants and rural labourers. ILC has now become, like IFAP, an important network working around land issues, but with perspectives and orientation significantly different from those of Vía Campesina.

127

In the Philippines, ILC's member, the Asian NGO Coalition (ANGOC), which has historically been led by Filipinos and headquartered in the Philippines, is also a key pillar in the global coalition. It is the main social-democratic coalition of rural NGOs in the Philippines, and PAKISAMA is its peasant base. Consequently, ANGOC has not had any actual land-related campaign in the Philippines since PAKISAMA shifted its focus to productivity issues. As a result, like IFAP, ILC is left without any connection to actual land-related campaigns in the Philippines.

In short, IFAP and ILC are high-profile, important and overlapping groups that claim global representation of the rural poor. Yet the reality is more complicated. Given the class identity of its mass base, IFAP does not have any direct or inherent interest in mobilizing for redistributive land reform; similarly, the ILC does not have any significant base among agrarian movements. Hence, neither global network can be said to directly represent the social classes that have the keenest material interest in land reform in the Philippines, namely landless peasantry and rural labourers.

Various movements within Vía Campesina By contrast, Vía Campesina is highly heterogeneous in terms of the class composition of its mass base. This includes landless peasants and rural labourers, mainly in Latin America and Asia but some in Africa; small and part-time farmers located in western Europe, North America, Japan and South Korea; a small but influential group of emerging small family farms created through successful partial land reforms, such as those in Brazil and Mexico; and a middle-to-rich farmers' movement in Karnataka, India.

The organizations from the Latin American and Asian sections are perhaps among the most vocal groups within Vía Campesina. They can easily claim to represent the most economically vulnerable and exploited groups among Vía Campesina's mass base; indeed, they cultivate an image of severe exploitation and make loud calls for social justice. Representatives from Brazil and Honduras have held critical leadership positions and exercised great influence within the global movement. While Asian networks are important in their own right, they are not as cohesive or powerful as the solid Latin American continental block, for reasons including extreme linguistic diversity and serious ideological differences. Nonetheless, together, the Latin American and Asian landless peasant and rural workers' movements were the main force behind the push for Vía Campesina to identify land reform as a strategic issue.

In the Philippines, three movements are connected to Vía Campesina, but in varying ways. All have a mass base, or at least formal claims to one, among the landless peasants and rural labourers. The first is Kilusang Magbubukid ng Pilipinas (KMP, Peasant Movement of the Philippines), a Maoist-inspired peasant organization whose ideological position on land reform gives premium to workers and campaigning for land nationalization (Putzel 1995). The second is the Democratic KMP (DKMP), which broke away from KMP in 1993 owing to ideological and political differences, taking a more populist position on land reform, and advocating for the cause of small family farms. But largely because of personality differences among its key leaders, DKMP ultimately failed to rally and consolidate its forces, which comprised the greater part of the mass base that had broken away from KMP in the early 1990s. By the second half of the 1990s, it had shrunk to a handful of peasant leaders and pockets of rice farmers in Central Luzon. Both KMP and DKMP remain official members of Vía Campesina, although KMP has fallen from grace within the movement in recent years, partly for ideological reasons (Borras 2008). As a result, one finds an ironic situation where one organization with a relatively significant mass base (KMP) has been politically marginalized within *Vía Campesina*, while another member organization without any significant mass base (DKMP) has been mainstreamed.

This becomes even more ironic when we consider the third group. A large chunk of the peasant movement that broke away from KMP did not find it conducive to rally under the banner of the DKMP, eventually regrouping as an umbrella organization, Pambansang Ugnayan ng Nagsasariling Lokal na mga Samahang Mamamayan sa Kanayunan (UNORKA, National Coordination of Autonomous Local Rural People's Organizations). Formalized only in 2000, UNORKA quickly became the largest group directly engaged in land reform in the Philippines, with its roots in nearly eight hundred agrarian disputes across the country. Its mass base is mainly among the landless peasants and rural labourers. UNORKA uses the state land reform law as the institutional context for its campaigns (Franco 2008b). Its ideological position on land tends to the eclectic: while taking a populist stance advocating for small family farms, it also has significant base among and advocates for rural workers at the intersection of trade union and agrarian issues. UNORKA would like to join Vía Campesina and the latter would like to take UNORKA in, but KMP objects. And because of a Vía Campesina organizational rule that allows existing members to veto any applicant from its own country, UNORKA's entry remains blocked. Recently, however, and despite KMP's objections, Vía Campesina has begun inviting UNORKA to important global gatherings – as an observer.[5]

Vía Campesina and other fraternal movements Fraternal relations within Vía Campesina are primarily defined along the lines of agrarian populism: 'peasant community' versus 'outsiders', and 'them' versus 'us'. Solidarity channels have been quickly forged between different classes of the rural poor – peasants, small farmers, fisherfolk and indigenous peoples – and discussions about land policy have broadened under the influence of this diversity in alternative civil society groups. Other land-related issues, such as indigenous peoples' rights and crises in food and energy, emerged as important. By 2006, the ranks of rural grassroots groups calling for progressive and pro-poor land policies had become far broader than Vía Campesina.

Perhaps this emergence of a broader fraternal global network of movements also helped instigate rethinking within Vía Campesina. The broader network, of which Vía Campesina is a member, is the International Planning Committee for Food Sovereignty (IPC). It is an ideologically, politically and organizationally broad network composed of some five hundred rural-oriented organizations worldwide, including rural social movements and NGOs, and was formed during the World Food Summit in Rome in 1996. Vía Campesina is a key pillar of the IPC, which also includes groups like IFAP and numerous ILC members. The IPC became more actively involved in land issues during the build-up to the ICARRD in 2006, during which it served as the anchor of the NGO parallel forum. It was during this process that the issues of other grassroots sectors linked to land were loudly and systematically brought to the surface, by pastoralists, nomads, indigenous peoples and subsistence fisherfolk, among others. The activation of the IPC in land issues also meant the ideological diversification of this political space.

The IPC's rise has broadened the conventional framing of land reform issues, transforming it into an interpretation that is based on the actual diversity of concrete conditions and the location of various groups in existing agrarian structures. Whether IPC will take on the more militant orientation of Vía Campesina, however, or sink politically to its highest common factor, remains to be seen. But one thing is certain: Vía Campesina's inclusion and participation in the IPC significantly politicize this particular space in an interactive way – perhaps transforming both the IPC and Vía Campesina.

The politics of intermediation

The politics of intermediation related to Vía Campesina can be seen from two broad perspectives: interactions within civil society, and interaction between civil society and (inter)governmental institutions.

Interactions within civil society Before Vía Campesina emerged, the global civil society space was cornered by IFAP and the NGO community, which is highly differentiated. In progressive circles, intermediary NGOs were seen to represent, and spoke on behalf of, the rural poor in global venues, and they came to mediate the representation and engagement of rural populations in global governance institutions and processes. Predictably, Vía Campesina started to question this situation, and not without basis (Borras 2009), arguing that only movements of the landless peasants and rural labourers could, or should, represent rural populations in international fora. Drawing this line was not then, and still is not, an easy task. In the aftermath of this confrontation, Vía Campesina has been able to carve out its own space internationally and occupy it.

Vía Campesina's emergence as a distinct voice and direct representative of landless peasants and small farmers has profoundly transformed the transnational civil society arena and global development and democratization agendas. Advocating for, creating and occupying a distinct citizenship space for poor peasants and small farmers – a space that did not exist before – the transnational agrarian movement has become the main intermediary between various local–national movements of the landless peasants and small farmers, replacing IFAP and the NGO community. Some NGOs resent the entry of Vía Campesina and have refused to back down; others have since tried to redefine themselves. Pre-existing groups have simply persisted in their own spaces, which sometimes overlap with Vía Campesina. IFAD's Farmer's Forum is an example of such a space: Vía Campesina succeeded in inserting itself, without dislodging the earlier occupants.

The relative share of each key civil society actor in the global governance terrain has not shrunk as a result of Vía Campesina's emergence. It was not a zero-sum but, rather, a positive-sum process: the space created and occupied by various civil society groups was expanded, broadening the democratizing impact on global policy-making processes. Moreover, not only was the space expanded with the entry of Vía Campesina, it was also rendered much more complex in an enriching way, with the subsequent creation of various layers of sub-spaces made up of new interactions between various civil society groups: between movements of poor peasants and small farmers and NGOs, intergovernmental institutions, funding agencies, research think tanks, and so on. These sub-spaces are important democratic blocks because they help facilitate multiple processes of issue-framing, demand-making and representation dynamics. Vía Campesina has been quite conscious of the spaces it has created and occupied, and puts a premium on alliances with politically like-minded social movements.

It is on the land struggle front that the transnational coalition's most solid alliance with an NGO network has been achieved. Over the past five years, Vía Campesina has built an alliance with the Foodfirst Information and Action Network (FIAN), a human rights NGO global network. FIAN is organized into country sections, with individual members coming from activist and human rights NGOs, people's organizations and academia, to struggle for the promotion of the right to food, a right which in turn requires the right to control over productive assets, especially land. In 1999, FIAN and Vía Campesina agreed to undertake a joint international campaign on land reform, the Global Campaign for Agrarian Reform. Since then, FIAN has steadily emerged as an important player in the global policy debate over neoliberal land policies and the promotion of a rights-based approach to land reform. A relatively high degree of mutual trust has been established between the two networks, notwithstanding some birth pains and persistent tensions. A global network of researchers later joined the initiative, and the three networks now formally constitute the Global Campaign for Agrarian Reform (Vía Campesina 2000).

Interaction between civil society and (inter)governmental institutions In dealing with (inter)governmental institutions, Vía Campesina has been quite skilful in combining 'expose and oppose' mobilizations, negotiation and critical collaboration tactics (Vía Campesina 2004). Internationalizing collective actions is not easy. The search for the most appropriate and effective tactics and forms of action depends on the nature of the particular global institution. In general, Vía Campesina tends to favour the UN system, which adheres to a one country, one vote representation mechanism; and they tend to be open to relating constructively with some of the other institutions with this kind of institutional representation, such as the FAO and IFAD, where serious efforts have been made to forge and consolidate an alliance with progressive and supportive top officials at the Policy Division, thereby partly directly challenging the traditional hegemony of ILC in this institution. Keen to preserve its autonomy, while facing limitations in logistical and human resources, Vía Campesina has maintained a degree of openness in working with some UN system organizations, but has yet to actually develop this front.

Meanwhile, it necessarily takes a confrontational stance against international financial institutions, including the World Bank, that are controlled by major capitalist countries, viewing them as the cause of, not the solution to, the problems of peasants and farmers. Some national movements have experimented with engaging the World Bank, but in the broader context of demanding accountability (Scholte 2002). This was what happened, for example, when the National Forum for Agrarian Reform, a politically and organizationally broad coalition of rural social movement organizations in Brazil, twice filed for the World Bank Inspection Panel to investigate the market-assisted land reform experiment there (Fox 2003). While the request was turned down twice owing to a technicality, the Brazilian land reform movements were able to deliver a powerful message that is captured in the words of Fox (ibid.: xi): 'For leaders of the dominant international institutions, the idea that they should be transparent and held publicly accountable was once unthinkable.'

Many of the large global (inter)governmental institutions, however, such as FAO and IFAD, are themselves contested arenas, made up of heterogeneous actors. The challenge, then, for transnational social movements such as Vía Campesina is to find ways to continue engaging with pro-reform actors *within* these institutions, rather than with the institution as a whole, aiming to create cleavages within these agencies, isolating the anti-reform actors, while winning over, expanding, consolidating and supporting the ranks of pro-reform actors.

Finally, while the engagement of Vía Campesina with some groups within FAO and IFAD has been quite significant, the absence of interaction with other multilateral and bilateral agencies working on land policies is equally notable. Land policies have become an important policy issue among multilateral and bilateral agencies in recent years. Important land policy frameworks and significant funds come from these agencies, especially from the bilateral agencies. And while ILC has been quick to move within and around these agencies, Vía Campesina has generally defaulted in this terrain. The bilateral agencies are among the best-funded and most aggressive on the land policy front, and Vía Campesina has never engaged – combatively or otherwise – with any of them. This default does not work well in favour of Vía Campesina's advocacy for two reasons: first, because bilateral agencies control the bulk of funds that support the land policies that get implemented in local communities in developing countries; and second, because a significant portion of funds controlled by multilateral agencies comes from bilateral agencies.

Knowledge politics

The experience of Vía Campesina's global campaign on land reform is illustrative of the dynamics of knowledge politics. This can be seen in at least two ways. On the one hand, the construction of alternative visions about land and land policies by key actors in the global governance scene is primarily based on competing knowledge about these issues. And so it is a struggle over which knowledge about land and land policies counts. For example, while the World Bank, using sophisticated econometric methods, would typically show how private, individual land property rights or land rentals lead to greater inflow of financial resources into the countryside, Vía Campesina, using its knowledge about particular rural communities, would invoke community land rights that work for the poor. The battle over whose knowledge is more sensible and truly pro-poor goes on.

On the other hand, knowledge politics is an important arena in which Vía Campesina challenges mainstream neoliberal thinking, makes citizenship claims, and constructs an alternative vision (McMichael 2008). Knowledge politics can also be seen in terms of the struggle over access to key information and in the ways such information is used. Most concretely, the transnational nature of the land reform campaign has partially eroded the traditional monopoly of the World Bank and other international institutions on access to and control over key information related to land and peasantry in different national and international locations. The exchange of information and experiences among different national Vía Campesina members has equipped them with the information necessary to directly challenge and confront the World Bank and other international institutions on controversial issues. For example, the World Bank used to boast about the success of its market-led agrarian reform in Latin America and South Africa – until Vía Campesina and allied groups in these countries and internationally, armed with empirical data, challenged the World Bank's claims.

Furthermore, the timing of changes in transport and communication technology over the past decade was auspicious for Vía Campesina's internal consolidation and global campaigns. When Vía Campesina started preparing the ground for its eventual formation in early 1990s, new technologies were just beginning to gain acceptance. During those early years, transnational communication within Vía Campesina was slow and expensive, relying on fax machines rather than electronic mail and telephones rather than text messaging or Skype, for example. This situation radically changed, beginning in the second half of the 1990s, with the emergence of faster and cheaper communication technologies and transportation facilities. As a result, more information and knowledge are being exchanged at a much faster pace, both within and between national–local movements.

Conclusion

Rural citizens involved in the global campaign for agrarian reform led by Vía Campesina have understood their rights in the context of two broadly distinct but inseparable areas: land rights and citizenship rights, or, more aptly, land rights as citizenship rights. The framing of their Right to Land campaign directly confronts the free market framework on land in mainstream development narratives. Vía Campesina's notion of citizenship rights takes a critical perspective: they did not simply accept the existing institutional spaces for citizen engagement at the global level, they created one; they did not simply accept the existing rules of engagement, they demanded new ones; they rejected the corporate-oriented governance structure of some institutions, such as the 'one share, one vote' system in the World Bank, but endorsed the 'one member, one vote' system of the UN; they do not consider the World Bank as a legitimate representative institution, and thus their attitude towards this institution is to delegitimize it. On the global terrain, the perceived duty holders are a variety of (inter)governmental institutions that have become increasingly involved in land policy-making, and have direct impact on what is or what is not carried out at the local and national levels. In its land reform campaign, Vía Campesina has constantly straddled the local, national and international arenas in trying to hold accountable, separately and collectively, various (inter) governmental institutions engaged in land policies.

Moreover, Vía Campesina represents both direct and mediated expressions of citizenships. In many ways it is a direct expression of citizenship, through the elimination of conventional mediators – wealthier farmers' associations and NGOs – and the creation and occupation of a new space. But in other ways, Vía Campesina's experience shows a mediated form of citizenship. Its elite leadership bodies have replaced the previous conventional mediators, but that does not always mean that the problems of not achieving full and real representation of local and national groups at the global level have been resolved. The politics of intermediation between the movement's global leadership and (sub-)national movements has become more dynamic and complex but also problematic at times. The global citizenship space created and occupied by various civil society groups expanded when Vía Campesina entered. Such space has also been rendered much more complex, with the subsequent creation of various layers of sub-spaces of interactions between civil society groups.

Furthermore, there are concrete ways through which Vía Campesina has shown how citizenship claims are made and practices changed in relation to the land campaign. The most concrete manifestation of this citizenship claim is when Vía Campesina, beginning in the late 1990s, barged into the global rural policy-making scene and questioned the way citizenship claims have traditionally been made and exercised there – that is, by representatives of rich peasants and big farmers represented by IFAP and by NGOs. It can be seen from the events of the World Food Summit in Rome in November 1996, the World Trade Organization (WTO) summit in Cancún and the 'confrontation' with the World Bank about market-led agrarian reform in Washington, DC, in April 2003, as well as through Vía Campesina's assertion of its political influence during ICARRD in March 2006, and its eventual insertion into the official 'Farmers' Forum' process at IFAD, among others. Vía Campesina's arrival on this scene brought with it a new, distinct citizenship claim: for and by poor peasants and their representative movements. Yet, as discussed in this chapter, the actual 'claim' and representation are never complete, smooth and static: they are always incomplete, uneven and dynamically changing. While Vía Campesina is the largest transnational agrarian movement, it remains absent in China and the former USSR, and has a thin presence in North Africa, the Middle East and sub-Saharan African regions. Movements rise and fall, and so will Vía Campesina's political influence.

Discourses aggregated at the global level do not always reflect completely and evenly discourse and practice of members at (sub-)national levels. For example, while Vía Campesina at the global level calls for the rejection of biofuels, important national members such as the Mozambican movement have taken a more calculated and nuanced position between outright rejection and uncritical support. The same can be said of different positions taken by national and local/individual peasant movement participants. A national movement may call for the rejection of GM crops, while some of its members are actually using them.

Meanwhile, Vía Campesina is well known for its autonomy and capacity to develop innovative and effective strategies in its campaigns. With the increasing involvement of global institutions in land policy-making, Vía Campesina has provided both an arena and an actor in itself for (sub-)national rural social movements to cross national borders and engage with global institutions linked to land policy-making. Moreover, Vía Campesina has employed its classic, time-tested strategy of combining agit-prop/expose-and-oppose tactics with a critical collaborative stance vis-à-vis (inter)governmental institutions. There remain several important challenges, though, including a sharper perception of and engagement with potential and actual groups of reform-oriented actors *within* global institutions, as well as the difficult challenge of engaging bilateral agencies.

As demonstrated in the chapter, the emergence of Vía Campesina on the global scene has resulted in the emergence of new identities and channels of solidarity. One of these identities is the broad and vague – but influential and powerful – notion of 'people of the land', very much in the tradition of agrarian populism's 'them' versus 'us', 'community' versus 'outsiders', and so on. In itself, this is not new. Having brought it so prominently to the global level, however, is arguably something new (Edelman 2005). Moreover, cross-class and cross-sectoral identities have also emerged in the form of alliances between Vía Campesina and other organizations and movements with different class and sectoral origins, as in the case of the much-diversified IPC, of which Vía Campesina is a member. The 'global agrarian community' – the 'global us' – is significantly broader today, and this is something new.

In some ways the global campaign launched by Vía Campesina has contributed to 'new' meanings of global citizenship. For one, (inter)-governmental institutions operating at the global level and framing policies that ended up being implemented in national and local settings can, and should, be held accountable. Another contribution made by Vía Campesina to 'new meanings' of global citizenship is that poor peasants and their movements have broken through enormous structural and institutional barriers and have become active and reasonable citizens, interpreting – and changing – their own conditions, giving concrete expression to the popular civil society saying of 'not about us without us'.

Notes

1 A longer version of this chapter appeared as an IDS Working Paper (Borras and Franco 2009).

2 It has to be noted that this representation is uneven within and between countries, and partial, because no single organization can fully represent the diverse sections and interests of the rural poor within and between countries (Borras et al. 2008).

3 For example, the land tenure block within the FAO and the policy division at IFAD.

4 It is largely based in Negros Occidental, one province out of eighty in the country, but a key area in sugar cane production where landlord opposition to land reform is very strong.

5 In October 2008, during the Fifth World Congress of Vía Campesina held in Mozambique, UNORKA was finally admitted as a 'candidate member'.

References

Borras, S. (2004) '*La Vía Campesina*: an evolving transnational social movement', TNI Briefing Chapter Series 2004/6, Transnational Institute, Amsterdam.

— (2008) 'La Vía Campesina and its global campaign for agrarian reform', *Journal of Agrarian Change*, 8(2/3).

— (2009) 'Revisiting the agrarian movement–NGO solidarity discourse', *Dialectical Anthropology*, 33.

Borras, S. and J. Franco (2009) 'Transnational agrarian movements struggling for land and citizenship rights', IDS Working Paper no. 323, Institute of Development Studies, Brighton, www.drc-citizenship.org/publications/Wp323.pdf, accessed 29 August 2009.

Borras, S., D. Carranza and J. Franco (2007) 'Anti-poverty or anti-poor? The World Bank's market-led agrarian reform experiment in the Philippines', *Third World Quarterly*, 28(8).

Borras, S., M. Edelman and C. Kay (2008) 'Transnational agrarian movements: origins and politics, campaigns and impact', *Journal of Agrarian Change*, 8(2/3).

Desmarais, A. (2007) *La Vía Campesina: Globalization and the Power of Peasants*, Halifax/London: Fernwood/Pluto.

Edelman, M. (2003) 'Transnational peasant and farmer movements and networks', in M. Kaldor, H. Anheier and M. Glasius (eds), *Global Civil Society 2003*, Oxford: Oxford University Press.

— (2005) 'Bringing the moral economy back in ... to the study of 21st century transnational peasant movements', *American Anthropologist*, 7(3): 331–45.

Edwards, M. and J. Gaventa (2001) *Citizen Global Action*, Boulder, CO: Lynne Rienner.

Fox, J. (2001) 'Vertically integrated policy monitoring: a tool for civil society policy advocacy', *Nonprofit and Voluntary Sector Quarterly*, 30(3): 616–27.

— (2003) 'Framing the Inspection Panel', in D. Clark, J. Fox and K. Treacle (eds), *Demanding Accountability: Civil Society Claims and the World Bank Inspection Panel*, Lanham, MD: Rowman and Littlefield.

Franco, J. (2008a) 'Peripheral justice?: rethinking justice sector reform in the Philippines', *World Development*, 36(10).

— (2008b) 'Making land rights accessible: social movement innovation and political-legal strategies in the Philippines', *Journal of Development Studies*, 44(7).

Keohane, R. and S. Nye (2000) 'Governing in a globalizing world', in S. Nye and J. Donahue (eds), *Visions of Governance for the 21st Century*, Cambridge: Cambridge University Press.

McMichael, P. (2008) 'Peasants make their own history, but not just as they please ...', *Journal of Agrarian Change*, 8(2/3).

Putzel, J. (1992) *A Captive Land: The Politics of Agrarian Reform in the Philippines*, London/New York/Quezon City: Catholic Institute for International Relations/Monthly Review Press/Ateneo de Manila University Press.

— (1995) 'Managing the "Main Force": the Communist Party and the peasantry in the Philippines', *Journal of Peasant Studies*, 22(4): 645–71.

Scholte, J. A. (2002) 'Civil society and democracy in global governance', in R. Wilkinson (ed.), *The Global Governance Reader*, London: Routledge.

Tarrow, S. (1994) *Power in Movement: Social Movements, Collective*

Action and Politics, Cambridge: Cambridge University Press.
— (2005) *The New Transnational Activism*, Cambridge: Cambridge University Press.
Vía Campesina (2000) 'Struggle for agrarian reform and social changes in the rural areas', Bangalore.
— (2004) 'Debate on our political positions and lines of actions: issues proposed by the ICC–Vía Campesina for regional and national discussion in preparation for the IV Conference', in *IV International Vía Campesina Conference: Themes and Issues for Discussion*.

7 · Spanning citizenship spaces through transnational coalitions: the Global Campaign for Education

JOHN GAVENTA AND MARJORIE MAYO[1]

Introduction

Globalization [...] has introduced a new space and framework for acting: politics is no longer subject to the same boundaries as before, and is no longer tied solely to state actors and institutions, the result being that additional players, new roles, new resources, unfamiliar rules and new contradictions and conflicts appear on the scene. In the old game, each playing piece made one move only. This is no longer true of the new nameless game for power and domination. (Beck 2005: 3–4)

In recent years, as Ulrich Beck's words indicate, a number of changes related to globalization and governance have challenged our assumptions about where power resides, and how and where civil society organizations (CSOs) can best engage to bring about significant policy changes. This chapter explores citizens' responses to these altered patterns of power and governance, highlighting the implications for citizens' changing perceptions of themselves and their identities. The case of the Global Campaign for Education (GCE), a civil society coalition that came together in 1999 to mobilize people across the world in a campaign for the right to quality, free education for all, demonstrates the potential for building global citizenship along two dimensions: a vertical dimension, in which people perceive global duty holders and are making claims against them, and a horizontal dimension, in which people are developing a sense of solidarity with others, locally, nationally and internationally.[2]

There are numerous challenges in building and sustaining inclusive and democratic coalitions which span multiple sites, spaces and identities of citizenship. Drawing upon the evidence from research in the UK, India and Nigeria, this chapter explores how these tensions may be negotiated in practice. When advocacy movements are able to mobilize effectively and across spaces, we argue, new – more multidimensional – identities and understandings of citizenship may emerge than are found in any single action space alone.[3]

Before focusing upon the case study findings, the first section of this chapter provides a brief overview of the changing governance landscape of education policies, which has given rise to the need for integrated advocacy movements, aiming to bring about mutually reinforcing changes at all levels of governance. This sets the context for considering how citizens have been mobilizing to express their citizenship and claim their rights in light of the changing global landscape, exploring how such mobilization across levels and spaces contributes to a changing sense of citizenship among those involved.

Who governs education? Power across boundaries

Though the United Nations Declaration of Human Rights (UNDHR) declared the universal right to education in 1948, the responsibility for ensuring the right has often been considered that of national and local governments. National governments sign international treaties, and they also often define education policies, implement programmes, provide finance and set standards that determine the reality of education at the local level.

Farther down the governance chain, educational rights are the responsibilities of state and local governments as well. It is at these levels, depending upon the legal frameworks and practices in different contexts, that local funds are allocated, teachers hired and fired, and mechanisms for citizen involvement such as parent–teacher councils established. It is also at the local level that ordinary citizens directly experience the consequences of educational decisions. As one experienced education activist told us, 'in many places, education is the last outpost of the state'.[4]

While education has often been thought of as the responsibility of states, education scholars increasingly argue that national education systems have been conditioned or affected by the international institutional context. Beyond the UNDHR, the right to education has been enshrined in multiple constitutions and charters, including the UNESCO Convention against Discrimination in Education (1960), the International Covenant on Economic, Social and Cultural Rights (1966) and the Convention on the Rights of the Child (1989). Examining this trend, McNeely and Cha argue that with 'an increasingly integrated global system, individual nation-states within the system became subject to world-level ideological prescriptions and structural properties and influences'. In the field of education, this consolidation of the system gave rise to a variety of international organizations through which 'the principles, norms, rules and procedures of the wider system are enshrined [...] and they have become the carriers of the culture of the world polity' (1994: 2). Indeed, a bewildering array of international agencies – including UNESCO, the Organisation for Economic Co-operation and Development, the World Bank and UNICEF – are mandated in formal international architectures to gather, monitor and support how the various rights to education are being realized, to exchange information, and to set global standards. It has only been relatively recently that these intergovernmental agencies have come together in a more coordinated way, joined increasingly frequently by non-governmental agencies.

The late 1980s was a turning point when four major international organizations – UNICEF, UNESCO, the World Bank and the United Nations Development Programme – began to work together towards hosting the World Conference on Education for All (WCEFA) in 1990 in Jomtien. The WCEFA 'harnessed together a relatively uncoordinated group of education specialists across these agencies in an effort to expose the deterioration of worldwide access to education in the poorest of developing countries' (Mundy and Murphy 2001: 98). It reaffirmed the importance of education as a priority for development, with the goals of universal access to primary education by the year 2000 and the reduction of adult illiteracy, particularly female illiteracy, by half. Following Jomtien, an interagency Education for All (EFA) commission was established 'charged with formulating a decade of EFA activities and overseeing the realisation of central WCEFA goals' (ibid.: 99).

At this stage the role of non-governmental organizations (NGOs) was relatively limited, focusing primarily on their contributions as providers of educational services, rather than as global advocates for the achievement of rights to education. There were 'no clear structures for NGO participation in post-Jomtien activities and there was no NGO representative on the EFA Inter-Agency Steering Committee until 1997' (ibid.: 101). On the other hand, the growing coordination of international agencies, and the development of international structures of deliberation, provided a political opportunity for many NGOs that were looking for a new role in global governance debates, based more firmly on advocacy. These new international opportunities led to the establishment of the GCE in 1999.

Once established, however, the GCE had to contend with the complex structures through which the right to education was mediated. Many poor countries rely on international aid to finance education. While the Dakar Framework for Action on EFA, signed by 160 countries in 2000, pledged that no countries seriously committed to education for all would be thwarted in their achievement of that goal by a lack of resources, the lack of finance for education in poor countries continues to be a serious issue. To deal with this problem a mechanism known as the Fast Track Initiative (FTI) was established in 2002. It was overseen by the World Bank and designed to coordinate education aid from over thirty agencies and banks for approved national educational plans.

Key decisions about who receives funding are made by the donors sitting on the FTI Trust Fund committees. Pressure to deliver is maintained on the FTI in a range of ways, including via the Global Monitoring Report, an annual 'report card' on progress towards achieving the Dakar EFA goals. Housed in UNESCO, the report is drafted by an international team of education experts, under the advice of an international advisory board. Several international NGOs, including the Global March Against Child Labour, Education International and ActionAid, hold seats on that board, whose annual reports have become crucial for influencing the global discourse and debate.

While the UNESCO-based Global Monitoring Report and the World Bank-coordinated FTI Report serve to monitor progress on international goals, and to ensure that funds for education reach national budgets, decisions made in these global policy spaces can be trumped by another global actor, the International Monetary Fund (IMF). Though national education budgets are set by ministries of education in most countries, it is usually ministries of finance which actually determine expenditures. In many countries, especially those with international loan agreements, IMF influence on macroeconomic policy has led in practice to establishing caps on public sector wages, which in turn limits the numbers and wages of teachers. This leads to an ironic outcome: in order to meet the Millennium Development Goal (MDG) target of getting children into classes with forty pupils or fewer, 18 million new teachers are needed, but caps are preventing these new teachers from being recruited (GCE 2005; ActionAid 2007). The World Bank has also promoted the use of para-teachers[5] as a way of increasing school places at the same time as holding public expenditure down – at the expense, critics argue, of the quality of education. Concerns about quality have been associated with school absenteeism, with poorer parents effectively deciding that schooling is not worth pursuing for their children. Alternatively, those parents who can afford to do so may move to private schooling to ensure better-quality provision.

While much more could be said about the international factors affecting the governance of education, the short account above helps to make the broad point: increasingly over the last two decades, the field of educational policy, like other sectors, has become increasingly crowded with international policy actors and networks, both formal and informal, which affect whether and how the right to education will be achieved. Often, power is diffuse and opaque: as one international activist commented, 'there are lots of dotted lines across all these spaces'. Yet at the same time, the emergence of the apparatus of global education governance points to the absolute necessity for action on the international as well as the national and local stages, if educational rights are to be realized.

The challenges of building transnational campaign coalitions

On the one hand, some theorists would suggest, the emergence of globalization gives rise to new types of spaces in which citizens can mobilize to claim their rights – what scholars of collective action have thought of as new political opportunities, contributing in turn to new forms of transnational activism. As Tarrow points out, 'today's international system offers a special challenge for activists because it opens conduits for upward shift and can empower national, regional and local contention with international models of collective action' (2005: 121). Tarrow goes on to explore various forms of transnational activism, ranging from short-term instrumental and event-based coalitions to enduring federations and campaign coalitions. He argues that 'campaign coalitions may be the wave of the transnational future. Their focus on a specific policy issue, their minimal institutionalization, their capacity to shift venues in response to changing opportunities and threats, and their ability to make short-term tactical alliances according to the current focus of interest make them among the most fruitful strategies for transnational collaboration' (ibid.: 179).

In many ways the GCE is a very good example of Tarrow's campaign coalition. Yet at the same time, like other international coalitions that try to span local-to-global spaces of engagement, there are many challenges. One set of issues involves the extent to which access to global structures and spaces is effectively limited to the 'acceptable' faces of civil society, typically represented by professional advocates from Northern NGOs. In international advocacy campaigns, who is actually being empowered to speak for whom – and who might be effectively disempowered in the process? Grassroots groups from the global South can feel used or abused when they consider that powerful outsiders are coming in with 'superficial understandings' of their reality (Bandy and Smith 2005: 11). If Southern voices are not heard, Clark argues, then people 'often feel like second-class citizens among their Northern partners. They feel welcomed as sources of information and legitimisation but not as equals' (2003: 24). The question of who legitimately speaks for whom also resonates among elite and non-elite groups within campaign movements in the South, which have their own internal hierarchies of voice and representation (Batliwala 2002).

While much of the literature points to the tensions involved for transnational campaigns when they try to span local and global, other literatures begin to point to the structures or relations that can help to overcome some of these tensions. In NGO and civil society circles, growing attention is being paid to ways in which NGOs and other international actors structure greater accountability to those with whom they work and for whom they often speak (Jordan and Van Tuijl 2006). Earlier work by Covey focuses on processes and relationships, such as 'inclusion in decision-making; access to alliance resources (especially information); and division of roles and responsibilities (for example, who the spokespersons are)' (1995: 86). Florini writes of the importance of 'rootedness', arguing that 'transnational civil society cannot float free in a global ether. It must be firmly connected to local reality' (2000: 217). That connection to local reality can give international campaigns legitimacy, and it can provide them with a representative base. Grassroots local groups can also benefit from the vertical links to global campaigns, finding solidarity with others fighting for the same issues. With international and outsider support, they can find an added weight in their efforts to pressurize their governments.

To be enduring, Tarrow (2005) argues, transnational coalitions must take into account a series of other factors. These include mutually acceptable ways of framing issues, the establishment of trust and credible commitments. It is also important to find ways of managing differences – including power differences – between coalition partners, and to have selective incentives which motivate coalition partners with short-term local gains as well as longer-term strategic goals. While such ideas are useful in theory, how are they actually put into practice?

The case of the Global Campaign for Education

Both the opportunities and the tensions of mobilizing transnational campaign coalitions may be found in the case of the GCE, which is now one of the longest-standing global campaigns on a poverty-related issue and has a positive reputation for the ways in which it has been able to build and maintain a strong, diverse, inclusive coalition across many countries. Yet, as we have seen, it does so in a changing landscape, and so it provides an illustration of the challenges of responding to the multilevel, diffuse nature of global governance today.

Since its inception, the GCE has operated in the international arena, monitoring and researching the role of international agencies, putting pressure on donors to maintain their commitments to the EFA and MDG, organizing the Global Week on Education each year, and compiling international reports from the field. And yet, perhaps unusually, the small international secretariat sees its role not only, or even primarily, as advocating for others in international arenas, but also supporting national and local voices to speak across levels of governance.

As a broad-based coalition, the GCE includes not only other international and regional networks, but also sixty-five national coalitions in both South and North. Supporting and building up from national-level work is critical to the character of the campaign. Over 80 per cent of GCE funds go to support national coalitions. In some countries, organized civil society action on education issues at the national level has a long history, pre-dating the GCE and the Dakar Conference. In other countries, the emergence of the GCE became an important opportunity for the development of national-level coalitions. For many of the international founders, supporting or helping to create these national-level organizations was an important task, even from the earliest moment of the campaign.[6]

While it is possible to see the importance of citizen engagement at each level, in the global, regional, national and local spaces, by looking more closely one begins to understand the complexity of what is occurring. The nature of the GCE is that it is simultaneously linking across all levels of action.[7] One veteran campaigner put it this way:

> Now anything which is just local is not going to solve the problem [...] The sites of authority and power have changed, and when the sites of authority and power have changed, the sites of struggle will have to be changed [...] The struggle for a just and democratic governance is not a linear struggle, it means being local, it also means being global [...] it's a simultaneous thing.[8]

Another Indian-based activist described the challenge: 'campaigns need to allow and encourage ways to link up-down, down-up and sideways'.[9]

A powerful example of the simultaneity of action is found in the GCE's annual Global Week of Action (GWA). This event is made up of a series of coordinated local actions – during the 2008 GWA, some seven and a half million activists participated in mobilizations in 120 countries. Operating under a broad theme, local campaigners mobilize children, parents and teachers, while at the same time actions aimed at UN or G8 leaders help to deliver campaign messages to international players. While thus involving action aimed at global targets, it is based upon coordinated actions situated nationally and locally. The GCE publishes an annual 'Big Book' highlighting a summary of the actions taken across the world, giving the sense of a global movement. For activists we talked to at every level, the GWA was a crucial moment – a created space which gave their voices visibility, and provided a sense of solidarity with others, and simultaneously linked the local, national and international in joint action.

Yet, at the same time, crossing the spaces of action posed challenges. There were potential tensions between the need to take action speedily and the need to consult and maintain inclusive democratic processes, and between the need for short-term achievements and the need to maintain longer-term horizons for the achievement of development goals. As with so many coalitions there was the potential for struggles emerging over branding and visibility – 'logos and egos'. And there were differences of ideology and organizational culture within such a diverse coalition, spanning civil society from NGOs to trade unions.

Despite the importance of working in and across many levels and spaces, while not privileging any one space as the primary source of change, the GCE faced the challenge of avoiding becoming a transnational coalition which reflected traditional, hierarchical, vertically nested forms of organizational structure. As one experienced NGO activist observed more generally about global campaigns, 'whatever is happening in the global gets reflected in the local. But unfortunately, this is organized vertically. The funds happen vertically and the institutions and negotiations are vertical. Our thinking and organizing models still remain vertical.'[10]

Given such views, as well as the discussions in the literature of these tensions in global campaigns, we expected to find similar views expressed within the GCE. In our fieldwork, however, we found a very different picture. Though there have been disagreements about framing and resources, we found remarkably constructive approaches to addressing and resolving tensions. There were few challenges from activists at one level about the legitimacy of actions at the other. What accounts for such a very different picture from what one might expect? What explains this apparent success in building legitimacy across multiple levels and diverse members?

Five factors that make a difference to success

One campaigner described the importance of trust as the glue across levels that allowed the campaign to function effectively.

Trust is key. Having trust means that GCE can respond quickly, when this is needed, knowing that the membership will be supportive, having confidence that the board is really rooted in the South. Trust takes time to build, though, and so do coalitions, as these need to be built upon trust. In addition, there have to be real pay-offs locally and globally, if people are to stay involved.[11]

While trust is clearly important, much more needs to be understood about how it is built, and how it relates to the other key factors that were identified as being involved in building successful campaign coalitions that stretch across boundaries. In interviews with GCE activists at various levels in India, Nigeria and the UK, five factors seemed to be particularly important. These were:

- strong national and local roots of the campaign;
- carefully built governance structures which reflect these identities;
- inclusive framing of the messages;
- recognition of and attention to the contributions and value added at each level;
- long-term resources for sustainability.

Throughout our interviews – in both North and South – we found echoes of these themes.

Representative structures Local and national roots and identities can be overshadowed by other factors. Predictably, perhaps, when the GCE first came together, there were fears that Northern NGOs might predominate, using their Southern partners to provide legitimacy for what would be in practice a Northern-led campaign. The international NGOs involved were clear that this was not to be the case. The campaign structures that were developed were designed to ensure that Southern voices would be effectively represented.

Although initially based at Education International in Brussels, the GCE swiftly moved to South Africa. The GCE president, Kailash Satyarthi, emerged from an Indian social movement. Since the 2008 World Congress in Brazil, the chair has been held by an Education International representative from Togo, with vice-chairs from Brazil and the Philippines. A sense of genuine Southern ownership of the GCE was widely expressed in interviews.

Unlike many campaigns, the GCE is not organized around a central structure with local branches. Rather it is built from national coalitions which are members; each of these is organized with its own name and its own agenda. In addition, international organizations and regional organizations are also members. Every three years, all members come together in a World Assembly to debate issues and priorities and to elect a board of thirteen members. Two seats are reserved for members from INGOs, two from the Global March against Child Labour, two from Education International and the rest from national coalitions. Thus, while linking national, international and regional voices, the structure of the campaign reflects its Southern roots and gives predominant weighting to nationally based coalitions.

In addition to structure, however, we would emphasize the importance of the contributions of specific individuals, based upon their personal values and their attitudes to issues of power, ownership and control. While they themselves would not have chosen to be identified in such ways, it seemed clear to us as outside observers at GCE events, including the 2008 World Congress, that key individuals were exercising democratic leadership qualities in significant ways. They were putting the needs of the GCE above the needs of any particular organization or interest, including their own, and facilitating and enabling Southern voices, particularly women's voices, to be represented effectively. There were a number of appreciative public reflections about how the board functioned, echoing those expressed during interviews in India and Nigeria. Extensive consultation before reaching positions on strategies and tactics was widely evident. When asked whether they had a voice in international decisions, a group of Indian teachers' union activists said clearly that they had their ways of getting their views across, employing informal as well as formal ties. Another national coalition member was adamant that 'we have a voice in GCE. It is a two-way process, with information flowing up and down'.[12]

Inclusive framing of issues and messages It is widely recognized in social movement literature that framing campaign issues is a critical factor for determining the legitimacy of a campaign, and who supports it. The ability to define the frame is a source of power. For global campaigns on poverty-related issues, there is often a deep frustration among Southern activists that the framing grows from a Northern perspective and that Northern organizations have the ability to define what is relevant for the rest of the world. As one Southern NGO leader observed from his experience in other campaigns,

> What is global? In the locational politics, global becomes Washington, New York, the cosmopolitan media hubs of the North. So when you organize something in New York, it becomes global. When you organize

something in New Delhi, it becomes local [...] Global as an identity category is a very deceptive category. Theoretically speaking, London is as local as New Delhi. Edinburgh [the Make Poverty History demonstration] was a local mobilization. There was nothing global about it.[13]

Choosing and framing the themes in global campaigns is critical for ownership. One of the biggest challenges, said one activist, is 'how to choose campaigns with local and national relevance. You can use global campaigns to strengthen local groups but they can backfire if they are not locally relevant. The greatest challenge is to aggregate something that is relevant.'[14]

This framing challenge is seen most clearly in choosing the themes for the GWA, which has become the global moment when national coalitions carry out actions. The GWA was seen as one of the processes in which local and national activists felt that they had a voice. The themes for GWAs were discussed at length, with lots of views expressed before reaching consensus. In both India and Nigeria, time and again, activists expressed the feeling that the GWAs were addressing themes that had been chosen for their relevance locally as well as internationally.

The structures and rootedness of the GCE thus allow it to develop locally relevant themes for global action, but this is not to say that there are not other tensions in the framing process. While EFA is now a widely recognized issue, and the right to education holds huge universal appeal and support in international discourse and agreements, how the issue of education is understood may quickly lead to conflicting opinions between differently positioned actors. This is particularly true of the degree to which some of the systemic reasons for the failure to achieve EFA are addressed.

For instance, defining poor quality of education as part of the problem was potentially difficult for teachers, who felt that they were being blamed, rather than being defined as part of the solution. And there was a legacy of potential suspicion on the part of some teachers' organizations, towards NGOs that had provided education in the past, provoking criticism that they were undermining the case for state provision.

There were differences, too, over some of the issues associated with child labour and its underlying causes. Some employers, under pressure to compete internationally, undercut wages and conditions, part of processes that have been described as the globalization of poverty (Chossudovsky 1997). Additionally, in India especially, there had been debates over the World Bank promotion of schemes leading to the development of private education, a position many activists in the coalition felt needed to be challenged. These themes took the subject of education into controversial political debates on international trade, trade justice and state service provision in the context of neoliberal economic policies.

There were tensions too when particular organizations pushed their own profiles and agendas, causing resentment among their coalition partners. Conversely, there were tensions for NGOs striving to balance their commitment to the collective interest with their own need for profile. As one NGO respondent explained, it was essential to keep their 'brand' from slipping, in order to maintain their fund-raising among their own supporters.[15]

While these tensions were present, what was notable in our fieldwork was that they were discussed and negotiated within the coalition. In other international campaigns, such disagreements over framing of issues have either been less effectively addressed and negotiated, or even contributed to the demise of the coalition.

There were significant differences between GCE coalition partners, however, in terms of their access to material resources, differences that were also impacting upon their capacities for international engagement. However carefully issues and campaign materials were negotiated to ensure maximum involvement, when it came to global advocacy events like the GWA, international organizations tended to have greater access to resources. For example, the cost of international flights to attend meetings in Geneva, New York or Washington was proportionately far greater for Southern organizations. As one respondent pointed out, 'rich countries find it far easier to send delegates to international meetings than poor countries'.[16] Whatever the equality of representation enshrined in formal structures, international campaigning can still slide into becoming hierarchical. This emphasizes the importance of having structures and processes that do all they can to counterbalance these potential biases and power imbalances.

Partly to deal with such issues, a special mechanism was established to make resources available for capacity-building that emphasizes supporting national coalitions, enabling them to provide key links between the local and the global levels, as well as maintaining pressures on their own national governments. This Commonwealth Education Fund (CEF), announced by Gordon Brown and administered by ActionAid, Oxfam and Save the Children Fund, has had a significant impact on the development and sustainability of work on education. As well as this external financial support, one of the key factors underpinning the GCE's international achievements has been the provision of resources from within the coalition itself, particularly from the international trade union movement via Education International.

The importance of such support emerged from a number of the discussions. Even the need for resources to travel to attend national, regional and international meetings poses serious financial challenges for so many organizations in the South, let alone the resources required to provide high-quality research and campaign materials and to campaign within and across national boundaries. As one commentator reflected on the situation in India, 'even meetings with MPs require resources'.[17] Similar points were made in Nigeria, where the sheer size of the country posed comparable challenges in terms of the costs of travel to meetings. Without such resources, participation in international advocacy becomes logistically beyond the reach of CSOs at national level, never mind at the local level.

There were expressions of appreciation at the ways in which the international NGOs centrally involved in supporting the development of the GCE were respecting the importance of ensuring that this was genuinely a Southern-led campaign. But, while there was similarly widespread appreciation of the resources provided by the CEF, there were also reflections on the problems associated with the fact that this was time limited, running out in 2008.

The CEF itself has engaged in a number of studies to examine the challenge of ongoing sustainability, especially for national-level coalitions, and has been seeking support for 'National Civil Society Education Funds' to address these concerns in some fifty countries in coming years (Tomlinson and MacPherson 2007).

Key lessons in spanning the global, national and local As earlier sections have identified, there has been widespread recognition of the potential tensions inherent in linking local, national and global citizen advocacy, just as there has been widespread recognition of the potential challenges involved in building coalitions between different types of organizations and agencies with complex power relationships, working in very varying social, economic, political and cultural contexts. While the research provided evidence of the extent to which these challenges were being recognized, there was considerable optimism about the GCE, in terms of the ways in which structures and approaches had been developed to working towards building more equal partnerships based upon mutual respect and solidarity.

The GCE's relative success in building legitimacy across levels and actors has been attributed to its well-developed roots in the South, and its development of structures that have ensured Southern representation and ownership. These structures were considered to have enabled differences of interest and perspective to be negotiated transparently, so that campaigns and campaign materials could be framed in ways that genuinely represented the priority concerns of activists in the South as well as the North. Over time, activists at every level have come to recognize the added value of their links through the GCE – of the complementarity rather than competitiveness of their actions and voices. Such complementarity has been supported by special attention to the allocation of material resources. All of these are factors which have enabled the GCE to develop trust, and to be sustainable over time. The long-term nature of its work – it has now been operating as an international campaign for a decade – has also distinguished it from other campaigns. As one Indian activist commented, 'the same thing being said over and over again [...] this makes a big difference'.[18]

This, then, brings our discussion to the final question: how might engagement in local–global advocacy coalitions impact upon the identities of participants themselves as active citizens?

Implications for citizenship

> Citizenship is a sense of belonging. Citizenship is a marker of identity. Citizenship is also a bridge, a sense of solidarity with the rest of the people, a sense of belonging to the world. So I call myself an Indian citizen, a citizen of Kerala, a citizen of my village, at the same time. I strongly feel about my village – I participated [in decision-making] in my village this morning. In India [as a national citizen] I sent another email about a friend of ours who is being jailed by the government. And then I am a global citizen. Today I was also talking about the world. Because I am a citizen when I am committed, when I have a claim, when I think I have a space, and then I think I have a sense of belonging. When I am concerned about the world, not my own country, then I am a global citizen. When I am committed to challenging it, I am a global citizen.[19]

As this quote indicates, in a world with multiple centres of power and authority, citizenship itself may become a multidimensional, multilayered concept, no longer considered only in the relationship of citizens to nation-states. In the final part of this chapter, we ask what happens to participants' perceptions of themselves as citizens when they engage together across borders.

The question is not an easy one to explore. Social movements have long been identified as sites for learning, both about the issues in question and more widely, about civil society and active citizenship. Getting involved can change actors' perceptions about active citizenship (Foley 1999). Citizenship education can emerge from practice, from everyday and lived experience (Merrifield 2002) at least as much as from formal teaching per se. Therefore, when people do participate in a global campaign – particularly in a case such as the GCE, which has been relatively successful and linking actions across spaces and levels of action – do they change their sense of what citizenship is about? Does it contribute to the emergence of a sense of global citizenship? And how might their experiences relate to the findings from other studies?

Reflecting upon this question of the extent to which the sense of global citizenship may be identified, Schattle has commented:

> like it or not, individuals all over the world are choosing to think of themselves as global citizens and to shape their lives as members and participants in communities reaching out to all humanities. [...] Indeed [...] the term 'global citizenship' is often used as a lever in public debate to evaluate the actions and policies of nation-states. (Schattle 2008: 24–5)

Archibugi has come to similar conclusions, on the basis of his review of the existing evidence. 'Surveys indicate that about fifteen per cent of the world's inhabitants perceive the supranational identity as the principal one, compared with thirty-eight per cent for the national identity and forty-seven per cent for the local identity' (Archibugi 2008: 78). How did such conclusions resonate with the evidence emerging from this research?

Across the board, activists expressed the feeling that being engaged did give them a sense of commonality and connection with a broader movement, which in turn they found to be important. Reflecting on her experiences of becoming involved in global advocacy, one activist summarized her feelings about international advocacy, contrasting these with her previous experiences working for a multinational company.

> Before [this] I worked for a multinational [...] I was connected with a global network but didn't feel very good about it. This [global advocacy] has given me another way to be connected, where I feel much better about what I am doing [...] You feel part of all this – you could influence this. That's very empowering.[20]

A Nigerian activist reflected similarly: participating in a global campaign 'increases my confidence that there are people somewhere struggling with the same issues'. This was about 'solidarity [...] recognizing that part of the solution lies outside my shore'.[21]

While many international NGOs and trade union activists had long histories of global advocacy and campaigning, there was also evidence to illustrate the impact of participation in some of the more recent transnational campaigns. Interviews time and again echoed the theme that getting involved in campaigning itself builds interest, understanding and commitment among activists. The

> very fact of being involved in GCE joint endeavours does change perceptions and increases members' sense of involvement. You do get a sense that you are actually part of something. This activity helps produce the 'glue' that builds the representation and accountability structures. This builds solidarity – giving the role of agency and active engagement to activists.[22]

It was suggested widely that when people see others engaging they get a sense of community and find it empowering. One international campaigner argued that these campaigns were creating 'genuine educational experiences which have changed people's understanding of power and of themselves as actors. It will also change their understandings of North and South.'[23]

But while connectedness across borders can provide a sense of solidarity, which contributes to more engagement, does this connectivity contribute to a sense of being a 'global' citizen, reinforcing or replacing a sense of local or national citizenship? Here views varied a great deal, especially across more globally located and more locally grounded actors. For some internationally located actors, being involved in global campaigns gave a sense of citizenship which they perhaps did not experience locally. One UK-based respondent reflected that 'I've changed [...] I've completely changed my sense of global community'.[24] In this person's view, a lot of people had 'learned a sense of global citizenship. We experienced a particular kind of feeling when we were all around the world talking together on the global teleconferences.' For another similarly positioned respondent, 'global citizenship is about looking into your own community, then linking issues to the outside world, finding commonality based on your issues. This is the direction.'[25]

While one could thus find evidence for a growing sense of connection among those involved in the campaign at the global level, this was not necessarily separate from their local identities, especially for activists with roots in local campaigns as well. In Nigeria, an activist emphasized, repeating an oft-used phrase, that 'yes, OK, we are global citizens [but] we are global citizens who act locally'.[26] But another added, 'we've run global campaigns in Nigeria [...] and we've contributed to global decisions, but I still see myself as very local'.[27] A third added that although the international context does 'broaden your views and understanding – it fires your zeal', it was important not to lose one's local roots.[28]

At the march for the GWA in Birmingham in 2007, discussion of similar themes was heard. A local councillor, responsible for lifelong learning, observed that, in such a diverse city, people in Birmingham are already 'linked to so many parts of the world'. So he felt that there was 'a duty to influence those with power and resources', so that people elsewhere could have the same opportunities. For him, 'citizenship is global', but demonstrating solidarity with others was also the basis for building greater social cohesion locally.[29]

Another participant in the Birmingham march, a teacher and union activist, argued that 'citizenship education is about gaining the skills and the knowledge to make a difference, locally and beyond. This is how you become a global citizen.'[30] Clearly, then, while engagement in global spaces changed participants' senses of belonging and solidarity, this could actually strengthen, and be grounded in, local identities as well. As Tarrow puts it in his discussion of 'rooted cosmopolitanism', 'what is new in our era is the increased number of people and groups whose relations place them beyond their local or national settings without detaching them from locality' (2005: 42).

There were, however, some potentially disturbing comments on global citizenship from the South. Although involvement in global campaigning was described as being about solidarity, as people elsewhere struggle with the same issues, there were contrasting comments that raised questions about the very notion of global citizenship. 'I can't say that I feel like a global citizen,'[31] reflected one GCE participant in Nigeria. Despite having extensive experience of international campaigning, the respondent explained that 'I feel like a second-class citizen outside Nigeria [...] you are made to feel [as if] you come from a developing country'. This feeling was perhaps compounded by some of the negative stereotypes that had been associated with Nigeria under military rule. Global citizenship based upon notions of solidarity, equality and respect still seemed a long way off here, implying important challenges for activists and for those concerned with development education and citizenship education more generally in the global North.

Conclusions

What, then, does the study of the GCE tell us about how citizens might most effectively mobilize to claim rights in the changing international context?

Reviewing the landscape of education policy illustrates that change on an issue like education must come at multiple levels – the local and national spaces of education governance are deeply affected and interact with the global polity. Though long considered the responsibility of states and localities, educational policies and realities are deeply affected by international institutions through which the 'principles, norms, rules and procedures of the world system are enshrined' (McNeely and Cha 1994: 6). Changing governance regimes, as Beck has observed, give rise to 'a new space and framework for acting' (2005: 3), in which new approaches to challenging and changing power need to be used.

Such a shift in the structures of governance has enormous consequences for how universally agreed rights, such as the right to education, are achieved. As the GCE illustrates, rather than being realized through duty bearers alone, citizen action and mobilization can be an important force in the struggle to ensure that formal governance institutions are held to account in delivering the rights to which they have formally subscribed. Support for such efforts will be very important in the efforts of international donors and NGOs to realize the MDGs related to EFA. Citizen pressure is no guarantee that such goals will be realized, but the chances seem much higher with effective citizen action than without it.

But to be effective, strategies of citizen action and mobilization must also change, and no longer be understood as needing to occur at only the local, national or international level – this case suggests the importance of simultaneous pressure at multiple levels which operate as potentially mutually reinforcing spheres. Such a view would be consistent with Scholte's perspective on the importance of understanding the interactions between the local, the national, the regional and the global (Scholte 2002) as the basis for effective advocacy.

As Tarrow (2005) suggests, the new political opportunities offered by the changing global landscape imply the need for transnational activists to shift the scale of contention. Yet the case adds further complexity to Tarrow's view of such shifts occurring along a vertical axis of upward or downward change. Rather, events in the GCE provide examples of spaces and strategies that transcend the vertical, which are moments simultaneously created by local and global action.

Despite this notion of simultaneity and non-linearity of the global to the local, campaigns are often organized along very vertical lines. Global campaigns have been critiqued for reflecting hierarchies of power, in which larger international organizations may fail to be accountable to those 'below', or may squeeze out local voices. Important questions have been raised about the legitimacy of global social movements, in terms of who they speak for, and how they are internally organized. New models are also needed of how voices may be linked across these levels, in more inclusive ways.

Relative to other examples of transnational campaigns, the GCE would seem to offer some clues as to how efforts for intentional change might be organized. Although, of course, there are tensions within the GCE, our interviews with actors at every level in the UK, India and Nigeria revealed a surprising amount of internal trust and legitimacy between actors at all levels, and a sense of inclusion and voice that is not always the case in transnational citizen mobilizations.

Could the GCE be considered a somewhat special case? This was the view of a number of those interviewed. While there were differences of interest and perspective within the GCE, these were less significant, it was suggested, than the differences involved in a number of other campaigns. Education is a relatively non-contentious issue, with which people across many settings can readily identify. The GCE was also seen as somewhat atypical in the nature and breadth of its supporters. In contrast, other campaigns were cited as raising far more problematic differences of ideology, interest and perspective.

The GCE offers an example of what Tarrow has defined as a campaign coalition. Campaign coalitions differ from event coalitions because of their duration, and also from shorter-term instrumental coalitions, or longer-term international federations, owing to the higher degree of involvement of participants.

> Campaign coalitions combine high intensity of involvement with long-term cooperation. [...] They emerge and endure successfully for three reasons: a) through seizing and making new opportunities, b) through institutionalization, but with 'cooperative differentiation', and through c) 'socialization': the combination of discovery and solidarity that is experienced when people with very different backgrounds, languages and goals encounter one another around a broad global theme. (2005: 168–78)

The GCE provides illustrations of all three. It has been flexible enough to take on new issues or themes – as reflected in the changing themes of each of its GWAs – and to raise challenges in different spaces – from the IMF to regional-level institutions and beyond to the local level. While it has developed an institutional structure, that structure recognizes the differing roles played by INGOs, trade unions and national members. And, as has been seen, this involvement has contributed to a widely felt sense of solidarity with others, giving a collective identity to the emerging movement.

This case study of the GCE also revealed several other factors which contribute to its relative legitimacy and durability. In summary, these included, first, deep pre-existing roots and forms of collective organization at the national level, particularly in the South, before the global campaign was formed. Second, once formed, the GCE was highly sensitive to building upon these existing organizations, especially in its inclusive and representative formal structures. Third, a great deal of attention has been paid to the collective framing of issues, across actors and levels of the coalition. Fourth, there is wide recognition of the differential roles that can be played by activists at each level in the campaign, with a high value placed on local actors, and ensuring complementarity rather than competition. Finally, there was attention paid to the material base of the campaign, especially in the distribution of the resources. The formation of a global funding mechanism, the CEF, was particularly important in helping to ensure that national-level organizations were able to access the funds they needed.

The case study also gives some interesting insights into the question of how involvement in a global campaign affects the identities of citizenship of those involved. We have very mixed answers to the question of whether transnational campaigns help to produce global citizens. Certainly, interviews with actors reveal the development of a strong sense of connectedness and solidarity with those across borders working on similar issues. While, for many scholars, global citizenship is a normative ideal, to the degree that citizens see global institutions as helping to shape their rights, and are raising voices in the global arena to claim their rights, one can argue that a sense of global citizenship may be emerging. Yet, for most activists, this was not replacing a sense of national or local citizenship, but was adding to it. As governance is increasingly multi-scaled, so citizenship can therefore also be multi-dimensional. The challenge is how to continue to build and sustain inclusive and democratic coalitions that span these multiple sites and spaces of citizenship in the pursuit of universally declared human rights, such as the right to education. In view of current anxieties about the likelihood of achieving the MDGs by 2015, in the context of international recession, the case for building and sustaining such citizen coalitions would seem likely to continue, at least for the foreseeable future.

Notes

1 The authors wish to thank members of the Global Citizen Engagements Working Group of the DRC on Citizenship, Participation and Accountability for their comments on earlier drafts, as well as comments received from Rajesh Tandon, Linda Waldman, David Archer, and members of the writers' circle in the Participation, Power and Social Change team. Many thanks to Kate Newman for her background report on Nigeria, and also to the many civil society activists and others who gave their time in the UK, India and Nigeria. The findings and conclusions here represent those of the authors alone. This chapter is drawn from a longer IDS working paper, Gaventa and Mayo (2009).

2 Four large NGOs came together in 1999 to establish the GCE. Two of these founding organizations – ActionAid and Oxfam International – are international NGOs. The third, Education International, is an international association of teachers' unions. The fourth, the Global March Against Child Labour, is an international movement concerned with children's rights, based in the global South.

3 During 2006, interviews were carried out with a range of stakeholders at national level, including CSOs participating in the GCE either directly or via its constituent member organizations. A few interviews were also carried out during visits to rural areas in Andhra Pradesh, India, and northern and western Nigeria, where there was also the opportunity to meet local teachers, parents and children, and to observe village meetings.

4 Interview, GCE campaigner and INGO professional, UK.

5 Para-teachers are minimally qualified, low-waged and employed by local governments on contract. They are often local; in some countries they are called community or volunteer teachers.

6 For a more complete report on the emergence and contribution of the national education coalitions, see Tomlinson and MacPherson (2007).

7 This challenges assumptions about a simplistic vertical or layered model of change, and gives credence to Scholte's (2002) new space of 'globality'.

8 Interview, Indian INGO professional based in Bangkok.

9 Interview, GCE participant and INGO professional, New Delhi.

10 Interview, Indian INGO professional, based in Bangkok.

11 Interview, GCE campaigner and INGO staff member, New Delhi.

12 Interview, national education coalition member, New Delhi, India.

13 Interview, Indian INGO professional, based in Bangkok.

14 Interview, GCE campaigner and INGO staff member, New Delhi.

15 Interview, INGO professional, UK.

16 Interview, trade union official, UK.

17 Interview, GCE participant, New Delhi, India.

18 Ibid.

19 Interview, Indian INGO professional, based in Bangkok.

20 Interview, INGO professional, New Delhi, India.

21 Interview, INGO professional, Abuja, Nigeria.

22 Interview, trade union official, UK.

23 Interview, INGO professional, UK.

24 Ibid.
25 Ibid.
26 Interview, GCE participant, Nigeria.
27 Ibid.
28 Ibid.
29 Interview, local councillor, UK.
30 Interview, teacher, UK.
31 Interview, GCE participant, Nigeria.

References

ActionAid (2007) 'Confronting the contradictions: the IMF, wage bill caps and the case for teachers', London: ActionAid.

Archibugi, D. (2008) *The Global Commonwealth of Citizens*, Princeton, NJ and Oxford: Princeton University Press.

Bandy, J. and J. Smith (2005) *Coalitions across Borders: Transnational Protest and the Neoliberal Order*, Oxford: Rowman and Littlefield.

Batliwala, S. (2002) 'Grassroots movements as transnational actors: implications for global civil society', *Voluntas*, 13(4): 293–309.

Beck, U. (2005) *Power in the Global Age: A New Global Political Economy*, Cambridge: Polity Press.

Chossudovsky, M. (1997) *The Globalization of Poverty*, London: Zed Books.

Clark, J. (2003) 'Introduction: civil society and transnational action', in J. Clark (ed.), *Globalizing Civic Engagement: Civil Society and Transnational Action*, London: Earthscan.

Covey, J. G. (1995) 'Accountability and effectiveness in NGO policy alliances', *Journal of International Development*, 7(6): 857–68.

Florini, A. (2000) *The Third Force: The Rise of Transnational Civil Society*, Washington, DC: Carnegie Endowment for International Peace.

Foley, G. (1999) *Learning in Social Action*, Leicester: NIACE.

Gaventa, J. and M. Mayo (2009) 'Spanning citizenship spaces through transnational coalitions: the case of the Global Campaign for Education', IDS Working Paper no. 327, Institute of Development Studies, Brighton, www.drc-citizenship.org/publications/Wp327.pdf, accessed 25 August 2009.

GCE (Global Campaign for Education) (2005) 'Missing the mark: a school report on rich countries' contributions to universal primary education by 2015', Brussels: GCE.

Jordan, J. and P. van Tuijl (2006) *NGO Accountability: Politics, Principles and Innovation*, London: Earthscan.

McNeely, C. and Y. Cha (1994) 'Worldwide educational convergence through international organizations: avenues for research', *Education Policy Analysis Archives*, 2(14): 1–11.

Merrifield, J. (2002) 'Learning citizenship', IDS Working Paper no. 158, Institute of Development Studies, Brighton.

Mundy, K. and L. Murphy (2001) 'Transnational advocacy, global civil society? Emerging evidence from the field of education', *Comparative Education Review*, 45(1): 85–126.

Schattle, H. (2008) *The Practices of Global Citizenship*, Lanham, MD: Rowman and Littlefield.

Scholte, J. A. (2002) 'Civil society and democracy in global governance', in R. Wilkinson (ed.), *The Global Governance Reader*, London: Routledge.

Tarrow, S. (2005) *The New Transnational Activism*, Cambridge: Cambridge University Press.

Tomlinson, K. and I. MacPherson (2007) *Driving the Bus: The Journey of National Education Coalitions*, London: Commonwealth Education Fund.

8 · Citizenship and trade governance in the Americas[1]

ROSALBA ICAZA, PETER NEWELL AND
MARCELO SAGUIER

Introduction

The question of who should govern the global economy, how and for whose benefit has once again been projected centre-stage. The financial crisis which intensified during 2008 has been viewed as a direct result of the lack of regulation of the financial sector at the national and international levels. For many, it is indicative of the broader failings of the assumptions that underpin contemporary neoliberalism: that markets self-correct and self-govern; that the wealth they create produces a 'rising tide that lifts all boats'; and that the appropriate role of the state is a minimalist one as facilitator of markets and enforcer of property rights. Amid dramatic and widespread state-led interventions in the economy in the heartlands of Anglo-American capitalism, including the renationalization of banks and the use of price controls as well as talk of a new global deal aimed at reforming the Bretton Woods institutions, it is not an exaggeration to say that contemporary neoliberalism is in crisis. Though finance has been the main focus of the debate to date, the growth of protectionism as countries seek to protect their industries from bankruptcy also pushes trade into the spotlight. This provides a timely backdrop to the struggles we describe in this chapter, which contest the relationship between state, market and citizen in debates about trade liberalization in Latin America.

Indeed, the social contracts that underpin existing obligations and duties between state, market and civil society have undergone important transformations as a result of the reconstitution of political and social power through globalization (Scholte 2000), producing competing claims about the changing nature of citizenship (Delanty 2000). For some, it is meaningful to talk about the existence of global citizenship as citizens acquire rights to hold foreign governments and firms to account for rights violations. This is true, for example, of panels and bodies set up under the North American Free Trade Agreement (NAFTA), which allow citizens to present evidence against firms from other countries, in theory allowing for transnational accountabilities and even granting rights that go beyond the state. Beyond the creation of these new global spaces for claim-making, others emphasize that the trans-state articulations of identity and solidarity that express citizenship in the making, ahead of and beyond formal legal recognition of such rights claims, are equally important.

Sceptics, meanwhile, reject the very basis of ideas of global citizenship. Michael Walzer argues:

> I am not a citizen of the world [...] I am not even aware that there is a world such that one could be a citizen of it. No one has ever offered me citizenship, or described the naturalisation process, or enlisted me in the world's institutional structures, or given me an account of its decision procedures [...] or provided me with a list of the benefits and obligations of citizenship or shown me the world's calendar and the common celebrations and commemorations of its citizens. (Walzer 1994: 29)

It is against this backdrop that we explore how ideas of citizenship are affected by the project of trade liberalization in the Americas: how trade policy impacts upon citizens' relationship with the state, and the state's ability to realize particular rights. But we also show how struggles over citizenship are being played out not only in a one-way, 'top-down', relationship. New solidarities and expressions of citizenship are also being articulated 'from below' by an increasing array of actors mobilizing simultaneously in multiple governance arenas linking local and global spheres and processes. Such practices often centre on the defence of existing rights as well as on demands for new rights that invoke duty holders within and beyond the state such as transnational corporations (TNCs). Social movements' resistance to neoliberal trade integration projects in the Americas has been associated with the emergence of new political spaces where citizens from across the region come together to protest, mobilize and express their concerns about trade liberalization. Through resistance to neoliberalism, 'old' social identities such as class are articulated alongside 'newer' identities and demands for gender and ecological justice in a common defence of democratic sovereignty.

The key question we address is 'how do changing patterns of power and governance in relation to trade affect the meanings and practices of citizenship in a globalizing world?' The patterns that we explore relate to trade politics and their contestation by the women's, labour and environmental movements in the Americas. The citizenship meanings and practices covered in this chapter emerge through transnational citizen mobilization around the distributional impacts of trade policies on entitlements and rights, and the procedural aspects associated with citizen participation and representation in trade decision-making processes. Research for this project was conducted over three years. Workshops were held with trade activists from the region, encouraging participants to define for themselves the relevant questions and topics for discussion within the parameters of the research project.[2] The idea was to create a safe space for activists to reflect on these themes and on the effectiveness of their strategies in tackling them.

The chapter is structured in the following way. The first section briefly explores the shifting landscape of trade governance in the Americas and reflects on the constraints that recent trade integration processes place on the possibility of a full realization of citizenship rights and entitlements. In the second section, we reflect on the politics of mobilization around trade, asking how this contributes to new expressions of citizenship in the Americas. In particular, we concentrate on the cases of the women's, environmental and labour movements as key social forces in relation to the trade agenda contained in the NAFTA, Free Trade Area of the Americas (FTAA) and Mercado Común del Sur (Mercosur, Common Market of the South) initiatives. Finally, the third section interrogates to what extent new expressions and practices of citizenship emerge from, and at the same reconfigure, the landscape of trade politics in the Americas.

The shifting landscape of trade governance in the Americas: implications for citizenship

The governance of international trade has undergone a considerable transformation. Efforts to consolidate the power of trade institutions brought about the creation of the World Trade Organization (WTO) in 1995. Alongside this, there has also been a resurgence of regionalism in the Americas. A new generation of trade rules led to the creation in the Americas of a series of trade initiatives during the 1990s supported mainly by the US government. These include NAFTA, an incomplete project to create an FTAA and the establishment of bilateral free trade agreements (FTAs) between the USA and Chile, Peru, Colombia and several Central American countries under the Central America Free Trade Agreement – Dominican Republic (CAFTA-DR). These agreements introduce levels of reciprocal commitment that go beyond existing commitments at the multilateral level, including rules on investment protection, competition policy, government procurements, trade facilitation and intellectual property rights. They raise concerns insofar as they restrict the policy autonomy of states to align international trade relations with their own national development strategies, needs and conditions (Gallagher 2005).

One of the key areas of concern has been that these trade agreements afford disproportionate rights to corporations without corresponding levels of responsibilities: regulation for, rather than of, business (Newell 2001). Under the state-firm provisions contained in investment protection rules, changes in national and local legislation that may affect foreign investments can make states liable for compensation. NAFTA's Chapter Eleven on rules of investment incorporates this provision, setting a precedent for later FTAs and for the CAFTA-DR.

Investment protections contained in the new generation of trade agreements serve to lock in the liberalization of trade, investment and deregulation that has already been implemented under structural adjustment programmes. They serve to discipline states by narrowing and constraining the space for the expression of democratic sovereignty over economic policy. Stephen Gill describes this as the 'new constitutionalism' which redefines the political 'limits of the possible' now and in the future and entails efforts to contain challenges to the neoliberalism project through 'co-optation, domestication, neutralization and de-politicization of opposition' (Gill 2002: 47). Viewed in this way, the current agenda of trade agreements is about the institutionalization of a particular model of trade governance that is consistent with limited forms of democratic participation and the exclusion of those subject to economic restructuring.

The distributional impact of the current trade agenda affects the possibility of realizing existing citizenship rights and claiming new ones. One way this occurs is through the liberalization of public services like education, health and the provision of water. Access to education and health constitutes a basic and in some cases constitutional right. The privatization of services, however, often creates a conflict between market-based and rights-based approaches to development whereby, while formally responsible for their protection, the state's means of realizing a right have been outsourced to the private sector (Mehta 2006). The recasting of citizens as consumers has produced widespread conflicts, such as battles over water privatization in Bolivia and Uruguay, and the creation of new alliances, such as the Reclaiming Public Water network (Balanyá et al. 2005).

In terms of their procedural dimensions, trade integration processes in the Americas have been criticized for their lack of transparency and accountability. In many Latin American countries national parliaments have played a minimal role in contributing to the definition of the agenda and the content of agreements. Where present, the participation of national legislatures in international negotiations is limited to the ratification or rejection of what the executive negotiates. Participation in a public debate about health rights in Peru revealed that parliament had not been consulted about key provisions on issues such as intellectual property rights, which impinge heavily upon government's ability to ensure poor people's access to essential medicines. The trend towards decreasing accountability appears to be consolidated by the latest extension of NAFTA, the so-called Security and Prosperity Partnership for North America (SPP). Decisions in SPP are exclusively made on the basis of executive agreements that do not even need ratification by the legislatures of the three countries involved.

Public hearings on current trade negotiations are rarely held. In Mexico, the internal regulations of the Mexican senate establish that public hearings are a discretionary duty of their members (Icaza 2004). When this is combined with a limited awareness among the general public about the nature and consequences of trade agreements, the accountability of decision-makers for the decisions they make is slight. This poses the question of what kind of mandate government officials have to negotiate agreements on behalf of their citizens.

To address such accountability deficits, the Confederación Parlamentaria de las Américas (COPA, Parliamentary Confederation of the Americas) was formed in 1994 in the wake of the First Summit of the Americas in Miami. COPA's aim is to contribute to the 'strengthening of parliamentary democracy and to the building of a community of the Americas founded on the respect for dignity and human rights, peace, democracy, solidarity between peoples, social justice and gender equity' (COPA 2008). In so doing, COPA aspired to 'represent to the executive authorities of the Americas, the interests and aspirations of the populations of the hemisphere with regard to the issues and impacts of the hemispheric integration process' (ibid.). Despite its noble ambitions, however, COPA has not so far been able to acquire an influential role in opening up trade decision processes to broader democratic debate.

Amid accusations of rich clubs of economic elites crafting the terms of trade agreements that serve narrow economic interests, it is unsurprising that there have been calls to democratize trade policy; to open it up to a plurality of participants, interests and agendas, to revisit fundamentally the question of who and what is trade for. The opportunities to participate effectively in such processes, however, have been reduced by the 'forum-shifting' strategies employed by powerful states and corporations, which allow them to move between decision arenas in order to secure the outcomes they desire. Sell (2003) shows this dynamic at work in the case of the struggles of some civil society organizations (CSOs) over the creation of a global regime for intellectual property rights. Contending coalitions prioritize the engagement in institutional arenas that are the most sympathetic to their interests, where the mandate most aligns with the outcomes they are pursuing and where they have the greatest degree of access.

When multilateral and regional trade negotiations break down, the liberalization agenda is often pursued through bilateral FTAs whose provisions often surpass those that were contested in regional and global fora. For example, the FTAs signed between the USA and Peru, Colombia, Chile and under the CAFTA-DR contain many provisions that some governments and their allies in civil society had opposed in the FTAA. Bilateral trade accords between unequal partners can be used to undermine social and environmental protection measures. For example, the bilateral investment agreement between the USA and Bolivia, said to have been 'negotiated on behalf of US mining companies to protect their investments in the mineral rich Andean country' (Cordonier-Segger 2005: 156), offers few openings for public input regarding the social and environmental impacts of mining, and there are no provisions for the public release of documents or stakeholder participation in investor-state tribunals. Likewise, the bilateral trade agreement negotiated between Peru and the USA opens the way for the entry of genetically modified organisms into a subsistence-based economy, which is a centre of origin for potatoes, by requiring Peru to synchronize its sanitary and phytosanitary measures with those of the USA, potentially undermining the policy autonomy conferred upon Peru by its membership of the Cartagena Protocol on Biosafety. There are also fears that measures to strengthen intellectual property protection in line with US demands will threaten the genetic resources and traditional knowledge base of indigenous communities in the country (TWN 2006).

For activists, moving between and across fora means combining mobilizations at national, regional and transnational levels with the construction of power 'from below' through informal initiatives. To adapt to this shifting landscape, civil society groups have sought to mobilize at each of the multiple levels of governance involved in trade policy decisions by crafting alliances with other social groups that may have better access to policy processes. For example, as Obach notes (2004: 63), 'although unions and environmentalists had distinct concerns in regard to NAFTA, the common threat the agreement presented created the impetus for labour–environmental cooperation'. At times working independently, at other times together, national coalitions such as the Citizens Trade Campaign and the Alliance for Responsible Trade were formed that included many of the major labour and environmental actors, who went on to work together in opposing fast-track trade authority for the administration of President Bill Clinton.

The technical, expert-led and legal nature of trade negotiations, combined with the reciprocal bargaining that is at the heart of trade deal-brokering, presents a high barrier to the meaningful engagement of citizens and organizations claiming to act on their behalf. Access to resources to train personnel with the kinds of skills required to make significant contributions to trade policy debates is critical. North–South cleavages are often reproduced between resource-endowed NGOs from the North and resource-deprived organizations from the South which find it difficult to keep up with the rapidly evolving trade development agenda (Newell and Tussie 2006). By contrast, large corporations with vast resources are in a position to employ professional lobbyists to represent their interests in the negotiations, and thus benefit from mechanisms of participation for CSOs which were originally deemed as means to open up trade processes to public involvement.

Interesting in citizenship terms is the way in which the corporations active in promoting the regional trade agenda have taken to using the language of 'citizenship' to describe what they perceive to be their values and obligations towards the society in which they operate. Various critiques have raised concerns about TNCs' practices of claiming citizenship rights without addressing corresponding notions of responsibility (Newell 2002). Clear definitions of citizenship – beyond being synonymous with neighbourly conduct – are rare amid generic claims by corporations to be behaving as a 'good citizen'. The notion of reciprocal obligations is often missing. The basic freedoms of capital around rights of mobility, to make a profit and to own property rights are protected even where they conflict with the pursuit of other social and environmental objectives (Blowfield and Frynas 2005). The citizenship that many firms are practising is, therefore, a partial one.

Indeed, the way in which processes of globalization enable companies to maintain a distance between the site of production and the site of consumption often makes it possible for producers to keep from public view the social and environmental impacts of their production processes. As Sachs argues, 'the emergence of the globe as an economic arena where capital, goods and services can move with little consideration for local and national communities has delivered the most serious blow to the idea of a polity which is built on reciprocal rights and duties among citizens. Through transnationalization, capital escapes any links of loyalty to a particular society' (Sachs 1997: 10). It is the disembedded nature of capital which fuels demands for the progressive re-embedding of economic actors in frameworks of social control over which citizens have some say. The following sections explore the role of civil society groups in contesting the current framing and contents of the regional trade agenda and the power that it affords to multinational capital in particular.

The politics of mobilization on trade governance

Practices of citizenship within invited spaces[3] In response to the changing nature of trade governance, there has been a transformation in the practices through which social demands are organized and mobilized in response to the democratic deficits of trade policy processes. There have been a number of attempts to involve CSOs in trade policy processes, often as the response of governments to a crisis of legitimacy facing a trade institution provoked by widespread social protest. Large-scale demonstrations such as the 'battle of Seattle' against the WTO's perceived power reflect the mounting objections to the secrecy in which decisions are taken. Many other local social uprisings have sought to contest the impacts of neoliberal trade initiatives, such as the Zapatista uprising in Mexico, which began on the day that NAFTA came into effect, and mass mobilizations against the FTAA, FTAs and CAFTA-DR.

Institutional responses have varied, but in most cases they have taken the form of initiatives to encourage public participation in trade negotiation processes. Yet, rather than serving as means to democratize the processes and agenda of trade integration, the following examples reveal that the participation of CSOs in formal mechanisms of consultation devised by governments has been largely instrumental to the purpose of obtaining legitimacy and social support for the negotiation process (Saguier 2007).

Where present, formal institutional channels of participation are separated from the trade negotiations and undertaken in an ad hoc manner. They include supporters of trade liberalization, while concerned groups that question the purpose, pace or appropriateness of trade liberalization are marginalized within the process. Furthermore, in many cases mechanisms for citizen participation agreed between CSOs and governing authorities remain subject to the discretionary whim of the latter. Moreover, mechanisms established for organizing public consultations have often had no enforcement capacity or resources, and are not widely known (Newell and Tussie 2006).

Some institutional innovations do allow for new forms of citizen engagement. The environmental side agreement of NAFTA, which activists lobbied hard for, created a Joint Public Advisory Committee (JPAC) to the North American Commission for Environmental Cooperation (NACEC), designed to provide input from NGOs and the private sector to the NACEC's governing council (Fisher 2002). The JPAC normally consists of fifteen members, with each nation appointing an equal number of representatives, and seeks public input and recommendations to help determine the advice it provides to the Environmental Council. According to Fisher (ibid.: 189), '[b]y consistently working to seek public input and incorporate the insights and expertise of civil society into its activities and projects, the NACEC's initiatives have been greatly enhanced'. Articles 14 and 15 of the side agreement provide that any citizen or NGO from the parties may send to the secretariat a submission asserting that a party is failing to effectively enforce its environmental law in order to promote exports or investment. In response, the NACEC's secretariat may be obliged to provide a factual record, though without legal value or the ability to trigger trade sanctions.

Certain efforts have been more serious in their outward attempts to create spaces for civil society, therefore, but all reproduce a liberal democratic version of participation as consultation about decisions already made, information about processes from which most groups are excluded, about agendas that have already been determined. This was the case, for example, with the Unidad de Atención a las Organizaciones Sociales (UAOS, Social Organizations Unit) established within the Mexican Ministry of Foreign Affairs in 2002, soon after President Fox's cabinet meetings held with Mexican CSOs. This has become one of the first liaison units at federal level interested in the institutionalization of dialogue with CSOs. The UAOS remained silent, however, in relation to mobilizations against the implementation of NAFTA's agricultural chapter in 2007, and since the end of that year has been reduced to an office within a sub-ministry for Multilateral Issues and Human Rights. Some sectors of civil society have remained sceptical about such top-down democratizing initiatives because they have tended to ignore the fact that some sectors of civil society are better positioned to participate than others (Domínguez and Icaza 2006). For this reason, invited spaces for civil society engagement tend to invoke a restrictive notion of the public realm, one which includes NGOs, business organizations, academics, think tanks and sometimes labour unions, but not broader movements; formally organized elements of civil society rather than its more unruly elements that are more difficult to manage.

Practices of citizenship in claimed spaces Many movements have shifted from engagement with institutions offering openings for citizen engagement to exit strategies and the construction of alternative 'outsider' approaches. Trade union organizations sought to influence the FTAA negotiation process by participating in a series of official consultations launched by the Committee of Government Representatives on the Participation of Civil Society (CGR) in 1998 and 2000. The CGR, however, proved to be an inadequate vehicle for the inclusion of social demands in the official process; its function was to 'transmit' the views of CSOs to the FTAA trade ministers. The limited scope of the CGR reflected the reticence of some Latin American governments towards establishing any kind of supranational initiative that could weaken the executive branches' control of the negotiation process[4] (Tussie and Botto 2003). Policy recommendations were submitted by trade unions and other social organizations via the internet to be incorporated in the negotiations. This input was not followed by any kind of feedback from the government officials, however, preventing a two-way political dialogue from taking place between trade ministers and trade unionists.

The underlying political purpose of the committee is made clear in the FTAA draft: 'The aim of the Committee of Government Representatives on the Participation of Civil Society is to build broad public understanding of and support for hemispheric trade liberalization by serving as a channel of communication between civil society at the regional level and the FTAA negotiations' (cited in Blum 2000: 6). It is also open only to those groups that express their views in a 'constructive manner', a device clearly intended to screen out critics. Issues such as human rights, gender and poverty, which are commonly treated by some officials as 'non-trade issues', were not brought into the trade discussions (Shamsie 2003: 16).

This led Global Exchange (n.d.) to reflect:

> Despite repeated calls for the open and democratic development of trade policy, the FTAA negotiations have been conducted without citizen input. A process has been set up to solicit citizens' views, but there is no real mechanism to incorporate the public's concerns into the actual negotiations. The public has been given nothing more than a suggestion box. At the same time, however, hundreds of corporate representatives are advising the US negotiators and have advance access to the negotiating texts. While citizens are left in the dark, corporations are helping to write the rules for the FTAA.

To broaden the base of citizen engagement in trade politics in the

Americas, beyond the realms of formal and invited participation, activists in the region organized their own plebiscites, and the national coordinating bodies of the anti-FTAA campaign organized a series of popular consultation initiatives between September 2002 and March 2003. The most successful of these experiences was conducted in Brazil between 1 and 7 September 2002, where more than ten million people in 3,894 municipalities from across the country voted in a popular plebiscite on the FTAA. The results of this consultation showed that 98 per cent of the people who participated were opposed to the signing of the FTAA, and that only 1 per cent were in support (Jorno do Brasil 2002). Material for popular education was also produced and widely distributed – 40,000 booklets, 5,000 videos, 15,000 books, 50,000 posters, as well as CDs circulated to local radio and 3,000,000 information leaflets on the FTAA. The massive turnout for the plebiscite was the result of a very successful information campaign, but also of the political momentum generated by an earlier popular plebiscite on foreign debt in 2000, in which 6 million people participated.

Consultations in other countries have been led by social organizations such as peasant movements and faith-based organizations, which are addressing labour issues outside the traditional form of trade unions. This was the case in Paraguay, where movements, organizations and NGOs working mostly on human rights and the environment organized relatively successful consultations in seventeen districts during 2003. Surpassing the organizers' expectations, 162,676 citizens participated in this consultation. A series of popular grassroots education initiatives were likewise held during the preparatory stages leading to the consultation: twenty-three workshops specifically targeted at community leaders in which 2,065 participated, while 182 general workshops reached 15,489 people. The Paraguayan campaign managed to introduce the FTAA as an issue for discussion in the press and in the national debate, which is considered one of the most important achievements of the movement against FTAA (Berrón and Freire 2004).

The contribution of these campaigns to the democratization of trade politics in the region is threefold. First, they permitted groups to raise public awareness and generate information about the FTAA throughout the region, at a time when the FTAA process was largely unknown to the public, being conducted almost exclusively by the executive branches of government. The opening up of public debate on trade issues at the national level accompanied (and perhaps contributed to) the change in the political climate in Latin America, which resulted in seven governments critical of the FTAA project coming to power. Each of them shared a growing consensus about the need to halt the FTAA process. The transition of movements into governments, however, has led to challenges for activists remaining outside government in maintaining critical distance and autonomy while playing a role that is supportive of those reform agendas of which they approve.

Second, the campaigns engaged broader publics, encouraging them to exercise their rights as citizens to decide whether or not to support the FTAA, compelling their national governments to hold official plebiscites. The possibility of participating in the popular consultations on the FTAA became an affirmation of democracy where citizens could claim their right to partake in decision-making concerning the fate of their communities (Saguier 2008).

Third, the ties that were developed among diverse movements and sectors in response to a coordinated effort to resist a neoliberal agenda in the FTAA are also important elements in the democratization of trade politics. The campaigns enabled a broad range of actors to mobilize in making the links between trade, development and citizenship rights. It also gave people confidence that it was possible to coordinate actions at a hemispheric level. Finally, the formation of heterogeneous coalitions requires that differences are acknowledged, negotiated and tolerated for the sake of solidarity. In this sense, multi-sectoral coalitions like the Hemispheric Social Alliance (HSA) have added to the possibility of democratization within the movements.

The significance of these initiatives in allowing citizens to express their views directly to political leaders, unmediated by civil society groups speaking on their behalf, should not be underestimated. When it comes to the definition and adoption of advocacy positions within coalitions, however, issues of power and hierarchy among groups have an effect on whose views count and which concerns are screened in and out of campaigns.

Axes of inclusion/exclusion In the case of the women's movement in the Americas, broadening participation has occurred through sustained trilateral cross-border campaigns on NAFTA's gendered nature and precarious democratic credentials. Diverse networks and groups have been mobilized around the negative impacts of trade liberalization on women's welfare, labour rights and employment opportunities in formal and informal sectors of the economy.

The incorporation of a gender perspective into civil society multi-sectoral alliances and networks, such the HSA, however, has not been an easy or automatic task. It has resulted from intense mobilizations of women from popular sectors allied to middle-class organizations in national and transnational campaigns (Domínguez 2002). For example, one representative of the Red Colombiana de Acción frente al Libre Comercio (RECALCA, Colombian Network against Free Trade) on the Women's Committee of HSA mentioned how difficult it was for them to promote their agenda on gender: 'the last time that we presented our priorities to the Hemispheric Council's representative, we were advised "compañera, wait, please don't distract us"'.[5] Another representative of the same committee reflected, 'within a multi-sectoral coalition like HSA the negotiation of differences is not exempt from power dynamics'.[6] The representation of different interests and agendas within the HSA has been addressed through the principle of equality in the right to vote, but this fails to take into account the inequality of power relations at work in relation, for example, to gender. As a multi-sectoral transnational network, the HSA faces a pressing need to 'democratize its own representativeness'.[7]

Civil society groups are clearly not immune from the asymmetrical relations that exist among their own members. In this sense women's organizations have confronted a double burden: that of opening spaces for gender concerns about trade governance within intergovernmental mechanisms, but also within civil society itself. For example, in the national campaign opposing the implementation of NAFTA's agricultural chapter, *Sin Maíz No Hay País* (Without corn there is no country), women played an important role as activists and peasants, but gender concerns about agricultural liberalization were not a prominent feature of the campaign.

The experience of the environmental movement also suggests different axes of inclusion and exclusion. Differences between groups were magnified by the creation of invited spaces by the state. During the NAFTA negotiations, for example, a split emerged within the environmental movement between those who viewed trade liberalization per se as antithetical to ecological sustainability, and those who took the view that under certain conditions trade liberalization can contribute to sustainability. Reflecting these differences, groups such as the National Wildlife Federation, the Environmental Defence Fund and World Wildlife Fund were able to support NAFTA, while the Sierra Club, Friends of the Earth, Greenpeace and Public Citizen took an adversarial position. The former constructed the Environmental Coalition for NAFTA, which sought to have the accord, complete with side agreement, accepted. The division made it easier for the US government to minimize the conflict caused by environmental issues by targeting key environmental groups willing to accommodate President Bush's economic objectives. Endorsement of NAFTA by the majority of national environmental organizations gave the administration, members of Congress and other pro-trade policy elites solid support for their defence of NAFTA on environmental grounds. The deal was reciprocated. Audley (1997: 130) notes, 'organizations supporting NAFTA were rewarded with a higher number of advisory appointments, thereby facilitating long-term participation in trade policy monopolies'. During key debates on fast-track decision-making on trade, for example, accommodating groups moderated their demands in exchange for formalized roles in trade policy and representatives of some environmental organizations were invited to join policy advisory committees (Hogenboom 1998).

Deepening and innovating democracy through trans-scalar practices of citizenship Trade issues have proved to be particularly relevant sites of contestation between formal representative democracy and informal direct participation. Rural workers, peasant and women's organizations, environmentalists, trade unions, faith-based organizations, indigenous movements and organizations of small producers have been salient forces in the development of novel repertoires of action to resist the exclusionary and undemocratic nature of recent trade initiatives. The involvement of indigenous peoples' movements in particular has strained traditional patterns of liberal politics and interest group representation (Yashar 2005).

Social movements have sought to deepen citizen engagement through efforts to encourage direct citizen engagement in politics, as opposed to participating in arenas and spaces constructed by policy elites for their own ends. This has taken the form of exposure tours, trade literacy work, publicizing educational materials and working with the alternative media. For example, diverse sectors of the women's movement have been actively involved in this strategy through academic analyses and economic literacy programmes on trade and gender, coalition-building, street protests and solidarity tours. The aim of these actions is to render more visible women's unpaid labour and to amplify the voice of those most affected by economic restructuring (Espino 2003; Espino and Azar 2002).

New arenas of deliberation have also enabled citizens to hold foreign economic actors to account through the construction of new fora. Examples include the Permanent Peoples' Tribunals on Transnational Corporations in Latin America. One tribunal, launched in Vienna in May 2006, focused on 'Neo-liberal policies and European TNCs in

Latin America and the Caribbean' and allowed an opportunity for environmental activists from Uruguay to bring cases against French and Spanish water companies, and Mapuche activists from Argentina to provide evidence of alleged illegal sales of their land to foreign investors such as the Italian fashion retailer Benetton.[8] Some such fora take on a generic form, while other parallel meetings and protests such as '*encuentros feministas*' (feminist encounters) and 'women's tribunals' open up spaces for specific sectors of society.

Often the intention is to draw excluded actors into the debate by creating new spaces or to demonstrate the gap between issues that concern broader publics and those which are being addressed (or neglected) in trade policy arenas. We see this in the case of crop biotechnology, for example, which has been the subject of international legal disputes before the WTO and the subject of aggressive attempts by exporters to penetrate markets in Latin America. In response to the limitations of formal channels of public participation around GM crops in Brazil, ActionAid Brazil, the Federação dos Órgãos para Asistência Social e Educacional (Federation of Social Assistance Agencies) and the Moviemiento dos Trabalhadores Rurais Sem Terra (Movement of Landless Rural Workers), among others, promoted two citizen juries targeting small-scale farmers, landless people and poor urban consumers in Fortaleza and Belem do Para in 2001 (Newell 2008). The juries were selected randomly from lists provided by a representative range of community-based associations. Hundreds of small-scale farmers, landless people and poor urban consumers attended the events, which took place over two days. A representative from ActionAid Brazil concluded that 'These people, always excluded from the process of policy-making in issues that affect them very much, had the opportunity to access all the information and to decide about it via members of the jury' (Campolina 2001: 29). Activists contribute, then, to deepening the democratization of trade policy through using the tools of democracy in novel, innovative and often informal ways.

Conclusions

In many ways the struggles that we have described in this chapter seek to democratize the institutions and policy processes through which trade agreements emerge and are managed. But they also aim to impact on the politics of knowledge production around trade by challenging the knowledge base and ideological underpinnings of the project of regional integration as it is manifested in these trade agreements. Ultimately, however, these also seek to challenge and exercise democratic control over the production process and material base which drive these processes in a direction that serves multinational capital in particular at the expense of alternative visions of development and regional integration by asserting that another production is possible (Sousa-Santos 2006).

It is certainly possible to argue that the processes of transnational mobilization described in this chapter produce new identities and solidarities around demands for social and ecological justice (Newell 2007). For some, however, this would not amount to evidence of transnational citizenships because the formal institutions active in the area of trade are insufficiently developed and without a mandate to recognize or process such claims. As Delanty argues:

> The modern state provided the institutional context in which citizenship developed so that modern society was not entirely shaped by the rule of pure democracy or by an unconstrained capitalism. The problem that conceptions of post-national citizenship, or more broadly, cosmopolitan citizenship, are faced with is that the institutions and social context on which citizenship rests do not exist in any substantive form in the global arena. (Delanty 2000: 4)

Though new identities are emerging through innovative forms of mobilization and accountability politics, we are cautious about claiming that new forms of global or regional/hemispheric citizenship are being practised in the absence of institutions with the mandate and resources to realize and enforce citizenship rights. It is often the case that regional and global solidarities are drawn upon in order to claim rights and justice from the state and other 'duty holders'. In this regard, symbolic expressions of citizenship as aspiration, intention and demonstration of solidarity should not be confused with the formal site in which competing citizenship claims are acknowledged, reconciled or denied. In most cases, this remains the nation-state. In the long run mobilizations around rights claims of excluded groups may succeed in bringing about the renegotiation of their formally granted citizenship rights and entitlements, but this is not the same as saying that such practices currently amount to actionable or concrete forms of citizenship.

We share the scepticism that others have expressed about the global or even regional exercise of citizenship when channels of accountability and participation at those levels are weak, direct elections do not take place and even national parliaments are often excluded from deliberations. Movements can work transnationally to democratize trade and other policy-making processes, invoking rights-based claims around the distributional and procedural aspects and consequences of the way in which trade politics is currently conducted. They can register concern about differential impacts upon poorer groups as well as mobilize demands for rights to information, transparency and participation. That does not mean that they are calling for a transnationalization of citizenship, even if they might desire stronger forms of accountability, participation and the existence of checks and balances within and upon economic institutions. There is a need for conceptual clarity, then, between notions of transparency, opening up and vertical accountability on the one hand, and the possibility of the exercise of citizenship in a trans- or post-state context on the other. The key features of citizenship for which movements have struggled for decades, if not centuries, at the national level in terms of recognition, legally enshrined and realized rights of access, recognizable and accessible channels of representation and electoral mechanisms that provide accountability, are unlikely to characterize regional economic or other institutions any time soon.

This is consistent with the claim that there is a need to 'ground cosmopolitan citizens' rights and duties in a constitution based on territoriality, and to create a public sphere for the discursive democratic governance of such a polity' (Crane et al. 2008: 177). Nevertheless, the idea of deliberation and discussion within a 'global public domain' is invoked by Ruggie, who finds evidence 'of an increasingly institutionalized transnational arena of discourse, contestation, and action concerning the production of global public goods, involving private as well as public actors' (Ruggie 2004: 504).

We can certainly find examples of such transnational arenas in the realm of trade politics. This is what leads others to contest the idea that citizenship can be understood largely in terms of formal political institutions (Mukhopadhyay 2004). They challenge the idea that transnational citizenship cannot be created because there are no transnational states. Citizenship, in this rendition, is also about identity and a sense of belonging to a particular (political) community or project that is not primarily defined by nationality. Feminist views on citizenship in particular have challenged the 'formal borders' of modern-patriarchal citizenship, for example (Espinosa Damián 2004; Yuval-Davis 2007). Likewise, the emergence of new and heterogeneous social movements pressing for social inclusion arising from the 'margins' of established society – such as urban unemployed workers, farmers and indigenous peoples, among others – challenges ideas about formal institutions being the only legitimate sites of political activity, including for the expression of citizenship rights and entitlements. An important characteristic of these movements is precisely their demand for greater autonomy from the state.

Returning to the start of the chapter, however, it is also the case that the latest wave of trade integration schemes promoted in the Americas since the 1990s has compromised the ability of governments to effectively implement previously granted political and socio-economic rights, whether to assembly, free education or water. It is defence of state capacity to realize these rights which characterizes many of the campaigns we have discussed in this chapter. While recognizing that activists make claims of duty holders beyond their own state and make use of openings in regional and international bodies to seek justice from their own and other states, one of the key foci of trade campaigning has been to defend the scope for autonomous state action by 'developmental' states aimed at prioritizing the needs of their poorest citizens rather than the investment needs of foreign firms. The aim has been to preserve policy space in the face of lock-in and pressure for conformity with neoliberal strictures (Gallagher 2005).

Practising citizenship in this context raises different challenges for each of the movements we have analysed here. Realizing ecological citizenship as a 'citizen of the world', or gendered citizenship as a basis for equal access to rights and entitlements, or citizenship as a worker based on class, each imply different challenges, scalar politics and political strategies. Shifts in the nature and sites of economic production, within the national, regional and global institutions that promote, manage and oversee this, and in the discourses that legitimize such shifts, have, if nothing else, created a richer and more multifaceted understanding of citizenship in a global age. The challenge remains for social movements and citizens to construct forms of citizenship that allow us to define a more just and sustainable form of globalization.

The coming to power of left-of-centre governments in Latin America from grassroots movements that were at the forefront of mobilizations against the FTAA – most notably in Bolivia, Paraguay, Ecuador and Brazil, but also to some extent in Uruguay, Venezuela and arguably Argentina – has opened up possibilities for rearticulating a new basis for regional integration. Their participation in the 'bottom-up' construction of social and environmental agendas of regional integration currently underpins efforts to build alternative models of integration as part of a South American Union process, the Alternativa Bolivariana para las Américas (ALBA) (Bolivarian Alternative for the Americas) and the Tratado de Comercio de los Pueblos (People's Trade Treaty). These developments suggest important implications for the issues we have discussed here. For example, the meeting of ALBA countries in April 2009 produced a declaration that included the following statement: 'Basic education, health, water, energy and telecommunications services should be declared human rights and cannot be subject to private deal or marketed by the World Trade Organization. These services are and should be essentially public utilities of universal access.'[9] The multiple citizenship claims that were voiced during the phase of resistance to neoliberal integration are now being articulated in national and regional reform proposals that suggest at least that there is an alternative to the claim that 'there is no alternative'.

Notes

1 We are grateful to a number of people in the Hemispheric Social Alliance and other social organizations who have facilitated access to information and contacts that were essential for this research. In particular, Gonzalo Berrón, Graciela Rodríguez, Marcela Escribano, Carlos Aguilar, Enrique Daza, Kjeld Jacobsen, Karen Hansen-Kuhn, Sheila Katz, John Foster, Juan Gonzalez, Carlos Coronado, Claudia Torrelli, Alejandro Villamar, Carlos Torres, Blanca Chancoso, Ximena Centellas, Renato Martins, Stephen Hellinger, Rafael Freire, Rick Arnold, Iara Petricovsky, Fatima Melo, Ivan Gonzalez, Dorval Brunelle, Jacobo Torres, Pierre-Yves Serinet and Tom Loudon.

2 Workshops were held during the Social Summit for the Integration of the Peoples in Cochabamba, Bolivia, in December 2006, the VI Hemispheric Encounter of Struggle against the FTAs in Havana, Cuba, in May 2008 and the Americas Social Forum in Guatemala in October 2008. We also participated as an observer at the Southern Peoples' Summit in Montevideo, Uruguay, in December 2007.

3 'Invited spaces' denotes the idea that the terms of engagement are set 'from above' by institutions opening spaces for those invited to participate; Cornwall and Schatten Coelho (2006).

4 The initiative to establish a CGR was supported by the governments of the United States, Argentina and other countries from the Caribbean, but was vehemently resisted by Mexico, Peru and some of the Central American governments.

5 This comment was shared with Rosalba Icaza during the meeting of the Women's Committee of the Hemispheric Social Alliance prior to Guatemala's Americas Social Forum of 2008.

6 From notes taken in the workshop 'Social mobilization and trade politics. Learning from civil society experiences in Latin America' that the authors of this chapter organized during the Social Summit for the Integration of the Peoples in Cochabamba, Bolivia, in December 2006.

7 Ibid.

8 Aborigen Argentino, 'Familia Mapuche enfrenta al grupo Benetton por tierra que le pertenece', www.aborigenargentino.com.ar, accessed 23 December 2005.

9 ALBA, *The Declaration of Cumaná*, 21 April 2009.

References

Audley, J. (1997) *Green Politics and Global Trade: NAFTA and the Future of Environmental Politics*, Washington, DC: Georgetown University Press.

Balanyá, B., M. Blower-Ailloud and K. Handlebar (eds) (2005) *Reclaiming Public Water: Achievements, Struggles and Visions from around the World*, Amsterdam: Transnational Institute.

Berrón, G. and R. Freire (2004) 'Los movimientos sociales del Cono Sur contra el mal llamado "libre comercio"', *Revista Observatorio Social de América Latina*, 5(13): 296–306.

Blowfield, M. and J. Frynas (2005) 'Setting new agendas: critical perspectives on Corporate Social Responsibility in the developing world', *International Affairs*, 81(3): 499–513.

Blum, J. (2000) 'The FTAA and the fast track to forgetting the environment: a comparison of the NAFTA and Mercosur environmental models as examples for the hemisphere', *Texas International Law Journal*, 35(3): 435–58.

Campolina, A. (2001) 'Brazilian small-scale farmers and poor consumers reject GMOs', *LEISA Magazine*, 17(4).

COPA (2008) 'Mission', www.copa.qc.ca/eng/who/mission.html, accessed 10 March 2008.

Cordonier-Segger, M. C. (2005) 'Enhancing social and environmental cooperation in the Americas', in M. C. Cordonier-Segger and M. L. Reyna (eds), *Beyond the Barricades: The Americas' Trade and Sustainable Development Agenda*, Aldershot: Ashgate.

Cornwall, A. and V. Schatten Coelho (eds) (2006) *Spaces for Change? The Politics of Citizen Participation in New Democratic Arenas*, London: Zed Books.

Crane, A., D. Fatten and J. Moon (2008) *Corporations and Citizenship: Business, Responsibility and Society*, Cambridge: Cambridge University Press.

Delanty, G. (2000) *Citizenship in a Global Age: Society, Culture and Politics*, Buckingham: Open University Press.

Domínguez, E. (2002) 'Continental transnational activism and women workers' networks within NAFTA', *International Feminist Journal of Politics*, 4: 216–39.

Domínguez, E. and R. Icaza (2006) 'Women organizing against restructuring and free trade: from Mar del Plato to Quito via Beijing', Latin American Studies Association 2006 Conference, San Juan de Puerto Rico.

Espino, A. (2003) *Los Impactos de Género en las Políticas Comerciales: Avances y desafíos para la investigación y la acción. Programa Economía y Género 2002–2004*, Havana: Fundacion Heinrich Boll.

Espino, A. and P. Azar (2002) *Comercio International y Equidad de Género*, vol. 2: *Quién gana y quién pierde en los acuerdos de integración economica*, Montevideo: UNIFEM.

Espinosa Damián, G. (2004) 'Cidudanías y feminismos. Entre el género y la clase', in R. Edmé Domínguez (ed.), *Mujeres, Ciudadanía y Participación Política en México*, Gothenburg University and Red Hanna.

Fisher, R. (2002) 'Trade and environment in the FTAA: learning from the NAFTA', in C. L. Deere and D. Sty (eds), *Greening the Americas:*

NAFTA's Lessons for Hemispheric Trade, Cambridge, MA: MIT Press.
Gallagher, K. P. (2005) (ed.) Putting Development First: The Importance of Policy Space in the WTO and International Financial Institutions, London: Zed Books.
Gill, S. (2002) 'Institutionalizing inequality and the clash of globalization', International Studies Review, 4(2): 47–65.
Global Exchange (n.d.) 'Top ten reasons to oppose the Free Trade of the Americas', non-exchangeable/campaigns/feta/topten.html, accessed February 2004.
Hogenboom, B. (1998) Mexico and the NAFTA Environment Debate, Utrecht: International Books.
Icaza, R. (2004) 'Civil society and regionalisation: a framework for analysis on transborder civic activism', Centre for the Study of Regionalisation and Globalisation Working Paper 150/4, University of Warwick.
Jornal do Brasil (2002) 'Dez milhões contra a ALCA', 18 September.
Mehta, L. (2006) 'Do human rights make a difference to poor people? The case of water in South Africa', in P. Newell and J. Wheeler (eds), Rights, Resources and the Politics of Accountability, London: Zed Books.
Mukhopadhyay, M. (2004) 'Introduction: gender, citizenship and governance', in M. Valk, S. Cummings and H. van Dam (eds), Gender, Citizenship and Governance: A Global Book, Amsterdam/Oxford: Royal Tropical Institute/Oxfam.
Newell, P. (2001) 'Managing multinationals: the governance of investment for the environment', Journal of International Development, 13: 907–19.
— (2002) 'From responsibility to citizenship: corporate accountability for development', IDS Bulletin, 33(2).
— (2007) 'Trade and environmental justice in Latin America', New Political Economy, 12(2): 237–59.
— (2008) 'Trade and biotechnology in Latin America: democratization, contestation and the politics of mobilization', Journal of Agrarian Change, 8(2/3): 345–76.
Newell, P. and D. Tussie (2006) (eds) 'Civil society participation in trade policy-making in Latin America: reflections and lessons', IDS Working Paper no. 267, Institute of Development Studies, Brighton.
Newell, P. and J. Wheeler (eds) (2006) Rights, Resources and the Politics of Accountability, London: Zed Books.
Obach, B. (2004) Labor and the Environmental Movement: The Quest for Common Ground, Cambridge, MA: MIT Press.
Ruggie, J. (2004) 'Reconstituting the global public domain – issues, actors, and practices', European Journal of International Relations, 10(4): 499–531.
Sachs, W. (1997) 'Ecology, justice and development', Development, 24(2).
Saguier, M. I. (2007) 'The Hemispheric Social Alliance and the Free Trade Area of the Americas process: the challenges and opportunities of transnational coalitions against neo-liberalism', Globalizations, 4(2): 252–64.
— (2008) 'Movimientos sociales transnacionales y la democratización del comercio en las Américas', Revista Pensamiento Propio, 28, Buenos Aires.
Scholte, A. (2000) Globalization: A Critical Introduction, Houndmills: Macmillan.

Sell, S. (2003) *Private Power, Public Law: The Globalization of Intellectual Property Rights*, Cambridge: Cambridge University Press.

Shamsie, Y. (2003) *Mutual Misgivings: Civil Society Inclusion in the Americas*, Ottawa: North-South Institute.

Sousa-Santos, B. (2006) *Another Production is Possible: Beyond the Capitalist Canon*, London: Verso.

Tussie, D. and M. Botto (2003) 'La internacionalización de la agenda de participación: el debate regional', in D. Tussie and M. Botto (eds), *ALCA y las cumbres de las Américas: ¿una nueva relación público–privada?*, Buenos Aires: Editorial Biblios.

TWN (Third World Network) (2006) 'US FTA likely to open Peru to GMOs?', TWN Biosafety Information Service, Kuala Lumpur, 2 October.

Walzer, M. (1994) *Thick and Thin: Moral Argument at Home and Abroad*, Notre Dame, IN: Notre Dame Press.

Yashar, D. J. (2005) *Contesting Citizenship in Latin America: The Rise of Indigenous Movements and the Post-liberal Challenge*, Cambridge: Cambridge University Press.

Yuval-Davis, N. (2007) 'Intersectionality, citizenship and contemporary politics of belonging', *Critical Review of International Social and Political Philosophy*, 10(4): 561–74.

9 · Mobilization and political momentum: anti-asbestos struggles in South Africa and India

LINDA WALDMAN

Although specialists have been aware of the dangers posed by asbestos for over a hundred years, in recent years widespread knowledge of asbestos's carcinogenic properties has led people to become more aware of the associated, and highly dangerous, occupational and environmental illness. As a result, new movements have surfaced across the world seeking to secure a healthier life through the banning of asbestos.

Focusing on these mobilizations in South Africa and India, this chapter asks how, in relation to asbestos activism, do changing patterns of power and governance affect the meanings, experiences and patterns of citizen mobilization (and vice versa) in a globalizing world? Anti-asbestos movements in South Africa and India have very different trajectories and consequences which have created different and new axes of inclusion and exclusion. In South Africa, activism has led to the banning of all asbestos use, whereas mobilization in India struggles for government recognition of asbestos risks against a powerful pro-asbestos lobby. This chapter explores these contrasting mobilization strategies, asking what has led to these outcomes and who stands to gain from the process. Although comparison tends, by its very nature, to highlight similarity and perhaps simplify a complex reality, it also provides an opportunity to explore what facilitates – or indeed obstructs – mobilization through global and local relations. Ultimately the chapter examines how anti-asbestos mobilization impacts on citizenship in terms of rights, values and accountability.

Common forms of asbestos (fibrous rock) are white (chrysotile), blue (crocidolite) and brown (amosite). The largest deposits are found in Canada and Russia, but it has been – and in some cases continues to be – mined in Australia, Brazil, Canada, China, India, Italy, Kazakhstan, Russia, South Africa and Zimbabwe. Because asbestos is fireproof, very durable and does not corrode, it has been used in an incredible range of products, including cigarette filters, mattresses, beer filters, brake linings, buildings and ships (McCulloch 2002). But microscopic asbestos fibres are carcinogenic and cause pleural effusion, pleural plaques, pleural thickening, asbestosis, lung cancer and mesothelioma. Pleural plaques are seen as benign and without physical symptoms, while mesothelioma is always fatal. All asbestos diseases have extended latency periods and people experience the symptoms only twenty to forty years after exposure. All forms of asbestos disease are untreatable. Given these dangers, the use of asbestos is regulated by global authorities.

The shifting nature of global authority

Many international organizations are involved in global health governance, which, although in its infancy, addresses health issues across national boundaries, across sectors and involving diverse actors and interests. The 'confusion of mandates' within global health governance is evident in the failure of any single organization to take the lead (Dodgson et al. 2002: 13). Because there is no formal authority offering a definitive view on questions of global health, the role of knowledge becomes critical. Global health governance is thus a form of 'soft' governance: the World Health Organization (WHO) can recommend actions but cannot compel states to comply. The World Trade Organization (WTO) relies on states to debate and agree on the dangers of certain industrial products, but cannot impose its judgement.

In relation to asbestos, international organizations have sought to mediate between corporate interests and health. For instance, the 1986 International Labour Organization (ILO) Asbestos Convention establishes guidelines for the safe use of asbestos, but does not forbid its use (Danish Confederation of Trade Unions 2005). During the late 1980s and 1990s Canadian asbestos corporations sought to influence the International Programme on Chemical Safety (IPCS), the WHO and the WTO through promoting the 'controlled use' of asbestos (McCulloch and Tweedale 2008). All these organizations relied heavily on industry-sponsored scientific expertise, and failed to support a ban on asbestos. Towards the end of the 1990s, however, wide-scale protest and social mobilization led to a reorientation of these global regulatory bodies. Industrial science and corporate voices were subsequently marginalized as mainstream scientists insisted on independent asbestos risk assessments by the WHO, WTO and IPCS (Castleman 2000). These international regulatory organizations then reached greater consensus, recognizing that all asbestos is carcinogenic, that there is no realistic way of controlling its use and that there are no safe exposure thresholds. This consensus has, however, not brought about an end to asbestos use; in part because these debates are too entrenched (McCulloch and Tweedale 2008) and, in part, because asbestos has to be banned by national governments, not international regulatory authorities.

Since the early 1990s, global social mobilization against asbestos has monitored and challenged these global authorities as it has sought to facilitate country-specific bans. Activists have created an interconnected network of anti-asbestos organizations in places as far afield as Japan, Korea, South Africa, Brazil and India (Castleman 2007). In 1999, the International Ban Asbestos Secretariat (IBAS) – formed in response to the growth of anti-asbestos movements – demanded a global ban on all forms of asbestos. Thereafter, country-specific movements, internationally networked through IBAS, challenged the WHO, the WTO and the IPCS on their industrial alliances and ultimately forced the consensus described above. IBAS's global forum for diverse anti-asbestos activists resulted in new campaigns starting in India, Malaysia, Canada and South Africa.

The asbestos industry

Initially a few large multinational corporations dominated the international asbestos market. In the 1930s these corporations formed a cartel which set prices, eliminated competition, emphasized asbestos's positive attributes and downplayed the health risks. The companies financed scientific research and invented new uses for asbestos, marketing it as quintessentially modern (McCulloch and Tweedale 2008). Asbestos production was cheap, primarily because production costs had been externalized on to workers and people located near production plants while ignoring its social and environmental effects (Castleman 2007).

The economic viability of large multinational corporations was undermined by social mobilization in the late 1990s, which resulted in many countries banning asbestos. In countries where asbestos awareness remained low, nationally owned, small-scale companies replaced the multinationals. In India, for instance, Everest was started by a multinational that dominated the UK and world asbestos market. In the mid-1990s, it became wholly Indian-owned. Everest still uses asbestos, ostensibly in a controlled environment and in accordance with national health and safety regulations. The degree to which it is monitored and meets national standards is, however, questionable (Tweedale 2008). In contrast, the South African company Everite was influenced by its Scandinavian connections and by the Scandinavian bans on asbestos in the 1970s. It introduced sophisticated health and safety procedures and worker training in the 1980s and stopped asbestos production in 2002 – both well in advance of South African national requirements.

These different ownership structures have also influenced how

TABLE 9.1 Schematic comparison of anti-asbestos activism in India and South Africa

	South Africa	India
Dynamics of mobilization	Grassroots mobilization rooted in poverty, unemployment and experience of asbestos disease	Mobilization of urban networks born out of exposure to international debates about asbestos hazards
	Unemployed mineworkers, some teachers and social workers	Professional networks of journalists, scientists, doctors, lawyers
Politics of knowledge	Asbestos disease recognized through the indigenous term *mynstof* and centralized state records	No local awareness of asbestos disease and no centralized state records
	Recruited specialized actors (lawyers, scientists, journalists)	Professional actors are activists mobilizing against asbestos
	No significant corporate challenge	Very powerful corporate challenge
Economic and social conditions of asbestos production	High unemployment, strong trade unions willing to challenge corporations	High unemployment, trade unions reluctant to advance job losses
	Multiple sources of compensation for asbestos diseases provide some financial support	Very little compensation for asbestos disease
	Asbestos embedded in houses viewed as problematic	Asbestos embedded in houses viewed as desirable and modern
Politics of intervention	Decentralized democracy	Decentralized democracy
	A supportive state seeking to address asbestos disease, environmental pollution and supporting activists' mobilization for compensation from former mining companies	An unsupportive state with legislative systems that advantage asbestos producers and erase evidence of asbestos disease or environmental pollution. Very little support for activists
	Participatory Forum with asbestos activists involved in policy processes, joint decision-making and a willingness to hear community perspectives	Environmental public hearings highly symbolic, local people's voices not heard
	All asbestos use banned in 2008	Asbestos privileged over substitutes and widely used
	All South Africans, especially workers and rural, unemployed town residents, emerge as possible winners	Asbestos corporations emerge as clear winners

companies engage with anti-asbestos mobilization. In the 1980s, after years of insisting that asbestos could be safely used, Everite stopped seeing anti-asbestos campaigners as adversaries and actively sought to engage with them. This 'helped the industry come to terms with the inescapable fact that the future of [...] its raw materials was uncertain' (Gibson 1987: 7). Everite then launched health and safety campaigns, an employee compensation scheme and a forum for South African asbestos production companies to consider alternatives. It engaged in national and international policy processes, working alongside trade unions and anti-asbestos activists for an asbestos ban. In India, Everest representatives argued that the company could make non-asbestos products, but they couldn't see the point in doing this because health risks were controlled during production, substitutes cost more and there was no market for non-asbestos products. Everite's approach, although ultimately driven by economic incentives, is accountable to workers, and it was able to ride a groundswell of public opinion and to position itself strategically within asbestos-related political processes in South Africa. Indian-owned Everest, however, sees anti-asbestos mobilization as stemming from a deficit of scientific knowledge, an ignorance of health and safety measures and lawyers' avarice. As such, Everest frequently takes 'containment action', responding defensively to activism and dismissing workers' health. It is accountable to the state and its owners through a version of corporate responsibility that promotes cheap, accessible, asbestos-ridden products in order to help India 'progress'.

Anti-asbestos mobilization

Despite similar experiences of British colonialism and industrialization, South Africa and India have had very different historical trajectories in relation to asbestos, with different mining activities, governance processes and social movements. The state is hostile to anti-asbestos mobilization in India, whereas in South Africa it has thrown its full weight behind international networking and mobilization. As a result, South African mobilization has led to new forms of citizenship, bolstered South African identities and shaped new citizen demands. In contrast, Indian mobilization has undermined a collective Indian identity and rights-claiming while creating more globalized identities for some activists. The following detailed comparison of anti-asbestos mobilization shows how these differential results came about and why.[1] It explores the four aspects of anti-asbestos activism summarized in Table 9.1, namely the dynamics of mobilization, the politics of knowledge, the economic and social conditions of asbestos production and the politics of intermediation.

The dynamics of mobilization South African anti-asbestos mobilization has been primarily grassroots oriented, arising out of poverty, unemployment and people's experience of asbestos disease. This is in stark contrast to Indian mobilization, where professional activists have been exposed to international debates about the dangers of asbestos. The source of inspiration for activism has significant ramifications for engagement in local and global mobilization, and for citizen identity.

In South Africa, Prieska, a rural town in the Northern Cape, was the centre of asbestos mining. Residents were exposed to asbestos for over a century, and many suffered from asbestos diseases. In 1979, heavily affected by the imminent closure of the mines[2] and by asbestos diseases, the town residents formed Concerned People against Asbestos (CPAA). The CPAA comprised former mineworkers, schoolteachers and social workers, born in and committed to Prieska. The CPAA organizers were immersed, through their work and their extended kin networks, in the community of Prieska, and they had first-hand experience of the manner in which former mineworkers had been left destitute and ill when mines closed. Thus, although generally comprised of better-educated people employed in relatively well-paid positions, the CPAA was a grassroots organization made up of local people and designed to improve local conditions.

The CPAA was initially concerned with improving town residents' access to government-issued compensation for asbestos diseases, challenging the Medical Bureau of Occupational Diseases (MBOD) to improve its services. Although the MBOD was concerned with the health surveillance of mineworkers and with compensation, it did not make it easy for injured or diseased workers to claim. The CPAA challenge was not directed at the mines' destructive and inhumane activities, or at the principle of compensation. Instead the CPAA tried to address local hardship, namely that access to compensation was hampered by long travelling distances, high relative costs of transport, lack of disposable income, low levels of literacy and general despondency brought about both by people's illness and by their perception that asbestos disease was 'normal'. The first battles the CPAA engaged in were thus focused on getting regulatory authorities to meet their legislative commitments, rather than seeking to directly challenge the state.

The MBOD's lack of cooperation and racism made the CPAA broaden its focus. It began to address environmental issues and to tackle the rehabilitation of abandoned mines and mills. CPAA meetings with diverse government officials tried to ascertain which departments were responsible and which would assist them. This resulted in high-profile national political interest and in the launch of a National Asbestos Summit. During this period of organizational expansion, the National Union of Mineworkers (NUM) became involved, issuing press statements supporting asbestos claimants' demands and public protest marches in Prieska. Alongside this, the CPAA expanded its organizational base to neighbouring towns where former mineworkers lived.

In addition to broadening its geographical remit, the CPAA – assisted by the NUM – expanded its knowledge base by finding scientists to collect data and assess the extent of pollution. A fortuitous meeting between a founding CPAA member and Dr Ahmon Randeree, who had been exposed to asbestos litigation in Canada, ushered in a new stage in the campaign. Working with doctors and community members, the CPAA facilitated the examination of more than a thousand Prieska residents. The results generated a computer databank of people suffering from respiratory problems and in need of further examination, which was, in turn, used to encourage medical professors from Johannesburg to get involved. As the CPAA made connections with international doctors and with prominent South Africans, new mobilization agendas evolved, particularly the idea that someone should be held accountable for gross abuse of human rights by the asbestos industry, and contact was made with international, Northern-based NGOs. In 1989 the British organization ACTSA (Action for Southern Africa) began publishing articles, bringing the CPAA's campaign into the international spotlight, leading to the involvement of both national and international lawyers. Ultimately this locally based campaign resulted in a transnational legal case in which 7,500 South African asbestos sufferers took Cape PLC, a British mining company, to court in the UK.

In contrast to the localization evident in the South African example, asbestos protest in India focused – almost from the start – on the activities of an international network of concerned citizens. The seeds of Indian asbestos mobilization are to be found in the National Campaign on Dust-Related Lung Diseases (NCDRLD) of 1984. Possibly the first occupational health struggle in India, this focused on the 'conscientization and leadership building of workers activists' (PRIA 2004: 1). Organized by an NGO in New Delhi, the campaign sought to encourage grassroots activists to initiate local responses to occupational health problems. Its successes include the NGO Kamdar Swasthya Suraksha Mandal (KSSM), born through the experiences of Haushala Prasad Mishra, a worker in a cotton mill in Ahmedabad, Gujarat. After thirteen years of employment, Mishra noticed that he and other workers were having difficulty breathing. His union activities allowed his investigations into workers' health to continue unnoticed. Mishra's meeting with members of the NGO Participatory Research in Asia (PRIA), who were campaigning for the NCDRLD, was a turning point because he learnt that he and his fellow workers were suffering from bysinnosis, a chronic lung disease caused by cotton. Mishra followed this up first with the National Institute of Occupational Health (NIOH), a state institution which ensures workers' health and had studied the prevalence of bysinnosis, and then by working his way through the bureaucracy for compensation. The Employers State Insurance Scheme (ESIS) made it difficult for illiterate workers to claim compensation and treated them disrespectfully, but Mishra secured compensation for eight workers. He no longer works for the cotton mill and now runs KSSM, an occupational health NGO, which educates workers in self-diagnosis and legal rights, and campaigns on their behalf, in 2006 winning a 'special civil application in the Gujarat High Court for the rights of sewerage workers' who were exposed to noxious gases and experienced chronic health problems (KSSM 2006: 9).

PRIA and KSSM have not, however, remained connected, and there has been no follow-up on the NCDRLD. PRIA experienced a shift from core to project-based funding, which meant its occupational health programme was replaced by development issues prioritized by the international donors who fund it. KSSM has retained its focus on local occupational health, although Mishra bemoans the lack of contact with PRIA and, with this, his inability to connect to the international world.

The combination of changing donor priorities and exposure to international networks working on asbestos stimulated new avenues of mobilization. During the NCDRLD, Barry Castleman, an environmentalist and researcher specializing in asbestos hazards with links to IBAS, visited PRIA. This visit established transnational links and facilitated the emergence of the Ban Asbestos Network India (BANI), an alliance of primarily urban-based scientists, doctors, journalists, public health researchers, trade union activists and civil society groups which 'condemns the government's continued pro-industry bias and lack of concern for the asbestos-injured' (Krishna 2006: 25). BANI's urban base was significant because, as Walsh (1988) has argued, the use of expert scientific information in toxic protests provides an important expert base; without this, BANI's arguments could be rejected as uneducated and unscientific. Using these professional skills, BANI has drawn public attention to hazardous and toxic products, rallied medical experts to demand the phasing out of asbestos, filed complaints to the National Human Rights Commission and pressurized the government to initiate studies on asbestos hazards. Like the South African MBOD, the NIOH initially supported government and industry concerns, despite aiming to identify and mitigate India's occupational and environmental health problems.[3] BANI highlighted the fact that the NIOH 'has compromised its credentials by taking the fiscal support from the chrysotile asbestos industry to do a study' (Krishna 2008: 43), challenged scientific understandings of asbestos diseases and raised urban and international support for their campaign.

To sum up, both BANI and the CPAA were initiated in the 1980s and mobilized against asbestos. The CPAA was a grassroots organization, while BANI, in contrast, stemmed from international mobilization processes and links with IBAS. Both organizations sought improvements in the state-run occupational health institutions as an initial starting point, wanting to get these institutions to work for workers. In South Africa this quickly developed into a more internationalized legal campaign which focused on British companies compensating workers, but retaining grassroots involvement throughout. In India, BANI forced the NIOH to recognize more cases of asbestos-related diseases, but only partially to align itself with workers.

As shown in this section, PRIA's broad-based mobilization was undermined by international funding priorities, while the CPAA's was characterized by grassroots, bottom-up pressure on the state. As discussed in the following section, however, other factors, such as understandings of science, also influence the possibilities of shaping grassroots movements. Both BANI and the CPAA have sought to challenge the politics of knowledge and different framings of asbestos dangers and disease as part of their campaigns.

The politics of knowledge As this section demonstrates, South Africa experienced broad recognition of the dangers of asbestos – through indigenous conceptualizations of asbestos disease and through centralized government recognition of disease and accompanying compensation. In India, in contrast, there was no local awareness of asbestos disease and no centralized system of recording and compensating it. Whereas South African grassroots activists recruited scientists to provide supporting evidence for the already widespread recognition that asbestos was dangerous, in India skilled activists, who were professionals in their own right, engaged in the politics of knowledge and science in order to challenge corporate science and to persuade the state and the public of the dangers of asbestos.

During the time of apartheid in South Africa (1948–94), research into asbestos hazards was suppressed by the mining industry and the apartheid state, which sought to protect the foreign exchange generated by asbestos production (McCulloch 2002). For people living near and working in the mines, there was widespread knowledge of the disease known as *mynstof* (mine dust),[4] but little awareness of the scientific or political processes that underlay it. Many people understood asbestos diseases to be 'natural', biomedical experiences;[5] Bergland (2001) argues that diseases understood as 'natural' need to be constituted in discourse before they can be recognized as a problem. Most of Prieska's adult population had worked in the asbestos mines, played on asbestos dumps as children or breastfed while their mothers hand-processed asbestos. They clearly linked *mynstof* to the mines, but initially did not connect the actions of the mining corporations to their own lack of well-being. It was, they believed, a disease about which nothing could be done. While medically accurate, the CPAA's actions laid bare the economic and political processes that caused asbestos exposure and reframed asbestos diseases.

As the CPAA's battles became more scientific and political, they recruited more specialized actors, mobilizing scientists and trade unions to assist in data collection and measuring pollution. It presented scientific evidence to the Ministry of Health and challenged it to do something about the exposed asbestos dumps, the limited involvement of the medical profession, doctors' inaccessibility, and asbestos hazards in houses. Working closely with the NUM and with medical professionals, it produced widespread evidence of asbestos diseases. Unlike in India, this mobilization around scientific and medical issues took the form of validating scientific claims rather than activists doing their own research.

Although the CPAA was instrumental in generating renewed interest in asbestos and pollution issues, and although it managed the research, it did not conduct its own science. This was not necessary because, despite the apartheid government's clampdown on research into and publicity about the dangers of asbestos, the MBOD had been compensating mineworkers for asbestos diseases since 1956 (McCulloch 2002). It had detailed medical records of all South Africans who had received compensation. This meant that there was widespread awareness of asbestos disease and a massive databank of information. In addition, because working in the Northern Cape mines was a family affair, the CPAA was talking to people who had grown up near the mines and were well versed in the experience of *mynstof*. At the end of apartheid, the political mood changed as the new constitution emphasized citizens' health and rights. South African scientists embraced the international position that asbestos was dangerous, and there was widespread support for the CPAA's campaign to address past injustices. In addition, because the global recognition of the dangers of asbestos had led to mine closures, companies withdrawing from South Africa or emphasizing worker health, there was little corporate challenge to the idea that asbestos was hazardous.

The same cannot be said for India. Here there was far less sense that workers had any awareness of the disease. For example, it was only after thirty-one years of working with asbestos, when his union initiated a health check, that one worker became aware of its dangers (Mohite 2008). There are many reasons why workers knew nothing about asbestos's hazardous properties: few workers grew up near mines where people had an indigenous name for the disease and knew of its effects; companies had never provided safety equipment or warned workers; casual labourers were not entitled to medical inspections or to unionize; workers had widely dispersed geographical origins and thus did not see others experiencing similar symptoms; very few workers have been compensated for asbestos diseases; and companies deliberately rotated workers and kept their periods of maximum exposure short, especially if they exhibited signs of disease (Tweedale 2008).

Medical categorization of disease and compensation structures also affected workers' knowledge. In South Africa, the MBOD categorized asbestos diseases into first- and second-grade damage to the lungs. It recognized pleural asbestosis, interstitial asbestosis, first-grade pneumoconiosis, pleural plaque and asbestosis as first grade and mesothelioma and pulmonary tuberculosis as second grade. Because the MBOD understood these diseases as progressing in a linear fashion from benign to malignant, workers received compensation in two bulk payments. There was thus a substantial body of literature, scientific recognition and documented evidence of the extent of asbestos disease in South Africa. These factors all benefited the CPAA, and when it finally went to court in Britain, it drew on 7,500 MBOD medical records to substantiate its claims. In India, the NIOH has been far less proactive in the registration and reporting of asbestos diseases. In the first place, formal recognition of asbestos diseases is confined to asbestosis, with pleural plaques, pleural thickening, lung cancer and mesothelioma not officially categorized as occupational diseases. Second, medical doctors are poorly qualified in occupational health, do not routinely take occupational histories and are actively encouraged not to diagnose asbestos diseases. Third, there is no systematic attempt to record the extent of disease and, as fewer than fifty workers have received ESIS compensation for asbestosis (Dutta 2008), there is no comprehensive evidence of the degree of asbestos disease. Instead, 'asbestosis is hidden in India. It does not sing on trains or beg on the streets. The disease is misdiagnosed, underreported and forgotten' (Dutta, cited in Daubs 2008).

This position – that the diagnosis of asbestosis and other related diseases is rare – is one which the Indian government is anxious to maintain. There are thus very few established records of workers getting ill. Although different BANI members have sought to bring together disparate recordings of disease (Daubs 2008), there is no official attempt to coordinate these records into a national register. This has critical ramifications for BANI's mobilization against asbestos, as it makes it substantially harder to prove to the general public and to workers that asbestos is a problem worthy of concern. In a recent attempt to record the extent of asbestos disease, the Occupational Health and Safety Centre in Mumbai conducted medical inspections outside an asbestos factory gate, demonstrating that 23 per cent of the workers tested suffered from asbestosis. In 2008, a Right to Information submission forced the Tata Memorial Hospital to provide the first official evidence of widespread mesothelioma. It reported that 107 cases of mesothelioma had been diagnosed between 1985 and 2005 (Dutta 2008).

Facilitated by the lack of data on asbestos diseases and the fact that it remains legal to use chrysotile asbestos, the Indian debate over the dangers of asbestos has become highly scientific. The Indian government – under pressure to ban asbestos – has conducted various research exercises to examine the dangers of chrysotile asbestos (ibid.). In 2004, the Indian Ministry of Chemicals and Fertilizers commissioned the NIOH to research the health and environmental hazards of chrysotile asbestos in preparation for the international Rotterdam Convention.[6] This study, however, is, as Lemen argues, one of 'smoke and mirrors', creating the illusion of scientific research (2008: 16). For instance, the study is based on current workers at asbestos cement factories that have been operating for ten to fifteen years, showing complete disregard for the well-known fact that there is a twenty-to-forty-year latency period between exposure and the onset of asbestos disease. The study uses sophisticated techniques to count asbestos fibres with an aerodynamic diameter greater than 5μm in length and smaller than 3μm, disregarding the fact that many chrysotile fibres fall outside these categories (ibid.). In addition, evidence of 'impaired lung function' is explained through alternative explanatory factors. The study will not be peer-reviewed by independent scientists, nor will workers or members of the public be given an opportunity to comment (Dutta 2008). The collusion between the national government and industry thus creates a set of scientific framings that exclude those most likely to exhibit signs of asbestos diseases. They also exclude people's accounts of disease. In stark contrast with the work of the CPAA in South Africa, the participants of these scientific debates have not been presented with dying asbestos workers' stories or graphic images of exposed mine dumps. Instead, they are blinded by seemingly 'scientific' evidence. As Lemen has argued:

> Overall, a reading of this study by the untrained reader would seem to support the safety of using chrysotile asbestos. However, the methods used [...] preclude the validity of any such conclusion. In fact, very little light is shed on the safety or otherwise of chrysotile use by this cross-sectional study because it focuses on active workforces. By their very nature such groups of workers are characterized by low latencies – particularly low in some of the workforces studied – so discovery of long-latent asbestos-related disease is virtually impossible. (2008: 18)

BANI has revealed this misuse of science, has questioned who funds these research projects and challenged the scientists' neutrality. Nonetheless, these scientific debates – flawed as they might be – provide support for the Indian government's argument that Indian asbestos is safe and that controlled methods of production protect workers. BANI has championed a growing body of Indian scientific research, published in peer-reviewed journals and reported in media articles, which demonstrates the presence of asbestos diseases (Murlidhar and Kanhere 2005). In addition to exploring epidemiological debates about fibre size and bio-persistence, BANI-aligned research has examined political and economic considerations for continuing – or banning – asbestos production. For example, Murlidhar and Kanhere examine the political reasons why asbestos disease diagnosis is so limited. They find workers experiencing difficulty in obtaining medical certifications; deliberate misdiagnosis; widespread medical naivety about occupational diseases; industrial management control over workers, over the factory space and over the results of medical surveillance, which means workers do not know about their own medical conditions and the 'healthy worker effect'[7] (ibid.). Similarly, the peripatetic nature of construction work and workers' temporary, migratory lifestyles mean they often have no written record of employment. These factors operate to keep disease rates down. As far as exposure to asbestos fibres and official records of asbestos diseases go, these workers are simply invisible. BANI's struggle therefore is far greater than that undertaken by the CPAA: it has to find widely dispersed workers without the assistance of any records; it has to persuade workers and medical experts to look for occupational diseases and encourage medical practitioners to officially recognize what they find; it has to convince the state and the asbestos industry that these are not simply isolated incidences but part of a widespread and under-recognized problem; and on the basis of this, it has to encourage the government to take decisive action that would threaten its economic potential. As Srivastava and Pandya argue:

> In a country of over a billion people where the majority of workers, many of whom are illiterate, belong to the unorganized sector, raising awareness of invisible hazards such as asbestos is not an easy task. People can visualise injuries from ladder falls and the collapse of scaffolding but explaining that an unseen fibre can cause a fatal disease in the far distant future is a very hard sell. (2008: 30)

India's institutional framing of asbestos as safe – coupled with the lack of worker organization, widespread poverty, illiteracy and unemployment – ensures that the treadmill of economic production continues unabated. Generally such an approach is modelled on the idea of an ignorant public which trusts governments and scientific experts to manage risk and protect their safety (Zavestoski et al. 2004). In India an extreme version is adopted where all evidence of risk and harm is erased. As demonstrated in the following section, debates about the science of asbestos also influence the production process.

Asbestos production Despite South Africa and India sharing high rates of unemployment and poverty, other conditions are substantially different and strongly influence the mobilization process of those working with and affected by asbestos. In South Africa, powerful trade unions were willing to challenge corporations, there were multiple systems of compensation for workers suffering from asbestos diseases, and asbestos embedded in houses was seen as problematic. In India, however, trade unions were very reluctant to challenge asbestos companies or to threaten workers' employment, there was almost no compensation for asbestos disease, and asbestos embedded in houses was seen as modern and desirable. These conditions bolstered mobilization in South Africa but provided additional obstacles for local Indian activism and undermined the possibility of grassroots support.

India's high unemployment rate restricts BANI's mobilizing opportunities and encourages people to hang on to their jobs, regardless of the conditions or potential risk. Many workers, supported by their trade unions, accept the government position that asbestos is safe. Those workers who believe in the toxicity of asbestos face an impossible choice as mobilization against asbestos would probably result in being fired: 'Then we will die [from starvation].' Instead, even those workers who know or suspect that asbestos is dangerous continue to work: 'at least we will die later [in twenty or thirty years when the disease develops] and our family will live'. Asbestos diseases, in particular, force workers into this binary choice because, as one trade unionist explained, 'it's a slow acting poison, that is the problem, the slow action and the fact that there's no treatment, so people don't take it seriously'. Workers themselves will not request medicals or compensation for fear of losing their jobs. Thus, although some trade unions work with BANI to ban asbestos, many prefer to demand improved safety devices, diagnostic tools and compensation.

South African trade unions debated similar issues in the 1980s, when industrial scientists were arguing that asbestos exposure was no more dangerous than coal smoke and car accidents. When the trade unions raised questions about European countries banning asbestos, the asbestos lobby cited other countries that had not banned it. After the end of apartheid in 1994, South African trade unions, supported by progressive doctors, readily followed growing international consensus that asbestos was dangerous. This led trade unions to evaluate workers' jobs in relation to workers' health. In contrast to Indian trade unions, they were determined not to facilitate workers' exposure to toxic products. Before the South African ban on asbestos, trade unions demanded that employers downscale their asbestos-containing production, allowing retirement and natural attrition to reduce the workforce exposed to asbestos. They also insisted that substitutes be found. This ensured that jobs were retained while workers' exposure was minimized. As one trade unionist recalled, 'it was very serious, we knew that employers would retrench anyway when under pressure. [We debated] do we wait and let people be exposed to asbestos or do we tackle it head on. We demanded that companies move out of asbestos production without job losses.' One factory found the substitutes so successful, it increased its workforce as it phased out asbestos. Nonetheless, several companies shut down production plants. Despite these losses, a Cosatu representative explained that they saw the struggle over asbestos as 'a victory for trade unions and for society as a whole. Trade unions have been losing members [as people die of asbestos diseases] who trust trade unions on occupational health matters.'

Mobilization against asbestos is thus a process of challenging a state-run system which allocates benefits to some people and, in so doing, disadvantages others. This means that processes of inclusion and exclusion created by the state and by the mobilization process benefit different categories of people. In India, the true costs of asbestos manufacture are externalized on to workers and, in particular, on to casual or informal workers. The disempowerment of workers in relation to the asbestos industry and the Indian state is perhaps most evident in the example of a retired asbestos worker who was diagnosed with throat cancer. A doctor explained that this disease stemmed from his work with asbestos and offered to provide an ESIS certificate so that he could claim compensation. The worker declined, stating that he 'knew the company' and knew that the certificate would not help him acquire compensation. In keeping with this, some of BANI's most recent work has focused more on the people affected by asbestos and demonstrates frightening parallels with apartheid South Africa: children play on asbestos heaps, artisanal miners work without respiratory equipment and eat their food in the mines, women hand-cob asbestos fibre, workers go home in their dusty clothes and use asbestos factories' rejects to build their houses. South Africa is still reeling from the effects of asbestos mining and still encounters rising rates of asbestos disease. India, however, continues to document minimal levels of asbestos disease, not least because, uninformed during employment and disempowered, 'workers return to their villages due to illness or after retirement, [where] they have no access to post-employment follow-ups or medical care for asbestos-related diseases' (Kamat 2008: 55).

In contrast to the situation in India, however, various South African systems of compensation make it possible for people diagnosed with asbestos diseases to survive and even to gain some prestige. In addition to the MBOD, which has paid out compensation to thousands of workers despite the difficulties they experience in claiming, there is a South African government disability grant, which all adult South African citizens are entitled to if medically certified and if their income is below a certain level.[8] This means that people who lived in the vicinity of asbestos mines, but were never employed, can receive a disability grant if they have more than 40 per cent damage to their lungs. This provides a small but steady monthly income which sustains extended families, because pensions are more secure than unskilled, informal jobs and provide more money. Indeed, Nattrass argues that, given the high levels of unemployment, the 'current disability policy is creating incentives for people to become and/or remain ill' (2006: 2). MBOD compensation, which can be claimed alongside the disability grant, provides large, lump sums of money, allowing individuals to extend their houses, erect gravestones, buy furniture and so forth. Ironically, then, asbestos provided jobs and a reasonably lucrative income between the 1960s and the 1980s, and asbestosis payments now provide similar financial security and status. In a context where it is impossible to secure well-paying jobs or save money, asbestos payments assume immense importance. These systems of compensation mean that workers in South Africa are both more knowledgeable about asbestos diseases (thereby providing a better starting point for mobilization against asbestos) and better – but not wholly – protected against the excesses of capital production.

In both South Africa and India, many thousands of people live in houses built from asbestos-containing products and, in particular, asbestos roofs. In India, these are constructed as desirable, cheap, long lasting and superior. Asbestos-cement roofs are seen as a sign of modernization and development. These roofs allow people to secure their houses and property in ways that are not possible with thatched roofing. Nonetheless, asbestos roofs are potentially dangerous and can release asbestos fibres. In other countries, research identifies residential properties as significant sources of asbestos contamination, identifying building workers as a significant high-risk group for mesothelioma. In India, there is no public recognition that working on asbestos-containing materials might be hazardous and, with the exception of BANI's work, no discussion about the dangers that construction and maintenance workers face. South Africa too has no data on how many people are likely to be exposed through the construction industry. It has, however, begun to address this through research and legislation. Research has shown that replacing asbestos roofs expanded the problem. This is because, once removed, asbestos roofing becomes desirable unwanted building material, and unless steps are taken to ensure that the asbestos-containing cement is immediately removed and appropriately disposed of, it often disappears overnight to be used in someone else's home. In terms of legislation, South Africa banned asbestos production completely in 2008, with strong penalties for anyone processing, manufacturing, importing, exporting or dumping asbestos-containing material. But asbestos remains in hundreds of thousands of houses, and this raises problems for the future. Given South Africa's problems of poverty and unemployment, trade unionists and government officials are asking themselves how they can demolish houses while others don't have homes to live in.

In South Africa it is now clear that, in material terms, no one really stands to win in relation to asbestos as workers continue to develop asbestos-related diseases and as society and government struggle with the legacy of unrehabilitated mines, exposed asbestos tailings and asbestos in houses, schools and other public buildings. In India, there is no doubt that big business benefits from asbestos production. It is subsidized by the Indian government through low import taxes, a lack of regulation and high taxation on asbestos substitutes. It is also subsidized by the workers on to whose bodies the real costs are externalized. As demonstrated above, workers' illness is largely invisible and worker mobilization severely constrained. In both South Africa and India, however, the state has implemented processes to address the contradictions between economic growth, societal well-being and environmental sustainability. The creation of fora, which allow actors to engage in matters of local concern and to participate in governmental policy-making, provide additional spaces for challenging asbestos use and production.

The politics of intermediation Both South Africa and India have a democratic government, yet the manner in which the state responds to mobilization is absolutely critical. In South Africa, a supportive state has facilitated anti-asbestos mobilization and encouraged activists' participation in formal policy processes, whereas in India state legislation works to actively encourage the continued production of asbestos products, and participatory processes are symbolic happenings which fail to incorporate dissenting voices.

In South Africa, the CPAA initially emerged in response to local community problems and it retained this focus. The CPAA's political credibility was bolstered by the ANC-led government which, after its election in 1994, sought to encourage local-level community participation through the 'constitutional requirements of transparent, accountable, democratic practices in all areas of governance' (Williams 2004: 20) and through communities' rights to participation in local development. Northern Cape stakeholders created a multi-stakeholder Asbestos Forum, comprising various government departments[9] to ensure joint consultative decision-making, rather than a fragmented approach to asbestos rehabilitation.[10] The CPAA participated in Forum decision-making and supported the policy process. The Asbestos Forum meetings thus created an invited space, characterized by regularity, deliberation and participation. Thus, community representatives 'exercised voice' and were expected to 'become empowered' through the process of participation (see Gaventa 2002). This has led to a broadened notion of risk which, to some extent, incorporates both science and community perspectives. As Leach et al. point out, however, community participation is particularly difficult to facilitate when dealing with scientific and technological issues as 'highly specialised professionalised knowledge and expertise' restricts participation, while scientific controversies create 'new demands and opportunities for concerted citizen engagement in decision making' (2002: 40).

The Asbestos Forum meetings dealt with medical screening, environmental rehabilitation and community development. The CPAA and Prieska's residents supported medical assessments, and scientific predictions of risk. Tensions arose, however, between scientists' understanding of risk in terms of disease modelling, statistical probabilities, microscopic fibres, wind direction and predicted deposition and community notions of harm, which focused on visible asbestos fibre disturbed by cloudbursts, strong winds and construction work. Local people thus recast and broadened scientific/medical risk in terms of moral judgements and emotions. Informally – beyond the confines of the Asbestos Forum meetings – Prieska's residents emphasized their asbestos-related experiences in terms of damaged bodies, family relationships and dependency on compensation payments. They thus interpreted harm in terms of emotions, bodily integrity and financial responsibility. The town residents were not concerned by the statistical risk that an isolated individual might face, but recognized the importance of networks of social relationships and how these are simultaneously threatened by asbestos diseases and sustained through government disability and compensation payments. Nonetheless, through people's participation in the Forum and collective action, these perspectives have become more closely connected. There has been greater accommodation of medical and scientific discourse and of the cultural interpretation of scientific knowledge in official local governance processes. Ultimately, however, the formal processes of participation were framed around medical expertise and knowledge. Despite official representation on the Asbestos Working Group, at no stage did any community residents or CPAA organizers point to possible disjunctures between scientific and informal beliefs about asbestos disease.

In India, public participation in asbestos-related issues centres around the Environmental Public Hearings (EPH), held before asbestos cement factories can be established. In theory, factories working with asbestos are subject to strict legislation, which includes transporting asbestos in sealed containers, no manual handling of bags of asbestos, emission controls, storage enclosures, monitoring of pollutants, the reuse or recycling of effluent and solid waste, and so forth. These hearings are open to anyone, although industrial actors are advantaged by their greater experience, technical knowledge and financial resources (Murphree et al. 1996). For example, when New Sahyadri Industries Ltd (NSIL) wished to establish an asbestos unit in Surat, Gujarat, surrounding communities were made aware of the dangers of asbestos and wrote letters protesting against the factory. They demonstrated at the EPH, holding placards stressing that asbestos is hazardous. In addition, scientific-based NGOs scrutinized NSIL's proposals and stressed, in the EPH, its failure to explain how the regulations would be met. For instance, the Safety, Health and Environment Association questioned the provisions for measuring airborne asbestos fibres, the types of occupational diseases possible and the safety-handling procedures. Public sentiment overwhelmingly stressed that it would be better to locate the asbestos plant somewhere else. NSIL countered this resistance with guarantees of strict precautionary measures, state-of-the-art technology and evidence from other NSIL plants that there was 'absolutely no problem regarding pollution or occupational health' because they used white (chrysotile) asbestos.[11] In closing the EPH, a committee member commended the local villagers on their environmental awareness, berated local women for their absence, and thanked everyone for their active participation. Despite local villager opposition during the EPH in the form of placards, protests, written submissions and signed petitions, and despite NGOs challenging the scientific arguments put forward by NSIL, the Ministry of Environment and Forests provided a 'No Objections Certificate', allowing NSIL to go ahead with the plant.

Citizen participation is thus highly symbolic and does not enable community representatives or BANI to engage successfully in policy processes. The factories still received environmental clearance based on assurances of scientific techniques and close monitoring of environmental and health conditions. 'Monitoring' is, however, equally symbolic. In India, it is the submission of company environmental audits, carried out every six years, which counts. When Paryavaran Mitra, an Indian NGO, requested details on 700 environmental audits performed in Gujarat, it was informed that there were no irregularities and all the companies had been granted an 'all clear'. The fact that there is no analysis of the environmental audits works to advantage companies, and submission of audits becomes equivalent to government monitoring of activities.

This has significant implications for villagers' effectiveness as citizens. As is clear from the above-described public hearing, their role is highly limited. Villagers are expected to be concerned about the environment and to partake in EPHs. Their opinions, however, are not heard by the officials, who readily accept the arguments made by industry. Not one villager supported the NSIL industrial plant, over two hundred villagers signed petitions against it, village leaders wrote letters and people protested outside the EPH. Yet this was insufficient to counter the industrial argument that asbestos is safe. As if recognizing these limits to citizenship, one village leader argued, 'We oppose the project near our village. If authority permit[s] this factory, we will never be heard by anyone. We would lose our chance to raise our voice.' Instead of being a positive experience of citizen action, the hearings served to channel opposition, creating a legitimate and administrative context for people to oppose industrial units but also acted to streamline and neutralize their resistance.

Conclusion: anti-asbestos mobilization and possibilities for citizen agency

The dynamics of mobilization, the politics of knowledge, the social and economic conditions of asbestos production and the politics of intermediation combine in a globalizing world to shape South Africa's and India's mobilization possibilities, creating new identities, new forms of citizenship, new axes of inclusion and exclusion and, in the process, shaping the nature of globalization. Emerging as potential winners out of the South African mobilization are workers, rural town residents and South Africans in general as all asbestos use is now banned and its disposal tightly regulated. Emerging – to date – in India as clear winners are the asbestos corporations, which have been able to authoritatively stamp their version of science and risk on to Indian asbestos debates. As is evident in both cases, mobilization strategies seek to bring together local and global solidarities, networks and dynamics to create new coalescences of power. In the South African case, the local/global relationship was mediated by professional doctors and human rights specialists based in South Africa and by international actors. IBAS, ACTSA and UK-based lawyers created the possibilities for the grassroots-based CPAA to link into global debates and networks. They assisted in keeping the campaign in the international spotlight, in facilitating protests and in providing legal specialization, technological equipment, financial backing and moral support for the CPAA. In addition, activists and trade unions had the backing of the state as they started to engage with a few asbestos corporations. Three things thus combined to facilitate anti-asbestos mobilization in South Africa: a strong grassroots orientation, the mediation of global networks through international actors and the cooperation of the state. This made it possible for the

CPAA to link very localized grassroots experiences of asbestos disease with international campaigns occurring at the global level. Nonetheless, although the CPAA engaged in these global networks during the course of the asbestos campaign, these relationships have not been sustained. A few CPAA members have subsequently joined a global environmental justice campaign, and are currently assessing how much public support there may be for another large-scale protest. The strength of CPAA's mobilization and the creation of new axes of inclusion are, however, to be seen at grassroots level and in local experiences. Anti-asbestos mobilization has been an empowering process which has created a deeper South African solidarity that crosses previous racial and class divides. For example, Prieska's residents have started to demand that businesses invest more in the town through educational scholarships, community resources and infrastructural projects. For many of the poor, illiterate and unemployed CPAA members, anti-asbestos mobilization was an empowering process which affirmed their citizenship by demonstrating that they had the right and, in conjunction with international networks, the ability to challenge corporate injustice.

Different axes of inclusion and exclusion are created through mobilization in India as BANI successfully engages at the global level. This has resulted in an affirmation and empowering process for BANI members, who have engaged in global intellectual debates, published papers, written media articles, attended international conferences and developed internationalized political profiles. Their success in the global arena has been possible because of their Indian citizenship, their democratic rights, and the protection that international networks have afforded specific individuals who challenge the Indian government. This internationalized form of networking has created new identities between BANI members and their international counterparts around the world and, in so doing, has shaped the identities of Indian professional activists in the cities of India. This new axis of inclusion has, however, also reinforced the distinction between these activists and the workers whose lives they seek to protect. Unlike in the South African case, in which grassroots experiences formed the basis of the mobilization campaign, BANI's inspiration stems from the global arena, and it has struggled to generate grassroots support, creating only weak linkages with the very people most exposed to asbestos. In addition, there are currently no mediating actors or structures that bridge the gap between global networks and local experiences. The Indian state, in contrast to the South African case, has facilitated a flourishing asbestos industry through lax environmental and labour monitoring, out-of-date legislation, poor workers' rights, ineffective surveillance and fiscal incentives. Its unsympathetic approach to anti-asbestos activists, coupled with its failure to document asbestos diseases and its insistence that asbestos is safe, controlled and monitored, obstructs BANI's ability to connect local experiences to global networks. This, in turn, creates new axes of exclusion – as BANI is increasingly absorbed into the internationalized, global networks, its social and economic 'distance' from India's workers increases. BANI's shared aims and commonality lie with the other international members of a global ban-asbestos movement, while its political cause is firmly located within India. Ultimately BANI seeks to improve living and working conditions in India and to secure all Indians' health. It has recently realized the necessity of bridging this gap between local experiences and global activism and has begun a process of highlighting Indian experiences of asbestos exposure. The extent to which this will be able to create new identities and solidarities within India will be critical.

Anti-asbestos mobilization brings together, in both the countries examined here, people who believe that citizenship includes the right to live a healthy life in an environment unpolluted by asbestos. Creating citizenship thus involves challenging the values associated with economic growth and liberalization and asserting that corporations should be accountable to workers and neighbouring residents. Ultimately it demands a form of accountability from the state which seeks to protect – rather than ignore – less powerful and vulnerable members of society through a combination of appropriate legislation, articulation of rights and dissemination of knowledge. Addressing asbestos issues thus becomes a means not just for people to shape their own experience of citizenship through the kinds of direct action described here, but also to expand the meaning of citizenship to one which is informed both through legal charters and through normative social values.

Notes

1 In South Africa, anthropological research was conducted in the Northern Cape towns of Prieska, Koegas and Griquatown in June/July 2003, May/June 2005, January 2007 and January 2008 in conjunction with the CPAA. Research in India occurred throughout March 2007, facilitated by PRIA. Methods included Participant Observation and semi-structured and open-ended interviews. A longer version of the findings of the Indian study appeared as an IDS Working Paper (Waldman 2009).

2 The Northern Cape blue asbestos mines closed when the asbestos seams were mined out or when US asbestos litigation expanded, highlighting the links between blue asbestos and mesothelioma (McCulloch 2002).

3 www.nioh.org, accessed 14 March 2009.

4 *Mynstof* is a broad category including pleural plaque and asbestosis, lung cancer and mesothelioma.

5 Asbestos diseases have been explained in terms of disease causality and the physiological action of the fibres. This obscures the relationships between workplace organization, legislation and disease (Braun and Kisting 2006).

6 The Rotterdam Convention is a multilateral agreement between country signatories that promotes shared responsibilities for importing hazardous chemicals. It became legally binding to its seventy-three country signatories in 2004. Prior Informed Consent (PIC) refers to a list of hazardous chemicals and pesticides recognized in international trade.

7 Companies employed healthy workers as full-time employees, while using part-time and casual workers for hazardous jobs. Workers voluntarily stop coming to work once they feel ill as they know they cannot perform satisfactorily and will not receive sick leave. This relieves management from recording illness and from retiring workers.

8 The disability grant is available to all mentally or physically disabled citizens, whether temporarily or permanent, whose assets are less than R500,000 and annual income less than R27,000. In October 2008, the grant comprised a monthly payment of R960.

9 Including the Departments of Environmental Affairs, Health, Social Security and Welfare, Minerals and Energy, Water Affairs, Housing, Labour and Nature Conservation.

10 Minutes of the Asbestos Forum meeting, 6 November 1997.

11 Letter to EPH committee chairman, 24 January 2006.

References

Bergland, E. (2001) 'Self-defeating environmentalism? Models and questions from an ethnography of toxic waste protest', *Critique of Anthropology*, 21(3): 317–36.

Braun, L. and S. Kisting (2006) 'Asbestos-related disease in South Africa: the social production of an invisible epidemic', *American Journal of Public Health*, 96(8): 2–12.

Castleman, B. I. (2000) 'The manipulation of "scientific organisations": controversies at international organisations over asbestos industry influence', Annals of the Global Asbestos Congress, Fiasco, Brazil, 17–20 September.

— (2007) 'The WTO trade disputer's impact on global efforts to ban asbestos', *World Asbestos Report: Bringing Together This Century's Asbestos Research*. Annals of the Global Asbestos Congress, Tokyo, 19–21 December 2004, worldasbestosreport.org/gac2004/PL1-01.html, accessed 25 May 2008.

Danish Confederation of Trade Unions (2005) 'ASBESTOS – in Denmark and at the global level', lo.dk/upload/LO/Documents/A/Asbestos%20in%20DK%20an%20globally_2773.doc, accessed 14 May 2009.

Daubs, K. (2008) 'Canada's asbestos time bomb. Part III: India's hidden epidemic', *Ottawa Citizen*, www2.canada.com/ottawacitizen/features/asbestos/story.html?id=e7fb6e00-c03f-4a5c-b92e-6205e68bf816, accessed 14 March 2009.

Dodgson, R., K. Lee and N. Drager

(2002) 'Global health governance: a conceptual review', Discussion Paper no. 1, Centre on Global Change and Health, Department of Health and Development, London School of Hygiene and Tropical Medicine, and World Health Organization, whqlibdoc.who.int/publications/2002/a85727_eng.pdf, accessed 26 May 2009.

Dutta, M. (2008) 'The Indian government's complicity in the asbestos scandal', in D. Allen and L. Kazan-Allen (eds), *India's Asbestos Time Bomb*, London: IBAS.

Gaventa, J. (2002) 'Exploring citizenship, participation and accountability', *IDS Bulletin*, 33(2): 1–11.

Gibson, B. (1987) '"Grasping the nettle": a review of the asbestos-cement industry's response to the asbestos and health issue 1965–1987', Unpublished paper presented at the International Conference on Air Pollution, Berlin.

Kamat, S. R. (2008) 'Asbestos-related disease in India', in D. Allen and L. Kazan-Allen (eds), *India's Asbestos Time Bomb*, London: IBAS.

Krishna, G. (2006) 'Asbestos: kill the people, protect the industry', Merinews, 17 October 2006, www.merinews.com/catFull.jsp?articleID=123573, accessed 4 June 2009.

— (2008) 'A government under an asbestos roof', *Indian Journal of Occupation and Environmental Medicine*, 12: 43–4.

KSSM (2006) *A Historical Judgement by the Gujarat High Court: A Ray of Hope for the Manhole Workers*, Ahmedabad: KSSM.

Leach, M., I. Scoones and J. Thompson (2002) 'Citizenship, science and risk: conceptualising relationships across issues and settings', *IDS Bulletin*, 33(2): 40–48.

Lemen, R. A. (2008) 'Smoke and mirrors: chrysotile asbestos is good for you – illusion and confusion but not a fact', in D. Allen and L. Kazan-Allen (eds), *India's Asbestos Time Bomb*, London: IBAS.

McCulloch, J. (2002) *Asbestos Blues: Labour, Capital, Physicians and the State in South Africa*, Oxford: James Currey.

McCulloch, J. and G. Tweedale (2008) *Defending the Indefensible: The Global Asbestos Industry*, Oxford: Oxford University Press.

Mohite, R. G. (2008) 'Preface', in D. Allen and L. Kazan-Allen (eds), *India's Asbestos Time Bomb*, London: IBAS.

Murlidhar, V. and V. Kanhere (2005) 'Asbestosis in an asbestos composite mill at Mumbai: a prevalence study', *Environmental Health: A Global Access Science*, 4(24).

Murphree, D. W., S. Wright and H. R. Ebaugh (1996) 'Toxic waste siting and community resistance: how cooptation of local citizen opposition failed', *Sociological Perspectives*, 39(4): 447–63.

Nattrass, N. (2006) 'Disability and welfare in South Africa's era of unemployment and Aids', Centre for Social Science Research Working Paper no. 147, University of Cape Town.

PRIA (Participatory Research in Asia) (2004) *Occupational Health in India: Making a Difference*, New Delhi: PRIA.

Srivastava, A. and V. Pandya (2008) 'Living with asbestos: a dangerous existence', in D. Allen and L. Kazan-Allen (eds), *India's Asbestos Time Bomb*, London: IBAS.

Tweedale, G. (2008) 'Asbestos multinationals in India: the experience of Turner and Newall', in D. Allen and L. Kazan-Allen (eds), *India's Asbestos Time Bomb*, London: IBAS.

Waldman, L. (2009) '"Show me the evidence": mobilisation, citizenship and risk in Indian asbestos issues', IDS Working Paper no. 329, Institute of Development Studies, Brighton, www.drc-citizenship.org/publications/Wp 329.pdf, accessed 28 August 2009.

Walsh, E. J. (1988) 'New dimensions of social movements: the high-level waste-siting controversy', *Sociological Forum*, 3(4): 586–605.

Williams, J. J. (2004) 'Citizenship, community participation and social change: the case of Area Coordinating Teams in Cape Town, South Africa', *IDS Bulletin*, 35(2).

Zavestoski, S., K. Agnello, F. Mignano and F. Darroch (2004) 'Issue framing and citizen apathy toward local environmental contamination', *Sociological Forum*, 19(2): 255–83.

10 · Hybrid activism: paths of globalization in the Brazilian environmental movement[1]

ANGELA ALONSO

Imagine a middle-aged man at Kennedy Airport. He is keen to read a paper about sustainable development in Brazil during his trip to Johannesburg, where he is expected to discuss global warming and deforestation with other activists from across the world. Besides the paper, he finds an overflowing email inbox on his laptop, including calls for demonstrations against World Bank policies in the developing world and proposals to collaborate with Southern environmental management projects. As he proceeds to his terminal, he recognizes someone whom he met at one of the United Nations summits. While catching his flight, he considers once more whether a true environmentalist should contribute to global pollution by globetrotting from one conference to another.

This story is not real, but it could be. Activists like this one continuously travel the world, carrying meanings, experiences and resources with them. At first glance, they are citizens without frontiers. The fiction lies in this statement rather than in my imagined scene. Is it possible to be a global activist without local roots? My research on activists from the two major Brazilian environmentalist organizations, SOS Rainforest and the Instituto Socioambiental (ISA, Socienvironmental Institute), indicates that it is not. Brazilian activists do not just 'globalize', they also 'localize', preserving deep local roots. In fact, they operate to connect two spaces. Within the global space, they build alliances with foreign groups, and in local space they deal with the nation-state, civil society and communities inhabiting the environments they aim to protect. This, however, is just an analytical distinction. In real life, the experiences of activists make these spaces virtually indistinguishable. As a result, their identities are a hybrid, being at the same time local *and* global. In this chapter, I will make the case for 'hybrid activism'.

Changing patterns of mobilization

The array of processes commonly known as globalization is generally associated with economic, political and cultural interdependence and exchange that supersede national territory and government, generating new social spaces, actors and conflicts. Transnational agencies such as the World Bank and the International Monetary Fund offer new quarry for social movements, who raise grievances beyond the national sphere. In addition, the spread of new technologies, especially the Internet, and of English as an international language, opens new spaces and opportunities for citizen political engagement in the international sphere.

Changes in activism follow. Protest crosses national boundaries, directed to multilateral institutions and international public opinion. New forms of organization arise: fluid global networks of activists, based on transitory solidarities. Movements become multi-issue, building what may be termed meaning packages (Tarrow 2005), the reframing and overlapping of themes and demands. Identity comes to be an issue at stake, continuously redefined. A new profile of activist emerges, circulating among local, national and global spaces.

These transformations of activism presented challenges to existing social movement theories. Political Process (PP) and New Social Movement (NSM) approaches, which emerged in the 1970s, defined social movements by virtue of their relationships to national political authorities and institutions (Tilly 1978; Touraine 1978), and had to develop and amend their theories in order to explain transnational activism.

The NSM tradition developed new concepts such as 'network society' (Castells 1996) and 'information society' (Melucci 1996), presenting democratization of knowledge, globalization and identity as the new main subjects of mobilization. It also fed theories of Global Civil Society (GCS), stressing the innovative character of transnational networks of non-governmental organizations. These were characterized as an empowering force for activists from Southern countries, a globalization-from-below, challenging the globalization-from-above carried out by Northern firms and national states (for instance, Falk 1999).

Meanwhile, PP theory developed into the Contentious Politics (CP) approach, broadening its definition of the field, and considering mobilization that crosses national state frontiers. Tarrow (2005), however, continues to focus on 'transnational' rather than 'global' activism. In this view, domestic claims projected on to international institutions and actors create transnational collective action. The process includes dissemination of global framing and the building of new identities among grassroots movements and national and international groups (ibid.). The rise of social movements would still take place, however, within and in relation to the nation-state.

Explanations of Latin American activism followed the first approach more than the second, reproducing the GCS focus on the innovative political culture of global social movements (Shefner 2004). Both approaches present limits, however. The concept of GCS is normative, considering only emancipating forms of activism, and ignoring violence, such as terrorism, and inequalities between Northern and Southern civil societies (Smith 2005). The CP approach lacks some cultural dimensions of globalization, such as knowledge. More important, both perspectives share the assumption that local and global are actual empirical realms.

McAdam et al. (2001) argued against the state–civil society dichotomy, insisting that there are no physical boundaries separating the two. The same can be said of the local–global dichotomy: they are theoretically constructed spheres. Individuals are embedded in local, national and global realms simultaneously. The globalization of economics and information makes any political action have repercussions at all scales at the same time. This is the novelty of contemporary social movements. They embody a new type of activism that does not operate by shifting from one sphere to another, but rather is local and global all the time, mixing the two in its own fashion: a hybrid activism.

In order to understand it, a new perspective is required. CP and GCS are essentially structuralist theories, facing difficulties in describing how transnational social movements emerge from meanings and actions of tangible individual agents. In contrast, I will focus on how individual biographical trajectories operate the exchange of meanings, knowledge and strategies (Jasper 1997; Polleta 2006) that build the process and structures of political globalization. These concrete social experiences are, as Gaventa and Tandon (2007) argue, constrained by the politics of intermediation (the standards of accountability between activists and local communities) and the politics of knowledge (forms of expertise used to frame contested issues) that they involve.

My cases show how hybrid identities, meanings and trajectories of mobilization are built through two mechanisms identified in Tilly's (2005) discussion of inequality. 'Emulation' takes place when local actors 'reproduce organizational modes already operating elsewhere, importing configurations' (ibid.: 156), while 'adaptation' happens when local actors use existing models, but also invent procedures (ibid.: 84).

Trajectories of mobilization

The global–local path: the case of SOS Rainforest Russell A. Mittermeier is a fifty-nine-year-old New Yorker, the son of German immigrants, who, as a child, dreamed of being a jungle explorer. He studied biological anthropology at Harvard and, while researching neo-tropical monkeys in the 1970s, he came to be interested in Brazil. He became acquainted with Brazilian environmental activists through the scientific route. He contacted Brazilian scientists working on natural conservation, such as Adelmar Coimbra Filho, member of the biggest Brazilian conservationist organization at that time, the Fundação Brasileira para a Conservação de Natureza (FBCN, Brazilian Foundation for Nature Conservation). The global–local connection was made.

Since 1977, when he was the International Union for Conservation of Nature chairman for primates, Mittermeier has travelled to Brazil as the representative of international organizations concerned with environmental protection. In the next year, he joined the World Wildlife Fund (WWF) as the Primates Programme director as a result of his link to Brazil. In the 1970s he and the organization grew concerned over the future of Amazon wildlife. This was not the priority for most Brazilian environmental activists, however, who were few at that time and were concentrated in the south-west of the country and more interested in the forest areas near São Paulo (Alonso et al. 2005).

Nevertheless, FBCN activists quickly understood the opportunities opened to them by the global–local connection Mittermeier initiated. Hence they began to emulate foreign conservationism, reframing the idea of tropical forest under the label 'rainforest', referring foremost to the forest areas they were already working in. The first joint initiative between Brazilian activists and Mittermeier was a study on this area, which lasted from 1979 to the late 1980s, and constructed the term 'rainforest' as a political issue. Local activists succeeded in shifting both Mittermeier's attention and the WWF's funds: 'I was always interested in the Amazon, but [Adelmar] Coimbra [from FBCN] persuaded me that the Atlantic Rainforest really was a high priority.'[2] This connection shows how local activists reaped the benefits of an alliance with global actors and how the reframing of meanings, organization-building and fund-raising come together.

Mittermeier worked as a broker. He obtained donations to the WWF from the United States and Switzerland, and then channelled them to the Brazilian rainforest, mainly to FBCN's projects, such as Coimbra's expedition to locate and create a natural reserve to protect the golden lion tamarin. By 1982, this global–local connection became part of the worldwide WWF campaign on tropical forests and primates, which started to fund many projects in Brazil. Another FBCN activist, Paulo Nogueira Neto, also benefited from the link, coming to be one of two Latin American representatives on the Bruntdland Commission (1983–86) and the president of UNESCO's Man and the Biosphere programme in 1983.

Despite his close relationship with FBCN, Mittermeier also paid attention to the many environmentalist groups emerging in Brazil at the time, formed by young upper-class activists concerned with urban and political problems (Alonso et al. 2005). Mittermeier encouraged them to start a new organization devoted to the rainforest. Fábio Feldmann was among them. A lawyer and administrator, he became involved with urban environmental activism and leftist parties in the late 1970s, campaigning against the building of an airport in the city of São Paulo, and came to be the main environmentalist lawmaker during the Constituent Assembly in 1986. Also involved was João Paulo Capobianco, a photographer, biologist and educator who specialized in environment and agriculture, and started in activism campaigning in defence of the Atlantic rainforest in the early 1980s.

These activists formed two alliances. They joined the pioneering Coimbra and Nogueira Neto, both engaged in the construction of the Brazilian environmental bureaucracy. They also attracted environmentalist sympathizers who had close connections to the market, such as Roberto Klabin and Rodrigo Lara Mesquita, both from families of entrepreneurs and businessmen themselves. Mittermeier's global links brought the material resources that allowed these activists to join one another and create a new organization, SOS Rainforest, in 1986, which Feldmann, Mesquita and Klablin would successively run until today. Mittermeier joined the SOS's advisory council, where he remains.

The decision to build an organization around the rainforest was primarily pragmatic, taking account of the available global funds: 'The first resources for organizing [SOS] were international. There was a project for [...] the rainforest's characterization [...] coming from the United States that [...] had resources from the WWF and other organizations.'[3] Mittermeier became Conservation International (CI) president, a position he still holds, which increased his capacity to raise financial support for Brazilian environmentalists and to work as a broker between Brazilian organizations and global donors, such as the MacArthur Foundation:

> I arrived here [in Brazil in 1989] with the Programme Director at that time, Dan Martin, to show him what there was here in the rainforest, like organizations, like priority projects [...] and based on our recommendations and meetings during these visits, the MacArthur Foundation decided to support our organization to work in Brazil, as well as three Brazilian organizations, which were Pronatura (which nowadays is not very active), SOS and the FBCN.[4]

Mittermeier was carrying out the politics of intermediation, since he controlled contacts, influences and access to resources. In 1990, CI released $80,000 for the conservation of Brazilian forests, part of it delivered according to the agenda of local activists,[5] who were thus able to channel some international funds to their area of interest, the Atlantic rainforest.

Despite the success of this connection, Brazilian activists also tried to forge an independent global link. Rodrigo Lara Mesquita, as SOS president, sent João Carlos Meirelles Filho, born to an important rural family, to the United States to learn how to raise funds from donor foundations. Lara Mesquita recalls, 'I got a scholarship in the United States, and he [Meirelles Filho] stayed there six months studying how American organizations related to the public to obtain recourses.'[6] This strategy reinforced the links Mittermeier had built, and through his mediation, in 1990 Meirelles Filho obtained another grant from the MacArthur Foundation, spent on organizing SOS Rainforest and starting projects in the rainforest. Throughout the 1990s, the MacArthur Foundation was the main sponsor of SOS:

> It was a support with a very important amount of money, more or less 700 thousand, 800 thousand for [...] three years. So this really helped a lot [...] the growth of SOS at that time. And after that we always had a very close relationship with SOS, which came to be much more formalized.[7]

The local–global alliance thus helped to stabilize SOS, while many similar groups, such as FBCN, just disappeared. SOS paid a price, however. Its local programmes had to be adjusted to fit the agendas of global environmental organizations. As a financial supporter, WWF pushed Brazilian activism towards issues of its own interest, such as wildlife, sidelining the priorities of local activists, originally concerned also with urban areas inside the rainforest – such as Feldmann's activism against air pollution in the industrial district of Cubatão (Alonso et al. 2005). The global–local link pushed Brazilian activists towards forest areas, since the WWF and CI grants were available for this,[8] and to the incorporation of the neo-conservationist frame, dominant among its international allies. If this made SOS eligible to receive global funds, it also created a dependency.

The WWF–SOS alliance began to weaken in 1990, when Brazil was chosen as the site of the United Nations Conference on Environment and Development (UNCED). Then WWF started a new politics of brokerage, trying to assume the role of intermediary between different sets of Brazilian activists, foreign groups, institutions and resources. Although WWF kept releasing funds to ongoing projects in the rainforest, support was also given to projects in other biomes.⁹ This change raised concern among Brazilian activists:

> When the WWF-Brazil established this strategy, it started to create a problem, because [...] we had environmental goals to achieve in forestry, in water, in management, in protection. If you did not reach these goals, the project [Brazilian activists presented] could be opportune, but [the answer for the grant requirement was] no.¹⁰

Being a donor, WWF influenced the local agenda and established formalized alliances with many local environmental organizations around focal projects. Furthermore, it created a local branch, WWF-Brazil, in 1996, decentralizing the management of financial resources and projects to Brazil and incorporating some local activists such as Eduardo Martins from FBCN, and Garo Batmanian, then at the World Bank. WWF entered Brazil as a supporter, but changed into an actor – and a competitor.

The new WWF approach forced a redefinition of SOS's own strategy:

> It dried out, I would say, one source of resources [...] this transition was very tough because at that time there was not too much money around, and people started to complain about WWF not giving money any more.¹¹

Nevertheless, SOS maintained support from CI, and Mittermeier consolidated the link, embedded in both organizations, which signed an 'Alliance for Rainforest Conservation' in 1998. In the following years, this meant 'the implementation of one action plan for conservation of the biome, based on a common strategy' (SOS Rainforest 2005: 44). Mittermeier defined this relationship as well balanced: 'it is a really mutual partnership; we can learn as much from the SOS and the techniques they have used successfully here in Brazil as they can learn from us'.¹² The global–local relationship, however, was not entirely an equal exchange. Rather, the link was increasingly one-way: SOS assimilated CI resources and emulated its patterns of activism.

This relationship between foreign and Brazilian actors that Mittermeier mediated gave origin to hybrid activism, in the sense that global and local spheres, meanings and actors are overlapping all the time. Nevertheless, there is a trajectory in this hybridism. Foreign actors initiated the contact, largely defined the agenda and provided the resources. In this sense, this path is global–local. This should not be taken to suggest, however, that local activists are passive instruments; they took the strategic decisions to emulate the global meanings and agenda, being able to push the grants to their own projects. Nonetheless, they were not strong enough to keep their original agenda. They emulated to survive.

The local–global path: the ISA case

Carlos Alberto Ricardo, son of a white-collar family, is from a generation of Brazilian social scientists that had no doubts about their political commitment. In the early 1970s, most of them joined the opposition to the military dictatorship running the country. In his undergraduate years at the University of São Paulo, Ricardo travelled around Latin America seeking elements for 'a diagnosis of local realities that would result in actions supporting concrete social claims: any kind of popular, participative and claim-making mobilization or organization was worthwhile'.[13] While enrolled in a master's programme in anthropology – never concluded – Ricardo obtained a position at the University of Campinas. In 1974, along with colleagues and students, he created the Centro Ecumênico de Documentação e Informação (CEDI, Ecumenical Centre of Documentation and Information), and received his first grant for indigenous studies. Since then, the activist has taken precedence over the professor.

CEDI was one of many social organizations that urban middle-class activists, protected by the Catholic Church, created during the crisis of the military regime. Thanks to this Catholic connection, CEDI linked to an international Christian funding network. For example, the Brazilian Indigenous People's Programme, which Ricardo created in 1978 in the Rio Negro area of the Amazon, benefited from the patronage of the Brot für die Welt (Bread for the World), a network of German evangelical churches, of Norwegian Church Aid and, mainly and durably, of the Netherlands-based Interchurch Organization for Development Cooperation (ICCO). CEDI activities consisted of 'working in this intersecting space between the ecclesiastical and the social movements',[14] comprised primarily of indigenous people and peasants.

In the following years, Ricardo used his anthropological knowledge in projects in Rio Negro, and was concerned with the production and dissemination of information about indigenous groups. Hence, CEDI rarely dealt directly with environmental concerns. 'CEDI was one typical social organization; they had nothing in environmental issues. They were working with the indigenous movement, the labour movement, the unions and the rural workers. They were entirely focused on social issues.'[15]

In 1981, Ricardo joined a campaign against the World Bank, which had released funds to the Polonoroeste Programme, a developmental project the military regime intended to implement in the Amazon. Ricardo worked as a broker between the global conservationist organizations – Environmental Defence Fund, National Wildlife Federation,

Greenpeace, WWF, Friends of the Earth, Survival International and Cultural Survival – that joined the campaign, and the local indigenous and rubber-tapper communities. During this mobilization, a new framework was created. 'Peoples of the Forest' embraced two meanings – the forest and the social groups living in it.

When Brazil returned to democracy, Ricardo used this framework in a movement to include indigenous rights in the new constitution, and in two other campaigns in 1989, one against the building of a dam on the Xingu river in an indigenous area, and another advocating Amazon preservation.[16] Its strategy was to include the claims of indigenous peoples and rubber workers in the international environmental agenda.

> We made a political bet: one strategic vision of linking the indigenous movements to the environmental issue, knowing that the indigenous [hadn't been] environmentalists since birth [...] We would have to persuade them to gather their agenda with society's aspiration [for environmental protection] into one strategy, and the socio-environmentalism fitted perfectly.[17]

This shift brought Ricardo closer to the environmental groups defending the Amazon. As McAdam et al. (2001) argue, during mobilizations political identities are detached, in the sense that actors may give prominence to characteristics that best suit the context. Ricardo did that, stressing the environmental dimension of his activism, until then focused on the welfare of local communities. The timing was fortuitous. With the UNCED being hosted in Brazil in 1992, global groups were seeking local partners and funds for environmental projects were abundant. Ricardo grabbed this new opportunity, building an identity as an 'environmentalist'.

Afraid of being overcome by international organizations interested in the Amazon, Ricardo went to see Capobianco, then frustrated by the lack of accountability in the relationship between SOS and global environmental organizations. Capobianco recalls that during a meeting in Vancouver,

> I felt [...] like this: 'Oh, here is the Brazilian. We must have someone from Brazil because the Summit [UNCED] will be there.' But, in fact, I did not say anything; there was no place on the agenda for me. Everything had been agreed beforehand [...] and I was called almost to legitimize [...] And I felt very uncomfortable.[18]

This dissatisfaction pushed Capobianco to join the local–global strategy Ricardo had started. Together they formed the Brazilian Forum of

NGOs and Social Movements for the Environment and Development, which attracted 1,100 other organizations, half of them without a record of previous environmental activism, and established a strong position at UNCED (Landim 1993).

In 1994, Ricardo and Capobianco formalized the alliance in a new organization, the ISA. It has three offices: in São Paulo, where they live; in Brasilia, for lobbying; and in São Miguel da Cachoeira, Amazon, to keep running the CEDI projects. ISA's creation was decisive in the local–global strategy. It framed the local agenda – the protection of indigenous and traditional communities – in terms that facilitated its national and global acceptance as part of an environmental agenda. Ricardo reflected:

> The creation of ISA had to do with the integration of the environmental dimension with CEDI's former concerns, but I think we imagined departing from a more organic concept in which the environmental question would not just be seen as one dimension but as *the* dimension. The very word 'socio-environmental' in ISA's name was not even used in Brazil at that time. Today it is everywhere.[19]

If SOS is an example of the emulation process, ISA shows how local activists adapted their agenda in order to be more attractive to potential global donors and institutions, without the intermediation of global civil society organizations (CSOs).

The 'socio-environmental' approach succeeded, disseminating the Peoples of the Forest framework on a global scale and allowing ISA to tap multiple donors. This has not changed Ricardo into a globetrotter. During 1997 and 1998, however, when ISA was being formed, many of its activists took part in international scientific seminars on the Amazon and on indigenous people, looking to give global visibility to their organization and seeking donors abroad.

The global links were largely established by Márcio Santilli, a co-founder of ISA, lawmaker during the Constituent Assembly and former president of the federal agency concerned with the protection of indigenous rights. As ISA executive secretary, he kept one eye on domestic politics and the other on the international sphere, seeking new global funds as well as maintaining CEDI's grants to ISA. In 1997, for instance, he had five meetings with World Bank representatives, drove ICCO members and British authorities to visit to São Gabriel da Cachoeira, a region ISA was keen to protect, granted an interview to the BBC to publicize ISA's activities, discussed an alliance with the Belgian government and participated in the Conservation and Development Forum in Istanbul. Activities like these become routine.

This strategy brought the ISA resources from many global quarters. In 1996, foreign funding constituted 75 per cent of its budget. Between 2000 and 2006, 74 per cent of its annual resources came from international donors, philanthropic, governmental and multilateral, as well as some funding from transnational CSOs. This pattern continues to this day. In 2006, ISA had support from more than thirty international institutions to maintain a monthly budget of approximately half a million US dollars.[20]

The People of the Forest framework, gathering local communities' lifestyle and natural resource protection under a single definition, explains this success. The framework allowed ISA to approach diverse international sources of funding, instead of being dependent on just one global CSO, as SOS was. ISA was thus able to channel global resources to its local choices.

Politics of intermediation

These two trajectories of activism, global–local and local–global, arose because there were global opportunities facilitating them. The siting of UNCED in Brazil in 1992 represented a watershed for environmental activism in Brazil in three ways.

First, it implied a shift of some decision-making processes on environmental issues from national to supranational levels and arenas. This meant an expansion of access to international spaces and resources for Brazilian activists. In terms of spaces, the UNCED allowed civil society actors to take part in discussions of the main documents, such as Agenda 21. Those spaces have expanded since then, with invitations to Brazilian environmental activists to take part in global environmental fora and conferences.

Second, the UNCED opened up an era of global funding programmes for environmental conservation. Since then, many international agencies have created programmes for biome protection, especially for the Amazon, which directed new and huge amounts of money to Brazil through programmes like the Pilot Programme for the Protection of Tropical Forest in Brazil and the Global Environment Facility, oriented to projects in developing countries. World Bank loans began to subsidize sustainable-development-oriented programmes run by the Brazilian government. Those funds offered opportunities to Brazilian environmentalists to work as managers of environmental areas, encouraging them to professionalize their activism to respond to the new global call for environmental management projects.

Third, UNCED brought global environmental actors to the Brazilian public space, improving the scope of strategies and alliances the Brazilian environment activists could count on. Greenpeace and WWF opened offices in Brazil, bringing with them new strategies of activism. WWF brought its technical know-how in terms of the management of environmental resources and its fund-raising strategy among entrepreneurs and governmental agencies. Greenpeace arrived with its repertoire of aggressive protest, intense use of media and gathering of huge numbers of adepts. WWF and Greenpeace also conveyed their professionalized pattern of activism, working like firms, with labour division, customized tasks and a globalized agenda. This configured a new model of activism that Brazilian activists could adapt or emulate.

Local activists responded to the opportunities brought by globalization by looking for professionalization and alliances. Activists did not circumscribe their action to the sphere of civil society; rather, SOS and ISA worked in close connection with both state and market. Further, they developed two strategies for approaching global partners: emulation and adaptation (Tilly 2005).

The emulation mechanism In shaping its activism, SOS activists emulated the global organizations' repertoire of styles of organizing, publicizing, fund-raising and acting. In the beginning, SOS assumed Greenpeace's strategy of aggressive proselytism, advertising in the mass media to attract individual contributors. This was facilitated by the links made by an SOS affiliate, the journalist Rodrigo de Lara Mesquita. After attending classes on 'eco-development', he started to write on the destruction of the rainforest, where his father kept a summer house,[21] for his family media conglomerate – including a radio station and one of the most respectable Brazilian newspapers. With this access to media and help from a marketing firm, SOS diversified its campaigns, with a logo (a map of Brazil with missing trees), a flag, a stamp, slogans and propaganda for television. It multiplied its affiliates from 5,120 in 1996 to 160,000 by 2006 (SOS Rainforest 2006). While it was still dependent on the Mittermeier connection to get global grants, until 2003 around half of SOS's resources came from individual contributions obtained through campaigns.

SOS also emulated WWF's style of organizing and raising money among entrepreneurs and local elites. Roberto Klabin, who had joined the environmentalist movement in the late 1970s, brought an entrepreneurial style of organization.

While all of them were dreamers, idealizing and shaping the movement

[...] I wanted everything to work. I was the guy that was always writing on a blackboard, making datasets, structuring activities, to know how many people we needed to gather and how much to spend.²²

Under Klabin, SOS, very informal until 2002, emulated the WWF's model of organization, gaining the features of a firm, with a formal hierarchy, division functions, full-time officials and a professional fund-raising strategy.

As an entrepreneur, Klabin attracted the support of firms. In 1992, his 'Conservationist Entrepreneur' campaign, asking for small annual grants, got more than fifty firms to contribute in just the first two years. From 2004 on, donations from big firms accounted for 45 per cent of its resources, and SOS also established partnerships to raise proceeds from the sale of toothpaste and magazines and credit card use. Hence, SOS used the fund-raising styles of global organizations to build up its financial independence from them. Nowadays half of its budget comes from thirty-three large Brazilian firms.²³ Because of this, SOS could keep focused on the rainforest while global funding turned to the Amazon.

In this politics of knowledge, SOS also emulated WWF's technical approach to environmental issues, seeing natural science and economics as instruments to achieve a rational use of nature. Mittermeier circulated this framework while helping to build up SOS. Also, WWF invested in knowledge transfer, distributing 136 scholarships to Brazilian environmentalists for master's and PhD degrees in the Nature and Society Programme at the State University of New York up until 2000.²⁴ In these ways, SOS incorporated a style of project design from global organizations.

SOS also assimilated international meanings of sustainable development. In 1993, WWF helped SOS in the creation of the Forest Stewardship Council. Since then, SOS has persuaded firms to support conservation projects in exchange for a certification of environmental responsibility (ISO 14000/14001). With CI, SOS also runs the Programme for Private Natural Reserves, a public–private partnership for management of conservation areas, combining funds from Brazilian entrepreneurs and foreign institutions. Through these joint programmes, SOS incorporated the sustainable development framework: to achieve environmental preservation by encouraging local communities and entrepreneurs to invest in environmentally oriented business projects: eco-tourism, small-scale agriculture, oyster production and certified extraction of wood. Bringing financial resources, institutional partnership and scientifically based guidance to local elites and entrepreneurs,

SOS built coalitions in nineteen municipalities in the early 1990s, and signed sixty partnerships with public and private entrepreneurs.

The sustainable development approach includes knowledge transfer to local communities through environmental education programmes. For instance, in the Lagamar project, SOS delivers courses on techniques for sustainable cultivation and natural resource management to teachers, families and children. Local traditional knowledge is incorporated where it matches the scientific requirement. SOS pursues a 'strategy of consciousness raising' (SOS Rainforest 2005: 25), envisaging a vertical pathway from activists to the community. SOS works as a mediator between donors and local groups, selecting which activities in the local communities are suitable to be funded by entrepreneurs and global agencies. Hence, SOS is a pathway for local communities to reach the national and global arena.[25] At the same time, however, being a representative of local programmes is vital for SOS in terms of maintaining its own relationship with national and global partners.

The SOS case shows that, in spite of its being originally an emulator of its global allies, local actors are able to adapt, producing not a boomerang but a ricochet effect: the meanings and practices brought by global actors are redefined and sent back. For instance, SOS first emulated sustainable development models, but now exports its own experiences, such as the environmental education project 'My World', disseminated across the world by CI. Mittermeier commented, 'I think it really worked for us and it is a model of how to work in partnership, [one] big NGO from one country connected and working very closely with an international NGO, both keeping also their independence.'[26]

In fact, SOS has to balance like an acrobat, being part of a global community by virtue of its style of organization, strategies of action, fund-raising, proselytism and meaning production, as well as part of a Brazilian public sphere, engaged with local actors and projects. With its feet at the local level and its head at the global level, SOS is an example of hybrid activism.

The adaptation mechanism ISA's politics of intermediation illustrate another path to globalization, from local to global. ISA is rooted in a national tradition of activism, and retained countercultural features from the Brazilian middle-class social movements. In its style of organizing, in contrast with the culture of the firm at SOS, ISA staff work as teams of ethnographers, using informal language, dress and sociability. Its founding staff was comprised of twelve social scientists, four geographers, four lawyers, three biologists, three engineers, two managers and one journalist; most of them have studied or lived abroad. It has around 150 members, divided between six offices, who are activist-experts working in patterns similar to those of academic research, by specialist areas, most of them rooted close to indigenous groups, in Manaus, São Gabriel da Cachoeira and Canarana. Relying on the expertise of these activists, ISA emulates the global environmental organizations' uses of scientific knowledge, developing a system of producing and disseminating information about indigenous and traditional groups living in the Amazon, using ethnographic case studies, datasets and socio-environmental maps and photos.

This expertise paved the way for alliances with the state. ISA has been required by federal agencies to run projects in the Amazon about plants, indigenous communities, ethno-politics, HIV/AIDS risk among indigenous people, diagnosis of environmental problems and even the demarcation of indigenous areas: 'ISA ended up by taking on this activity, which is typically a government function [...] Hence, in fact, there are moments ISA did work in close relation with the state.'[27]

Around 20 per cent of ISA's budget comes from governmental sources.[28] Also, when Marina Silva, a People of the Forest leader, became minister of environment in 2003, she named Capobianco as Secretary of Biodiversity and Forests, and in 2007 he became her executive secretary, bringing ISA activists and ideas to the formulation of federal environmental policies.[29]

ISA is also a global organization, however, gathering financial support from three different sources. First, ISA was the heir to CEDI's international network, retaining grants from the Ford Foundation and from global Christian organizations.[30] Second, ISA's alliances with the state facilitated access to global spaces, such as environmental and indigenous fora, and global grants. In this way, ISA itself became a broker between local and global arenas and actors on biodiversity in the Amazon.[31] Furthermore, ISA benefited from global appeals, adapting its projects to fit donor requirements.[32] Because of this, ISA, in contrast to the SOS, is unreceptive to contributions from national firms. About 80 per cent of ISA's budget comes from international sources – around eighty donors and a hundred projects.[33]

Unlike SOS's, most of ISA's relationships with global environmental organizations are conflictive – despite episodic collaboration. In the 1990s, ISA had a conflict with Greenpeace about staff,[34] and when WWF started projects in the Black River, a conflict about meanings arose between conservationism, represented by global organizations, and ISA's socio-environmentalism: 'we believe that there is a diverse environmental landscape in Brazil because there is a diversity of cultures

[... while] this organization [the WWF] brought a mediator that imposed [...] priorities that had no relation to the inter-culturality'.[35]

These conflicts had two outcomes. ISA's grassroots activism in the Amazon forced the global organizations aiming to work there to adapt: 'they come with formulaic standards, [...] but [...] their dogma is eroded; [...] they are forced to mix with local actors, local communities; they are submitted to a powerful influence through this process'.[36] ISA also had to adapt to face global competitors, assimilating global formulae, such as on climate change. It imbued these with local meanings, however, as in the case of its environmental education programmes in Black River and Xingu, which are, in fact, indigenous education programmes, based on local traditions, with tutorial materials in native languages, and training of native teachers. The aim is to transmit knowledge to build autonomy.[37] Its 'sustainable development' programmes are also seen as a capacity-building strategy, with training of leaders in technical and administrative skills, and encouraging local communities to organize.[38]

In its politics of knowledge, ISA also combines science and local experiences, as in its socio-environmental maps. This knowledge construction is politicized, including a defence of intellectual property in local uses of biodiversity, and is seen as a path to local independence. Besides this participatory emphasis, however, ISA still works as a broker, showing local communities the sustainable economic activities that would suit the global donors and facilitating the connection between them.

ISA is the inverted image of SOS: its feet are planted in the global, since its funding comes from there, but its head remains at the local: 'ISA has a root and an antenna.'[39] The side effect, however, has been ISA's dependence on global funds and agencies. It has local roots, but it is unable to survive without its global antenna.

The SOS and ISA cases highlight the fact that there are two paths in the connection between global and local, but in both there is an intertwining of the local and the global, a hybridism.

Hybrid activism

From the cases presented, some conclusions can be drawn on local–global activism. Instead of 'activists without borders' and 'rooted cosmopolitans', the Brazilian cases show an intermingling of local and global as two sides of the same coin. What makes local and global exist are activists' biographies. They live in both spheres, and as they move, they carry with them meanings, knowledge, forms of action and organizing.

This process, however, creates two paths of hybrid activism, according to two mechanisms. SOS is an example of the global–local hybrid identity, built through emulation. In this case, a Northern CSO looked for local allies to implement its agenda, ideas and strategies in the South. Local activists responded, emulating Northern frameworks and selecting local ideas, agendas and strategies amenable to them. In the resulting global–local alliance the foreign activists gained entrance to local projects and arenas, while the local activists gained access to global ones.

ISA shows another path, a local–global hybrid identity, born of adaptation. In this case, local activists grasped the opportunities brought by globalization, making strategic alliances with global institutions. They had to adapt the meanings, agendas and strategies they already worked with, however, reframing local issues under new labels to gain access to global fora and resources. Hence, local activists used foreign channels to globalize and finance their own agendas.

Tarrow (2005) suggests that contemporary mobilizations are multi-issue, aggregating diverse demands. Brazilian activists did more – they built meaning packages, combining local and global meanings in frameworks, such as sustainable development and Peoples of the Forest, which make possible the building of alliances with global activists and donors.

The compromise between local and global appears also in the politics of knowledge, combining traditional and scientific knowledge. SOS emulates global meanings at the local level, in a vertical politics of knowledge, while ISA reshaped local knowledge to carry it into global discourse. Despite this difference, both gained access to global spaces as representatives of and experts on local communities. Their power comes from this intermediation.

The cases shed doubt on the frequently raised opposition between state and globalization. The market is usually seen as a globalizing force, but SOS's choice to engage with market actors did not lead to the strengthening of a global activism; quite the opposite – it reinforced its local action and financing. Conversely, ISA's connection with the state worked as one path to access global grants and spaces.

GCS theories stress accountability in relationships between local and global civil society actors. This view, however, is normative. The Brazilian cases show that CSOs can combine a discourse of horizontal accountability with a vertical politics of intermediation vis-à-vis local communities. Besides, there are power asymmetries between Northern and Southern civil societies, and since the financial resources come from the first, patron–client relationships can be generated. This means a hierarchy inside 'civil society', challenging the optimistic view of global civil society held by many analysts.

The relationship, though, cannot be seen as simple domination by global over local actors. Local activists have their own resources to manage in trading with global actors. Belonging to a stratum of highly educated liberal professionals and to national elite networks, they have privileged access to national government and local communities living in the areas targeted by global environmentalists. Hence, they benefit from the intermediation they do, being fully able to shuttle between local and global spaces. As Tarrow (ibid.) argues, political participation on a global scale remains the business of few.

The GCS perspective does not acknowledge that activism is a double-edged sword. It can be a resistance to asymmetries as much as a reinforcement of them, deepening the gap between common citizens and professional activists, restricting the benefits of globalization to the latter.

Keck and Sikkink's (1998) 'boomerang theory' suggests that transnational activism is very much concerned with the ability of local activists to grasp global allies and, strenghtened by them, to pressure their own government. This argument stresses transnational networks, but neglects the local links activists maintain. The Brazilian cases show that activists access global spheres, make links and obtain resources outside their home country, precisely because of – and not despite – their roots in local contexts and in concrete national interactions. The image of a conflict between the national state and global coalitions orchestrated by 'activists without borders' is false; indeed, the ISA case shows how the national state can operate as an ally and as a channel to promote issues at the global level.

Instead of a boomerang, a better image to describe the process would be a ricochet. Meanings and practices coming from global actors are emulated or adapted by local actors, who modify them and send them back. This is a continuous movement, in which the global is not merely imposed on the local or vice versa. Rather, the two realities mingle and are lived by activists as part of a single experience, encompassing scenes like the one at JFK airport I imagined at the opening of this chapter. The man waiting for his flight is not just a global activist. To keep his activism working he must return home. His lived experience, his meanings and strategies, are made of a mix of local and global. That is why 'hybrid activist' seems the best way to designate him.

Notes

1 This chapter is based on three years of interviews and research carried out within the Environmental Conflicts team at the Centro Brasileiro de Análise e Planejamento (CEBRAP). Information on biographical trajectories of local–global environmental activists and the two main Brazilian environmental organizations was gathered from autobiographical accounts, earlier interviews with CEBRAP researchers and interviews in other media; published sources are given where these are directly quoted in the chapter. I am grateful for suggestions from Debora Maciel, Valeriano Costa, Denise Milstein, John Gaventa, Rajesh Tandon and Ian Scoones.

2 Beth Quintino and Rodrigo Godoy, Interview, Russell Mittermeier, *Portal Bioclimático*, 25 February 2005, www.bioclimatico.com.br/pdf/entrevistas/SOS%20Russell Mittermeier.pdf, accessed 21 August 2009.

3 Interview, Mário Mantovani, 26 July 2001.

4 Interview, Russell Mittermeier, 25 February 2005.

5 Interview, Peter Seligman, *Gazeta Mercantil*, 15 June 1990.

6 Beth Quintino and Rodrigo Godoy, Interview, Rodrigo de Lara Mesquita, *Portal Bioclimático*, 20 December 2004, www.bioclimatico.com.br/pdf/entrevistas/SOS_%20 RodrigoMesquita.pdf, accessed 21 August 2009.

7 Interview, Russell Mittermeier, 25 February 2005.

8 'There were the resources coming from the United States from the WWF but it had to be used to research the environmental questions in the Vale do Ribeira.' Interview, Mário Mantovani, 26 July 2001.

9 Especially to the Amazon, such as the Amazonic Victory Foundation and the Institute of Amazonic Man and Environment.

10 Interview, Garo Batmanian, 31 August 2004.

11 Ibid.

12 Interview, Russell Mittermeier, 25 February 2005.

13 Philippe Léna, Interview, Carlos Alberto Ricardo, January 2002, www.lusotopie.sciencespobordeaux.fr/ricardo-lena.rtf, accessed 21 August 2009.

14 Interview, Carlos Alberto Ricardo, January 2002.

15 Beth Quintino and Rodrigo Godoy, Interview, João Paulo Capobianco, *Portal Bioclimático*, 21 March 2005, www.bioclimatico.com.br/pdf/entrevistas/SOS_%20 Capobianco_OK.pdf, accessed 21 August 2009.

16 Formally entitled the Peoples of the Forest Alliance, this is known to the world as Chico Mendes's campaign.

17 Interview, Carlos Alberto Ricardo, 22 July 2008.

18 Interview, João Paulo Capobianco, 21 March 2005.

19 Interview, Carlos Alberto Ricardo, January 2002.

20 Interview, Enrique Svirsky, *Revista Eletrônica do Terceiro Setor – Integração*, April 2006, integracao.fgvsp.br/ano9/04/opiniao.htm, accessed 21 August 2009.

21 Interview, Rodrigo de Lara Mesquita, 20 December 2004.

22 Beth Quintino and Rodrigo Godoy, Interview, Roberto Klabin, *Portal Bioclimático*, 18 January 2005, www.bioclimatico.com.br/pdf/entrevistas/SOS_%20RobertoKlabim.pdf, accessed 21 August 2009.

23 SOS Rainforest Bulletins, 1992–2007.

24 pdf.usaid.gov/pdf_docs/PDACA222.pdf, accessed 21 August 2009.

25 The Condé Nast Traveller Prize which the Lagamar region won for best eco-tourist destination in the world in 1999 certainly would not have been achieved without SOS's actions in the area.

26 Interview, Russell Mittermeier, 25 February 2005.

27 Interview, Carlos Alberto Ricardo, 22 July 2008.

28 ISA Activities Reports from 1997 onwards.

29 For instance, in 2003 ISA produced a document on the deforestation in Amazonia, which was integrally incorporated by the ministry.

30 ISA Financial Reports, 2006 and 2007.

31 For instance, in the Biodiversity Programme in Indigenous Areas, formed in 2003 in a collaboration between the Global Environmental Facility, the Ministry of Environment and the National Indigenous Foundation.

32 ISA even created an Institutional Development Section to look at appeals for proposals.

33 Interview, Carlos Alberto Ricardo, 22 July 2008.

34 'They [Greenpeace] took lots of folks from us.' Ibid.

35 Ibid.

36 Ibid.

37 www.socioambiental.org, accessed 21 August 2009.

38 ISA helped at least thirty-nine indigenous and fourteen Maroon people's organizations to be born, as well as a federation linking them.

39 Interview, Carlos Alberto Ricardo, 22 July 2008.

References

Alonso, A., V. Costa and D. Maciel (2005) 'The formation of the Brazilian environmental movement', IDS Working Paper no. 256, Institute of Development Studies, Brighton.

Castells, M. (1996) *The Power of Identity – the Information Age: Economy, Society and Culture*, Baltimore, MD: Johns Hopkins University Press.

Falk, R. (1999) *Predatory Globalization: A Critique*, Cambridge: Polity Press.

Gaventa, J. and R. Tandon (2007) 'Citizen engagement in a globalising world: emerging synthesis of findings', Unpublished working paper, Development Research Centre on Citizenship, Participation and Accountability, Institute of Development Studies, Brighton.

Jasper, J. (1997) *The Art of Moral Protest: Culture, Biography, and Creativity in Social Movements*, Chicago, IL: University of Chicago Press.

Keck, M. and K. Sikkink (1998) *Activists beyond Borders: Advocacy Networks in International Politics*, Ithaca, NY: Cornell University Press.

Landim, L. (1993) *Para Além do Mercado e do Estado? Filantropia e cidadania no Brasil*, Rio de Janeiro: ISER.

McAdam, D., S. Tarrow and C. Tilly (2001) *Dynamics of Contention*, New York: Cambridge University Press.

Melucci, A. (1996) *Challenging Codes: Collective Action in the Information Age*, Cambridge: Cambridge University Press.

Polleta, F. (2006) *It Was Like a Fever: Protest and Politics*, Chicago, IL: University of Chicago Press.

Shefner, J. (2004) 'Introduction: current trends in Latin American social movements', *Mobilization*, 9(3): 219–22.

Smith, J. (2005) 'The uneven geography of Global Civil Society: national and global influences on transnational association', *Social Forces*, 84(2): 621–52.

SOS Rainforest (2005) Activities Report.

— (2006) Activities Report.

Tarrow, S. (2005) *The New Transnational Activism*, Cambridge: Cambridge University Press.

Tilly, C. (1978) *From Mobilization to Revolution*, London and New York: McGraw Hill.

— (2005) *Identities, Boundaries and Social Ties*, Boulder, CO and London: Paradigm Publishers.

Touraine, A. (1978) *La Voix et le regard*, Paris: Éditions du Seuil.

11 · Caught between national and global jurisdictions: displaced people's struggle for rights

LYLA MEHTA AND REBECCA NAPIER-MOORE

Modern politics is a spatial politics. Its crucial condition of possibility is the distinction between an inside and an outside, between citizens, nations and communities within and enemies, others and absences without. (Slater 1997: 261)

Citizenship and displacement in a globalizing world

Arjun Appadurai talks of different 'scapes' to describe the new global world. By ethnoscapes he is referring to:

> Landscapes of people who constitute the shifting world in which we live: tourists, immigrants, refugees, guestworkers and other moving groups and persons constitute the essential feature of the world, and appear to affect the politics of and between nations to a hitherto unprecedented degree. This is not to say that there are not anywhere relatively stable communities and networks, of kinship, friendship, of work and of leisure, as well as of birth, residence and other filiative forms. But this is to say that the warp of these stabilities is everywhere shot through with the woof of human motion, as more persons and groups deal with the realities of having to move, or the fantasies of wanting to move [...] (Appadurai 2002: 158–9)

Indeed, mobility, displacement and emplacement have become defining features of our times. While we, in part, share Appadurai's celebration of the shifting world and its moving inhabitants, we are concerned with the phenomenon of forced displacement that compels a displaced person to leave her home, family, loved ones and livelihood, maybe never to return.

As long as there are wars and large-scale development projects, forced uprootedness is here to stay. At the end of 2008, globally 42 million people were in situations of forced displacement. Of those 15.2 million were refugees, with the rest asylum seekers with cases pending, and internally displaced people (IDPs) (UNHCR 2009). Some estimate that, owing to intractable conflicts, about eleven million people lack citizenship or effective nationality worldwide, situations which violate Article 15 of the Universal Declaration of Human Rights (UDHR), which upholds that every person 'has a right to a nationality' (Frelick and Lynch 2005). Many of these are also displaced people.[1]

The problem of displacement is here to stay, meaning that the rights of refugees are at risk (Grabska and Mehta 2008). States, which should be rights providers, are failing refugees, and international actors are often de facto bearing their responsibilities, at times failing miserably to mediate between host states and refugees. Where citizenship is not granted or where neither the state nor international agencies are acting as duty bearers, many refugees are defining what rights are important and are reshaping what citizenship looks like, through the very fact of their movement, through mobilization or through the realization of rights locally. How does increasing displacement pose challenges for citizenship 'without nation-states'? How do refugees understand their rights and whom do they see as duty holders with respect to these rights – national or global actors? How do refugees claim their rights? Who is accountable to them? How do refugees force us to rethink conventional understandings of citizenship, and can they be considered to be 'global citizens'? These questions are the focus of the chapter.

We begin with a brief review of how refugees[2] are challenging conventional understandings of citizenship and how displaced people are realizing rights without having access to formal citizenship and rights. We go on to show how displaced people are participating in protest and mobilization efforts to have formal rights granted and abuse of rights stopped, and how transnational alliances across global–local spaces take place in efforts to change citizenship rights. We conclude with an examination of what global citizenship means for refugees.

Who is responsible anyway?

Who is supposed to protect the rights of these 'international orphans' and those crossing international borders? In principle, by 'voting with their feet' (Hathaway 1991: 120), refugees fleeing from oppressive state regimes and the abuse of their human rights can expect protection from international law and from host countries. Legislative frameworks that embrace protection for refugees are based on the framework of the UDHR (1948)[3] and specific conventions such as the 1951 Convention relating to the Status of Refugees. Under international law, states are obliged to protect non-citizens and those residing within their national borders, giving refugees a strong basis for protection against the abuse of their civil and political rights. But official duty-bearing states do not always step up to meet their obligations – or meet them fully. And the social, economic and cultural rights of refugees[4] – including the right to development and self-determination, food, health, education, participation and livelihood – remain very neglected, often viewed as 'second generation' rights. Host states are reluctant to award them to refugees, as we shall demonstrate.

In reality, refugees often cannot claim entitlements from host states that deny them their basic rights and often abdicate responsibility to international organizations, primarily the Refugee Settlement Commission of the League of Nations, the United Nations Relief and Works Agency for Refugees in the Near East (UNRWA) and the United Nations High Commissioner for Refugees (UNHCR). But UNHCR, for instance, is not supposed to provide direct assistance, and instead has a mandate to lobby for states to meet refugees' rights. UNRWA, which works only with displaced Palestinians, has the mandate to provide direct assistance but not to lobby states.

Moreover, there are broad and narrow definitions of who is a refugee, and many would-be refugees are denied this status. The power of categorization and awarding status is linked to the 'right' to have 'rights'. Owing to the strict requirements for refugee status provided in the 1951 Convention and the 1969 Organization of African Unity Convention Governing the Specific Aspects of Refugee Problems in Africa, being granted refugee status is difficult for most displaced people. In fact, the strict legal criteria and status determination procedures often employed by either host governments or on their behalf by UNHCR mean that many remain outside the protection of international refugee law.[5] In other cases, governments simply choose not to apply the definition, whether narrow or not. For example, refugees in Egypt are treated like mere 'foreigners' in terms of access to rights (Grabska 2008). Perceived as temporary guests on their way to resettlement in a Western country, refugees from Sudan, Somalia and Palestine are not provided with access to formal citizenship, even though Egypt is a signatory to several refugee conventions. Egypt turns to UNHCR to protect and assist refugees; they in turn see UNHCR as the guarantor of their rights.

At the same time, however, the category 'refugee' or 'displaced person' establishes rights and entitlements. For example, illegality and lack of refugee status mean limited and disadvantaged access to jobs,[6] lack of access to education for children,[7] lack of access to health services, and the inability of refugees to claim their other rights in the host society,[8] including freedom of movement.[9] Rights, however, are granted to refugees temporarily, pending a durable solution to the refugee 'problem'.[10]

Regional bodies such as the Association of South-East Asian Nations (ASEAN), the European Union, the South Asian Association for Regional Cooperation, the African Union, and the Mercado Común del Sur (Mercosur, Common Market of the South) can also play a large part in determining whether refugees originating from elsewhere can enter a region, and whether states will be pressured by the regional body to recognize them as such. For instance, ASEAN does not exert and has not exerted pressure for the recognition of different groups of Burmese fleeing the Myanmar military regime as 'refugees'. Instead, Burmese entering Thailand or Malaysia are summarily arrested, detained and deported upon discovery. In contrast, regional bodies such as the African Union and Mercosur have broadened the refugee definition in their regions, working to help more people access rights.[11]

Thus several actors play a part in the landscape of authority that governs recognition of refugee rights – ranging from states to UN agencies to regional associations of states. Others, at a local level (below the state), also play a part, including citizens of a host country who either work to meet or to obstruct the rights of refugees through non-discrimination, through employment or through assistance with education. Local civil society groups play similar roles. Actors at all levels – local, national, regional, global – populate the landscape of authority in which refugees find themselves – aiding or taking away access to rights. Of course, as we show in what follows, refugees also have a role in this 'authority', taking some of it for themselves, in ways that make rights real.

How do displaced people defy conventional notions of citizenship?

The practices of the state are premised on the normality of citizenship and the state, but they also produce the 'accident' of the refugee (Nyers 2007). Refugees, displaced from 'authentic political identities, communities of citizenship, etc. are seen as a temporary aberration to the norm, as hiccups, that disturb "the national order of things"' (Malkki, in Nyers 2007: 9). But their disturbance is precisely the catalyst and foil that induced states to make their boundaries and identity firm, using the displaced person as the marker for what defines the outsider and what defines the insider (see ibid.; Malkki 2002; Tuitt 2008). In this section we look at several aspects of the 'citizenship problem' for refugees, ranging from refugees rupturing norms of territory, political participation, and single versus multiple citizenships.

Large-scale population movements, as well as the host of reasons that will continue to compel people to flee and move, suggest that there is no turning back to an ideal of a state with a bounded and sedentary group of citizens, and it is best to expand the notion of citizenship. The division of people into full citizens and non-citizens perpetuates racism and social tensions, drawing lines and labelling insiders as differentiated from people with partial or no rights (Castles and Davidson 2000: 101). Special protection for one group may ironically mean exclusion for another. Thus, inclusion becomes the crux, as labelling in a category often is what displaced people want or need in their struggle to claim rights. For example, the case of stateless Palestinian refugees in Lebanon is a significant example of displaced people whose formal rights in their host state have gradually been worn away over their many years in exile. Jaber Suleiman (2008: 103) describes how Palestinians' right to own property and to work, for instance, continues to decline with decree after decree, changing previous laws:

> Despite the fact that Decree 927 refers specifically to 'Palestinian refugees', Lebanese legislators make no attempts to distinguish us from foreigners. Ordinance 319 of August 1962, which regulates the situation of foreigners in Lebanon, considers Palestinian refugees as one of five classifications of foreigners, that is, a 'special category of foreigners', despite our protracted residence in the country and our exile as refugees. So on the one hand we are denied basic rights that Lebanon granted to its nationals, and on the other we are not guaranteed the refugee rights accepted and recognized in relevant international instruments.

Thus, refugees break the state–nation–territory triad that conventionally and formally defines citizenship in refugees' home and host states (Nyers 2007: 41). Their belonging is thrown into question in both home and host countries. Refugees have a twofold lack with respect to citizenship. Without citizenship in host states, they are denied not only basic rights but also the capacity to speak politically and the right to be heard. In many parts of the world, host countries fail to live up to international human rights standards, or meet basic provisions of the Refugee Convention that they have signed. Hannah Arendt sees refugees representing a problem not of geographical/territorial but of political space. They are people denied rights because they are denied access to a political space that allows for a meaningful political presence (see ibid.). Being a refugee thus becomes an aberration. This is because conventional understandings of citizenship are made out to be the only authentic political identity of modern political life. Refugee aberration vis-à-vis political space is our first break in conventional notions of citizenship.

Furthermore, the fact that millions of people have multiple citizenships and split lives also challenges the conventional notions of citizenship and belonging. This suggests new rules of conviviality. Some argue for dissolving the 'nation part' of the nation-state (Castles and Davidson 2000: viii), replacing it with flexible and open belonging and a democratic state. Citizenship should be derived from residence on a state's territory, cultural participation and economic involvement. It should no longer be determined by belonging to certain cultural groups. Yet this argument poses questions of political involvement for refugees, who have crossed international borders but are still active, or think it is their right still to be active, in home-country politics. Tibetan refugees protesting against the Chinese government from India, France or Nepal are doing so as part of belonging to what Castles and Davidson say are cultural (rather than territorial) groups. Rainer Baubock (2007) talks of 'external citizenship', in terms both of a right to return and external voting rights, and of citizenship duties of military service, taxes and compulsory voting. Saskia Sassen (2004: 191) argues that the destabilizing of hierarchies of power of the nation-state has led to new political forces and actors which signal a 'deterritorializing of citizenship practices and identities'. Transformations inside the nation-state have also led to changes in the institutions of citizenship, and post-national citizenship can be distinguished from denationalized forms of citizenship (ibid.: 192). Neither geographical nor political space notions in traditional citizenship hold up any more without significant challenges.

Globalization's effects on displacement have also contributed to new problems and challenges to citizenship. Globalization has created a 'citizenship gap which puts noncitizens and "second class citizens" at risk' (Brysk and Shafir 2004: 3). So, vulnerable displaced people cannot even rely on the few formal rights they thought they had. Globalization can be seen as the acceleration and intensification of flows (cultural, financial, of people, information and so on). As described above, states play a key role in interpreting and enforcing citizenship based on combinations of birth, descent, residency, cultural characteristics and so on. But globalization intensifies these discrepancies and disparities as well as the numbers of people in dual or overlapping status. It has led to a growing number of non-citizens such as refugees whose lives are affected by market trends, conflicts and policies in the North that impact unfavourably on Southern lives and livelihoods.

There is also a big disjuncture in what is laid out in international human rights conventions and the actual experiences of refugees. There is, for one, a big gap in perceptions of what rights displaced people should be given. Social, economic and cultural rights continue to be viewed as 'second generation' rights, despite the great strides made by the 1969 African Union Convention Governing Specific Aspects of Refugee Problems in Africa to include their violation as cause for flight and thus refugee status in host countries. Nonetheless, leading forced migration scholars, such as Hathaway (2005), argue that there are some rights for refugees that are immediate, whereas others – including economic rights – are seen as progressive. This argument is also used by host states which use the level of development of a country to get out of being responsible for providing and protecting the social, economic and cultural rights of refugees. But as we shall shortly see, this view is not shared by refugees, who view rights in more all-encompassing ways.

The difference between the statist view and that of this chapter is summed up by Kurtz and Hankins (2005: 2), who talk of the differences 'between state-centred definitions of the rights, obligations and membership requirements of citizenship and the discursive and active practices of citizenship as they unfold in different times and spaces'. Few in the academic literature are asking how displaced people are viewing their own citizenship and struggling for the rights that they see as their own. Even though refugees are largely excluded from formal citizenship and are often caught between both local and global jurisdictions in their struggle to realize rights, in this chapter we move away from the 'sedentary' perspectives of governments and intergovernmental bodies (Malkki 1992) to adopt a migrant or displacement lens to demonstrate how refugees are living citizenship and seeking in multiple ways to negotiate the complex realities discussed above. We do this by using an actor-oriented lens that 'privileges the experiences of the poor and marginalised groups and their own understandings of rights, but without denying the importance of formal sources of rights. The approach enables the pushing of the boundaries of formal legality when this is necessary for justice' (Nyamu-Musembi 2005: 48). This understanding sees the interaction between the formal and the subjective understandings of rights. We now go on to demonstrate different ways in which refugees are realizing their rights and experience 'lived citizenship' by realizing rights quietly and informally, by mobilizing and publicly claiming rights and by building transnational action or solidarities with others.

Realizing rights ... informally When rights are not formally available to refugees, they often seek to realize them informally, engaging in the same practices as formally defined citizens. Thus, informal social contracts emerge between the 'community' and immigrants (Sassen

2004). Marginalized groups move between powerlessness and the condition of being an actor, thus acquiring a presence in a broader political process. This presence entails the possibility of a politics that, while centred in specific localities, is transnational (ibid.).

Kibreab (2008) discusses a similar scenario when talking about Eritrean refugees in his research on decisions to repatriate or stay in Sudan, the country of asylum. He shows that though denied formal rights from the Sudanese government, through social networks with the host populations based on religion, ethnicity and language, some Eritrean refugees have informally and de facto been able to enjoy economic and social rights nearly on a par with Sudanese. They accessed economic and social rights even though they formally lacked 'the right to have rights'. They own houses and access healthcare even though they are not supposed to; they live in urban centres even though their mobility is supposed to be restricted to designated zones; and by different means some have acquired Sudanese nationality or residence permits. Those who have been able to enjoy these rights have not repatriated to Eritrea when the causes for displacement were no longer a threat to them. Those who did not realize these rights largely returned (ibid.). In another example from one of the authors of this paper, during 2006 work with Liberian refugees in Ghana, several displaced Liberians explained they did not want to go back to Liberia because the unemployment rate in the Ghanaian camp (located close to the country's capital) was 30 per cent; in Liberia it averaged 70 per cent. Formally displaced Liberians are not supposed to work in Ghana without a work permit, which few people have. Nonetheless, the reality is that they are informally realizing (and prioritizing) their right to employment by giving up formal citizenship rights that they would have, or at least are supposed to have, in Liberia. By contrast, at the same time in 2006, Liberian refugees who had been encamped in reputedly worse conditions in Guinea (Human Rights Watch 2002) were flocking home to what they hoped would be a better realization of rights than what they were experiencing in displacement. UNHCR held up the closing of Guinean camps as a shining example of successful refugee repatriation (UNHCR 2006). From a displacement, actor-oriented perspective, however, in this case refugees' agreement and desire to move home was a strong sign that rights in exile were not being realized. This voice was not heard, or at least not in media representations.

We see growing acknowledgements of the failure of 'equal citizenship' – rendered visible through processes of claim-making on the part of refugees and other migrants. Indeed, displaced people are even questioning the value of traditional citizenship. For instance, Palestinian refugees are demanding the right to return, rather than citizenship in exile:

> [T]he Palestinian community in Lebanon is not looking for citizenship, and its demand for basic human rights does not entail the right to citizenship. In fact, the right of return is the highest priority for Palestinian refugees in Lebanon. But obtaining basic human rights while in exile would serve to mitigate our destitution and alleviate our day-to-day suffering. Thus, in order to accommodate our isolation and neglect, we are seeking greater economic, social and cultural rights in the local Lebanese context. (Suleiman 2008: 95)

This is a strong message about Palestinians placing value on one right, and the inability of citizenship in a host country to meet it.

Another example is self-settlement, rather than camps, as a way for displaced people to realize rights on their own. Take self-settlement success in Guinea, where villages that welcomed refugees received international development and aid support (Van Damme 1995). Epidemics were fewer, especially in comparison to extreme examples like the Goma camps in Zaire which experienced a cholera epidemic, killing an estimated 50,000 people. Yet, as Van Damme (ibid.: 360) says, the '[m]ixing of refugees with the host population complicated targeting of food aid intended only for refugees; consequently this liberal policy has been changed and new arrivals are now concentrated in camps'. Camps were, in the end, preferred for the sake of targeting and efficiency. Yet self-settlement can provide aid to whole communities in which displaced people settle. Though the literature largely lacks a refugee voice, it lacks it here especially. Do refugees want to be in camps or would they like to self-settle? Malkki's classic *Purity and Exile* describes two refugee situations: first, a camp in which refugees actively claim 'refugee-ness' and 'Hutu-ness', and second, self-settled refugees in townships who refuse to be categorized as refugees. Theirs is a 'subversion of identification' in which they 'manage a series of different identities'. Both situations involve refugee agency, whether it be taking on the refugee narrative wholeheartedly or defying all essentializing categories. They prove that they are not just objects (blank slates to be written upon) but subjects 'creating their own refugee-ness' (Malkki 1995: 3, 4, 11, 153, 235). Some prefer the refugee label and encampment, seeing that as their way to get the rights they want, especially in terms of affiliation with a home-country political voice. Others see self-settlement as the way to blend in, realizing rights that citizens in the host country are receiving. These examples highlight the fact that often refugees find both national and global institutions and processes inadequate and unhelpful. Instead, they exercise agency to realize their rights informally.

Mobilizing for rights, protest Displaced people are struggling for, enacting and making real rights that they see as important, with or without a state's official consent. They identify different duty bearers for the realization of their rights, depending on what entity they perceive to be responsible or actually capable of ensuring the rights that they think are most important. Refugees are often viewed as passive beneficiaries of welfare, aid and charity instead of agents of change (Mehta and Gupte 2003) or, as others have posited, they can be seen as agential 'warrior communities' (Nyers 2007). Take the case of refugees in Egypt. Owing to the restrictions imposed by the Egyptian government on several articles of the 1951 Convention, refugees have very restricted access to education, employment and so on. Egyptian officials use the high unemployment rate in Egypt as an excuse and refugees need to apply for work permits which are notoriously difficult to get. After some struggle, Sudanese refugees have now managed to lobby for a new decree that allows them to gain access to Egyptian public schools, but they need to present valid documents to do so. Those children lacking 'official' refugee status (which is very restricted and difficult to obtain from UNHCR) cannot have these documents (Grabska 2008). Several NGOs have stepped in to meet refugees' immediate needs and help them with the resettlement process. But they do not have the funds or resources to help refugees protect their rights and maintain secure livelihoods.

Grabska (ibid.) describes a lack of clarity in Egypt among the refugees, NGOs, the government and UNHCR regarding who is responsible for the guarantee of refugee rights. Because UNHCR is responsible for conducting refugee status determination and provides direct assistance, many refugees turn to it to realize their rights, especially their social and economic rights. But UNHCR maintains that it can provide them only with legal protection, not the right to work or their social integration. But from the viewpoint of a refugee, protection is multilayered, and encompasses both freedom from persecution and the right to livelihood, health, education and so on.

Often refugees in Cairo and elsewhere see UNHCR as the state provider of rights, and therefore make direct protests to UNHCR rather than to governments (Harrell-Bond 2008). In many situations refugees are right: UNHCR is the most likely entity to take any action or to hear their voices on rights provision. Can the 'country of UNHCR' (Moulin and Nyers 2007) provide citizenship rights? It has at the least a remit for rights advocacy, but whether it hears and then acts on requests for change made by refugee voices 'from below' is another question. A good case in point is the 2005 Sudanese protest in Cairo.

For three months in autumn 2005, hundreds and then thousands of Sudanese refugees staged a sit-in in downtown Cairo, protesting against violations of their rights by UNHCR. Many saw the 'local integration' option they were experiencing as problematic because their rights to education, work, housing and lack of discrimination were severely curtailed (Forced Migration and Refugee Studies 2006). Many were also angry about their petitions and appeals for refugee status being rejected, leaving them without any formal legal status. This mobilization of refugees was unprecedented and large. It was striking that the government refrained from using force over the three months of the sit-in. After increasing pressure from UNHCR, the local media and residents, however, the Egyptian state eventually intervened, not least owing to a clear failure of negotiations between the protesters and UNHCR (ibid.). The demonstration ended on 30 December 2005, with a forced removal of all those protesting in the park in front of the UNHCR office. The police used excessive force in removing the protesters, not offering any allowances for women, children and the elderly. The removal was brutal, and twenty-eight Sudanese died. Many were injured and arrested. Those with official papers were released within a few days, but 600 without formal status remained in detention for longer (ibid.).

Those who have analysed this protest and its tragic outcome argue that much of the blame rests with UNHCR, which adopted a hostile and confrontational attitude towards the protesters (ibid.). It did not initially allow its staff to interact with the refugees directly. It also sided with the Egyptian government and took a lot of risks concerning the safety of the protesters. Unfortunately, there is no way to hold UNHCR to account for the failures and miscalculations that help compound this tragedy. Finally, the leaders of the protest are also partly responsible. Some commentators feel that the number of demands was unrealistic (Harrell-Bond 2008). When some leaders accepted a package from UNHCR, other dissenting voices in the park decided to continue with the protest, even though it meant putting the lives of the protesters at risk. Thus the protesting Sudanese refugees in Egypt were caught between UNHCR and the Egyptian state, with both failing to deliver on the refugees' basic rights. They were also caught up in the politics of mediation and representation with confusing and hostile messages coming from UNHCR, Egyptian authorities and mediators.

Another example of protest took place in Ghana's Buduburam refugee settlement. In 2008, not wanting to accept what they felt was becoming a forced repatriation back to Liberia, refugees held a five-week sit-in on a field next to the highway by the settlement. They felt they were not being given enough financial support to build a new life in Liberia, and they still held on to the hope of being resettled to the USA. At the end of the five weeks, Ghanaian authorities began arresting hundreds of people, saying that some had been protesting naked (BBC 2008). Within days, thirty people had been deported, an action that violated refugee law and enraged remaining refugees (International Herald Tribune 2008). Liberian refugees see several entities as responsible for providing and ensuring their rights. The Ghanaian state and UNHCR are two obvious ones, but many Liberians also see the United States government as responsible for provision of their rights. Liberia's history is one of 'founding' by former US slaves, and some people in the refugee settlement told Napier-Moore that Liberia is seen as the fifty-first US state. With that, they hold hope that the USA will come to the rescue, taking them in as refugees and then as citizens. Realpolitik, however, suggests otherwise, and their subjective view of citizenship rights is very unlikely to be met by the USA.

A graphic and media-attracting angle to protest is that taken by Abas Amini, an Iraqi asylum seeker in the UK, who sewed his eyes and mouth closed to point to lack of rights, maltreatment and unjust denial of asylum by the UK Home Office. His action manifest also as a hunger strike, Amini attracted a further hundred protesters, who gathered outside his residence (BBC 2003). Protesters in Woomera detention centre in Australia also sewed their lips shut in 2003, highlighting poor conditions and lack of rights in detention. Not all is well in the North, as those not granted formal rights fight to attract attention to injustice.

Protests have been going on as long as displaced people have experienced rights violations. We hear more about them only thanks to journalists increasingly picking up the stories (Harrell-Bond 2008). Consider images of:

- Sudanese refugees in Cairo defiantly withstanding Egyptian police water hoses, some with fists raised, and some who had fallen to the ground showing peace signs with their hands (photograph in Sylvan 2005);
- Bhutanese refugees marching peacefully in Nepal protesting about their confinement to camps and lack of right or ability to secure livelihoods. Many wanted repatriation and tried marching home, but

were stopped by Indian authorities as they passed through Indian territory on the way (ibid.);
- Sudanese refugees working in camp schools alongside Ugandan nationals. Sudanese were paid a pittance 'incentive' wage by UNHCR's implementing partners, while Ugandans received a very different national wage. The Sudanese, with support from Ugandan colleagues, formed a union in 1993. Both Sudanese and Ugandan teachers went on strike over the wage differential in 1997, and Sudanese were threatened with being fired from the job. UNHCR was not following the labour laws of host countries. Refugees want and should be paid on a par with citizens, under international and national law requiring equal pay for equal work (Harrell-Bond 2008).

These stories of public protest as a means to secure rights are seemingly countless, in both South and North (see also Lewis 2006). They demonstrate how displaced people are protesting and questioning the top-down policy frameworks through which displacement, repatriation, integration and resettlement are characterized. In some cases, they are successful. In others, their demands are not entirely met owing to the politics of mediation and to the sheer lack of accountability on the part of global and national agencies. We have seen in this section examples of displaced people realizing their rights independently, or in spite of formal state legislated restriction to rights. And we have seen examples of protest, identifying not only host states but international agencies and home or third states as perceived duty bearers.

Building transnational links A transnational citizen is an activist and an idealist, looking to 'a future to be created' (Falk 1994: 139). Forced displacement is a powerful arena for transnational citizens and struggle. We have already discussed the powerful protests of Sudanese refugees in Cairo, Liberians in Ghana and Sudanese in Uganda. Fighting transnationally for both rights in exile and for rights for fellow Tibetan 'stayees', Tibetans exiled across the globe followed the 2008 Olympic torch and used the media attention devoted to it to enhance their claims and protest. As many Tibetans attempt protest against the Chinese government, 'crackdowns' and detention are rising in China and abroad. Yet displaced Tibetans have held the attention of both the international media and NGO activists. Foreign governments debated their participation in the China 2008 Olympics as a consequence. Protest from a wide diaspora of forced migrants, as well as from many non-Tibetan NGO allies and state governments, united behind the calls of the Government of Tibet in Exile for meaningful self-rule for all Tibetans under a single administration (Government of Tibet in Exile 2008). Transnational alliances demonstrate increasing local–global linkages and a global citizenry appealing to international entities as well as states as duty bearers.

For the aforementioned refugee protests, the battle is also transnational, identifying duty bearers including and beyond their country of residence. Sudanese refugees in Cairo, for instance, are also fighting for the right to be resettled by UNHCR in order to move on to a third country, usually Canada or the USA. While protesting, however, displaced people are doing what they can to informally realize as many rights as possible. By sewing his lips together in the UK, Amani realizes his right to a voice as he gets media attention. Despite the problems discussed with the park protest, Sudanese refugees did realize some of the rights they were demanding from UNHCR. Schafer writes:

> While consistently demanding that the UNHCR and international community give them 'their rights' and improve their situation, the sit-in itself temporarily assuaged many of the hardships they faced. The park was transformed into a relatively autonomous community of refugees who created their own sense of security and provided mutual support and solace for each other. The constant uncertainty and frustration associated with life as a refugee was eased as they were able to take back some control over their present lives. (2006: 2)

Transnational links through refugee protest are built as diaspora groups unite across the globe or a region. They are also arguably built as refugees call on transnational duty bearers to help them realize rights. Many refugees turn to UNHCR for that, but others link with refugee rights advocates across the globe to get their stories heard in hopes of betterment of their situations. These include calling on academics, journalists, international NGOs or individual advocates with whom they might have contacts. Often these people might take their message to UN or regional meetings where crucial, rights-impacting changes can happen.

Global citizens?

> The consul banged on the table and said;
> 'If you've got no passport you're officially dead':
> But we are still alive, my dear, but we are still alive.
>
> W. H. Auden, quoted in Malkki (1995: 495)

In this chapter, we have demonstrated how displaced people are performing citizenship, living citizenship, in situations where their own state and most often their host state deny them citizenship rights. Given the way citizenship is normally understood, we are left wondering 'is citizenship a useful concept for exploring the problems of belonging, identity and personality in the modern world?' (Schotter, quoted in Sassen 2004: 195). As reviewed above, the migration, forced migration and citizenship literature has conceptualized some new understandings of citizenship, calling them: external; multilayered or multiple; territorially defined or deterritorializing; denationalized; and global.

Some scholars argue that dual and multiple nationality will one day become the norm (see ibid.: 194). As demonstrated, when the state does not step in, displaced people are either self-realizing rights, or looking beyond the host state as the sole duty bearer. They are creating lived multiple and multilayered citizenship experiences, beyond or beneath the state. Sorensen suggests the notion of membership, rather than citizenship, because membership can be more multifaceted, with several layers:

> [C]itizenship is a straightforward category. One is either a citizen, or not, of a particular state. Membership on the other hand is more convoluted; it is not an all or nothing category. One can be more or less a member; one can be a member in one aspect but not in another. Membership is therefore a broader and more inclusive category than formal citizenship. (Sorensen 1996: 76)

Earlier in the chapter we looked at disruptions to territory, political space and national concepts of citizenship and how displaced people are realizing rights informally where they are not granted citizens' right to have rights, or when they are caught between national and international jurisdictions. We looked at protest and mobilization efforts to secure formal rights, and we saw transnational alliances across global-local spaces. These actions from people making claim to formal or to lived citizenship can be thought of as external citizenship, as multilayered or multiple citizenship, as membership, as territorially defined or deterritorialized citizenship, and as post- and de-nationalized citizenship. Each of these concepts offers a way of explaining changes as well as projecting the future of citizenship. Refugees push the boundaries of the citizenship concept, unsettling our norms, asking for change, and making change happen. The concept of global citizenship presents yet another powerful reconceptualization of citizenship. It is one that is already made real through displaced persons' expressions of agency.

A historical look at 'global citizenship' includes Nansen passports, internationally recognized identity cards first issued by the League of

Nations to stateless refugees. They were designed in 1922 by Fridtjof Nansen (Holborn 1939), and fifty-two countries were honouring them by 1942. The first refugee travel documents, these passports are today recognized as one of the greatest achievements of the League of Nations. The World Service Authority, a non-profit organization that promotes 'world citizenship', issues a 'World Passport' (purportedly under the authority of Article 13, Section 1 of the UDHR) with the de facto acceptance of 170 countries that offer stamped visas, of which six countries – Burkina Faso, Ecuador, Mauritania, Tanzania, Togo and Zambia – recognize it *de jure* (World Service Authority 2007).

In Nansen's age, borders were not as tightly controlled, and the 'refugee problem' concept was largely a European one. Global citizenship for refugees could mean a return to the Nansen passport whereby refugees could be free to travel to a range of countries. It could also mean that governments respect the basic right of all individuals to a nationality. It could mean they adhere to international standards and reduce 'statelessness' by facilitating acquisition of nationality, allowing equal rights and registering every child at birth. These are perhaps more formal aspects. At the informal level, it could be an increasing presence, a multilayered sense of belonging and rights-claiming in global institutions. Not only global institutions, but states should recognize the 'multiple citizenships' of peoples within their borders and of people who have left them. Communities and displaced individuals, of course, already experience and 'live' these multiple citizenships, and many are asking for formal states and institutions to formally recognize their rights as citizens.

Louise Arbour, former UN High Commissioner for Human Rights, when interviewed on global citizenship, said that the foremost global citizens are refugees (Schattle 2005: 124). Benequista and Levine identify three discourses for global citizenship: '1) a *civic* republican discourse that emphasizes concepts such as awareness, responsibility, participation and cross-cultural empathy; 2) a *libertarian* discourse that emphasizes international mobility and competitiveness; and 3) a *legal* discourse that emphasizes legal rights and responsibilities of transnational actors' (2006: 3). In forced migration debates, all three discourses feature. In particular, attention has been paid to the civic republican and legal discourses. These are generally views 'from above', prioritizing the civic republican discourse of moral responsibility (see Nussbaum 1996) towards an 'other'; or the legal discourse, which is often a more statist view. The libertarian discourse, on the other hand, which has an emphasis on international mobility, has the potential to take into account views 'from below'. It only gets a meagre showing, however, if that – indicating global citizenship has not been well defined in terms of international mobility – especially for those displaced and forced to move. Further, international mobility in the libertarian discourse usually refers to upper-class expatriates (Schattle 2005) rather than those forcibly displaced. What Malkki (1992) describes as a 'sedentarist metaphysics' remains the bias. Can we move to a displacement lens or a migrant metaphysics as our norm? The displaced are demanding rights through protest and through international mobilization. From an actor-oriented view of citizenship, we have seen that displaced people are claiming what they see as citizenship rights, or as much of them as they can, in a myriad of ways – whether informal realization locally or by demands to international entities when states are unresponsive.

Would it be possible to transform the rights of forced migrants into a new form of global citizenship – membership of one or more political communities with institutions for participation, distribution and enforcement? Along with others, we argue that multilevel citizenship may allow marginalized peoples, forced migrants included, to be able to enhance rights access by appealing to levels above and below the state (Brysk and Shafir 2004: 212). The key problem is the lack of accountability of key political actors at those different levels. States are not accountable to UNHCR, and UNHCR is not accountable to refugees. 'Who could monitor the monitor?' ask Verdirame and Harrell-Bond, referring to absence of monitoring of UNHCR (2005: 17). In many cases, refugees do de facto 'live in a country of UNHCR' without any citizenship rights, as the Sudanese refugees in Cairo said. Their 'lived' citizenship starts with UNHCR, and so does their protest.

Non-citizens, refugees and others have little knowledge of and access to accountability mechanisms. Other problems of global institutions include weak enforcement, excessive bureaucratization and corruption. But in an era when asylum seekers are deported back to hostile situations, when the global recession is creating ever more protectionism and xenophobia, and when states are cracking down on non-citizens and citizens under the guise of the war on terror, multilevel citizenship could provide rights on different geographical levels (local, district or urban, state, regional and global). This would allow for national, sub-national and supranational identities along with different levels of loyalty. Global citizenship would be based on membership of a global political institution, and the dilution of sovereignty could provide a positive stimulus for enhanced civic engagement. International law should de facto ensure the global right to rights.

'In the world of nation-states, in an era of globalisation, people out of place will always be at risk. While new forms of membership cannot yet grant them a place, evolving institutions can give them greater voice and protection' (Brysk and Shafir 2004: 215). This needs appropriate global governance and the elimination of unaccountable global decision-making. Is it unrealistic to believe in global institutions to uphold rights? Perhaps. Will countries, especially rich ones, submit willingly to processes of global governance to open their doors to strangers in need? Perhaps not. Despite our doubts concerning the feasibility of global citizenship, we acknowledge that the displacement issue cannot be addressed within the current paradigm of the nation-state. In sum, global citizenship may be very hard to achieve in the coming decades, and millions of refugees may have to wait a long time for a Nansen type of passport. These may, however, be normative projects towards which to strive.

Notes

1 Stateless people – including millions of Palestinians who are both stateless and refugees, and about 250,000 Biharis or 'stranded Pakistanis' languishing in Bangladeshi camps since the early 1970s – do not benefit from the protection and assistance of governments, donors and the UN. They are 'international orphans' (Frelick and Lynch 2005: 24).

2 It is beyond the scope of this chapter to examine the situation of internally displaced people or those affected by development-induced displacement (see Grabska and Mehta 2008). Instead, we focus on refugees, whom we take to be people forced to move across borders for fear of political, social, religious, racial or national persecution, those individually recognized under the 1951 UN Convention; those recognized en masse under the 1969 African Union Convention governing the specific aspects of 'Refugee Problems in Africa'; Palestinians specifically excluded from the 1951 UN Convention; those displaced but denied refugee status owing to stringent application of the 1951 Convention; and displaced people in South and South-East Asia where few countries have signed the 1951 Convention.

3 In 1948 the United Nations General Assembly adopted the UDHR, which was endorsed by virtually all states. It is premised on the inherent dignity and worth of all human persons, regardless of background, class or race.

4 Falling under the Covenant on Economic, Social and Cultural Rights (ICESCR) of the UDHR.

5 Hence, it is important to question narrow legalistic definitions and adopt a more encompassing definition of refugees, including those who either have officially applied for refugee status in the country of asylum or who do not feel safe to return to their country of origin.

6 The 1951 Convention lists a number of rights which should be guaranteed for refugees by the host

government; Articles 13, 14, 17, 18 and 19 refer to various labour and property rights in the country of asylum.

7 Article 22 guarantees access to public education for refugee children and Article 23 deals with access to public relief.

8 Article 3 addresses the issue of non-discrimination and Article 16 talks about access to courts.

9 Article 26 directly talks about freedom of movement and Article 28 deals with travel documents.

10 According to the UNHCR, there are three possible outcomes: voluntary repatriation, local integration or resettlement to a third country.

11 See Mercosur Declaration information at unhcr.org/3ae6b82358.html, and the Organization of African Unity 1969 Convention Governing Specific Aspects of Refugee Problems in Africa at www.africaunion.org/Official_documents/Treaties20Conventions20Protocols/Refugee_Convention.pdf.

References

Appadurai, A. (2002) 'Disjuncture and difference in the global economy', in S. Schech and J. Haggis (eds), *Development: A Cultural Studies Reader*, Oxford: Blackwell.

Baubock, R. (2007) 'Political ethics of external citizenship', Lecture in the Sussex Centre for Migration Research Seminar Series, University of Sussex.

BBC (2003) 'Protest as refugee sews eyes up', *BBC News*, 28 May, news.bbc.co.uk/1/hi/england/nottinghamshire/2942602.stm, accessed 26 June 2009.

— (2008) 'Liberians suspend Ghana protest', *BBC News*, 24 March, news.bbc.co.uk/2/hi/africa/7311507.stm, accessed 26 June 2009.

Benequista, N. and T. Levine (2006) 'Literature review on local–global citizen engagement', Prepared for the Local–Global Citizen Engagements Working Group, Development Research Centre for Citizenship, Participation and Accountability, Brighton, www.drc-citizenship.org/publications/Local_Global_Literature_Review.pdf, accessed 26 June 2009.

Brysk, A. and G. Shafir (2004) *People out of Place: Globalization, Human Rights, and the Citizenship Gap*, London: Routledge.

Castles, S. and A. Davidson (2000) *Citizenship and Migration: Globalization and the Politics of Belonging*, London: Macmillan.

Falk, R. (1994) 'The making of global citizenship', in B. van Steenbergen (ed.), *The Condition of Citizenship*, London: Sage.

Forced Migration and Refugee Studies (2006) 'A tragedy of failures and false expectations: report on the events surrounding the three-month sit-in and forced removal of Sudanese refugees in Cairo, September–December 2005', American University, Cairo.

Frelick, B. and M. Lynch (2005) 'Statelessness: a forgotten human rights crisis', *Forced Migration Review*, 24.

Government of Tibet in Exile (2008) 'His Holiness reiterates firm commitment to the middle-way policy', www.tibet.com/News-Room/dharamsalatibetday1.htm, accessed 26 June 2009.

Grabska, K. (2008) 'Brothers or poor countries? Rights, policies and well-being of refugees in Egypt', in K. Grabska and L. Mehta (eds),

Forced Displacement: Why Rights Matter, Basingstoke: Palgrave.

Grabska, K. and L. Mehta (eds) (2008) *Forced Displacement: Why Rights Matter*, Basingstoke: Palgrave.

Harrell-Bond, B. H. (2008) 'Protests against UNHCR to achieve rights: some reflections', in K. Grabska and L. Mehta (eds), *Forced Displacement: Why Rights Matter*, Basingstoke: Palgrave.

Hathaway, J. (1991) *The Law of Refugee Studies*, Toronto: Butterworth.

— (2005) *The Rights of Refugees under International Law*, Cambridge: Cambridge University Press.

Holborn, L. (1939) 'The League of Nations and the refugee problem', *Annals of the American Academy of Political and Social Science*, 203: 124–35.

Human Rights Watch (2002) 'Liberian refugees in Guinea: refoulement, militarization of camps, and other protection concerns', reliefweb.int/rw/rwb.nsf/8b7d0954 31371f6e 852567cb008396bb/8f 104cfe 1909c76449256c7d0008d20d?OpenDocument, accessed 26 June 2009.

International Herald Tribune (2008) 'Liberian refugees in Ghana deported', 22 March, reprinted at economictimes.indiatimes.com/PoliticsNation/Liberian_refugees_in_Ghana_deported_/articleshow/2890269.cms, accessed 26 June 2009.

Kibreab, G. (2008) 'Access to economic and social rights in first countries of asylum and repatriation: a case study of Eritrean refugees in Sudan', in K. Grabska and L. Mehta (eds), *Forced Displacement: Why Rights Matter*, Basingstoke: Palgrave.

Kurtz, H. and K. Hankins (2005) 'Guest editorial: geographies of citizenship', *Space and Polity*, 9(1): 1–8.

Lewis, M. T. (2006) 'Nothing left to lose? An examination of the dynamics and recent history of refugee resistance and protest', Paper presented at the 4th Annual Forced Migration Postgraduate Student Conference, University of East London, 18/19 March, www.aucegypt.edu/ResearchatAUC/rc/cmrs/reports/Documents/Lewis.pdf, accessed 26 June 2009.

Malkki, L. H. (1992) 'National geographic: the rooting of peoples and the territorialization of national identity among scholars and refugees', *Cultural Anthropology*, 7(1): 24–44.

— (1995) 'Refugees and exile: from "refugee studies" to the national order of things', *Annual Review of Anthropology*, 24: 495–523.

— (2002) 'News from nowhere: mass displacement and globalized "problems of organisation"', *Ethnography*, 3(3): 351–60.

Mehta, L. and J. Gupte (2003) *Whose Needs are Right? Refugees, Oustees and the Challenges of Rights-Based Approaches in Forced Migration*, Working Paper T4, Development Research Centre on Migration, Globalization and Poverty, University of Sussex, Brighton.

Moulin, C. and P. Nyers (2007) '"We live in a county of UNHCR" – Refugee protests and global civil society', *International Political Sociology*, 1: 356–72.

Nussbaum, M. (1996) 'Patriotism and cosmopolitanism', in J. Cohen (ed.), *For Love of Country: Debating the Limits of Patriotism*, Boston, MA: Beacon Press.

Nyamu-Musembi, C. (2005) 'An

actor-oriented approach to rights in development', *IDS Bulletin*, 36(1): 41–9.

Nyers, P. (2007) *Rethinking Refugees: Beyond States of Emergency*, London: Routledge.

Sassen, S. (2004) 'The repositioning of citizenship', in A. Brysk and G. Shafir (eds), *People out of Place: Globalization, Human Rights, and the Citizenship Gap*, London: Routledge.

Schafer, S. (2006) 'Solace and security at the Cairo refugee demonstration', Paper presented at the 4th Annual Forced Migration Postgraduate Student Conference, University of East London, 18/19 March.

Schattle, H. (2005) 'Communicating global citizenship: multiple discourses beyond the academy', *Citizenship Studies*, 9(2): 119–33.

Slater, D. (1997) 'Spatial politics/social movements: questions of (b)orders and resistance in modern times', in S. Pile and M. Keith (eds), *Geographies of Resistance*, New York: Routledge.

Sorensen, J. M. (1996) *The Exclusive European Citizenship: The Case for Refugees and Immigrants in the European Union*, Aldershot: Avebury.

Suleiman, J. (2008) 'Refugees or foreigners? The case of Palestinian refugees in Lebanon', in K. Grabska and L. Mehta (eds), *Forced Displacement: Why Rights Matter*, Basingstoke: Palgrave.

Sylvan, L. (2005) 'The phenomenon of refugee protest in the Global South: 2005 developments', *World Refugee Survey*, US Committee for Refugees and Immigrants, www.refugees.org/data/wrs/06/docs/refugee_protest_in_the_global_south.pdf, accessed 26 June 2009.

Tuitt, P. (2008) 'The time of the refugee', Westminster School of Law lecture, 'A murky relationship: human rights and UK immigration and asylum policy' seminar, 21 February.

UNHCR (2006) 'UNHCR ending operations in Kissidougou region of Guinea', UNHCR Briefing Notes, www.unhcr.org/news/NEWS/451cf7d92.html, accessed 26 June 2009.

— (2009) '2008 global trends: refugees, asylum-seekers, returnees, internally displaced and stateless persons', www.unhcr.org/cgi-bin/texis/vtx/search?page=search&docid=4a375c426&query=2008%20global%20trends, accessed 26 June 2009.

Van Damme, W. (1995) 'Do refugees belong in camps? Experiences from Goma and Guinea', *Lancet*, 346: 360–62.

Verdirame, G. and B. Harrell-Bond (2005) *Rights in Exile: Janus-faced Humanitarianism*, Oxford: Berghahn Books.

World Service Authority (2007) 'WSA passport acceptance', *World Government of World Citizens*, www.worldgovernment.org/visas.html, accessed 26 June 2009.

About the contributors

Angela Alonso is a professor in the Department of Sociology, University of São Paulo, and coordinator of the Environmental Conflicts Area, Brazilian Centre of Analysis and Planning. She has written books on environmental conflicts in Brazil and the Brazilian reformist movement in the nineteenth century, as well as a biography of the leader of the Brazilian abolitionist movement. Currently she is a Guggenheim fellow and a visiting fellow at the MacMillan Centre in Yale University, researching the ideas and strategies of the movement for the abolition of slavery in Brazil.

Saturnino M. Borras is Canada Research Chair in international development studies at Saint Mary's University, Nova Scotia. He has been deeply involved in rural social movements internationally since the early 1980s. He is a fellow of the Amsterdam-based Transnational Institute and the California-based Food First. His research interests include land issues, agrarian change and (trans)national rural social movements, and land governance and agrofuels. His books include *Pro-Poor Land Reform: A Critique* (2007), the edited volume *Critical Perspectives in Rural Development Studies* (2009) and the co-edited *Transnational Agrarian Movements Confronting Globalization* (2008, with M. Edelman and C. Kay). He is editor of the *Journal of Peasant Studies*.

Rebecca Cassidy is a doctoral student at the Institute of Development Studies, University of Sussex. Her research focus is on the social context of antiretroviral treatment and support for people living with HIV in the Gambia, looking at the dynamics of treatment and support, in support groups, clinics and in the national context of Global Fund programmes. Her wider interests are in medical anthropology, HIV-related stigma and support, negotiations over disclosure of HIV status within family and community, antiretroviral treatment, and how people living with HIV navigate the politics of programmes and projects.

Jennifer C. Franco is an independent social science researcher who has worked with a number of academic institutions and activist organizations in Europe and in the Philippines. Since 2006 she has been affiliated with the Transnational Institute, where she is currently leading an international team investigating the social and environmental assumptions and impacts of European Union agrofuels policy. Her main research interests are rural social movements and the challenges of democratization, rural politics and rule of law processes, and the variable meanings of rights and resistance across time and across and within national boundaries.

Rosalba Icaza is an international studies scholar who specializes in the international political economy of trans-border civic activism on regionalism, democracy and gender, with a particular emphasis on Latin America and Mexico. She currently holds the European Commission Reintegration Grant for a two-year research programme on alternative regionalisms in Latin America, exploring the principles and institutional structures of governance that have informed the alternatives to neoliberal/open regionalism policies promoted by indigenous social movements and anti-capitalist networks. Her recent publications include 'Regionalism in the Americas' for the *Encyclopaedia on Globalization and Security* (2009) and *Networked Activisms and Regionalism. Power and Resistance across Borders* (forthcoming).

Melissa Leach has directed the Economic and Social Research Council's Social, Technological and Environmental Pathways to Sustainability Centre since 2006. Professorial fellow at IDS and leader of the Knowledge, Technology and Society team, she originally trained as a geographer (MA, Cambridge) and social anthropologist (PhD, London). Speaking four African languages, over the last twenty years she has been closely involved both in ethnographic fieldwork and in extensive interdisciplinary research. This has combined anthropology with historical, ecological and science and technology studies approaches, as well as working with foresters, agricultural and medical scientists. Her recent work has explored the politics of science and knowledge in policy processes linked to environment and health; addressing vaccine controversies, scientific uncertainties, citizenship and public engagement; cultural and political dimensions of vaccine delivery; medical research trials, emerging infectious diseases, and ecology–health linkages.

Marjorie Mayo is professor of community development at Goldsmiths, University of London, and joint head of the Centre for Lifelong

Learning and Community Engagement. She has worked in the community sector, and local government, and has experience of working internationally. Her publications include *Imagining Tomorrow: Adult Education for Transformation* (1997), *Cultures, Communities, Identities: Cultural Strategies for Participation and Empowerment* (2000), *Global Citizens* (2005) and *The Dilemmas of Development Work* (2008, with Paul Hoggett and Chris Miller).

Lyla Mehta is a research fellow at the Institute of Development Studies, University of Sussex. She is a sociologist, and her work has focused on the gendered dimensions of forced displacement and resistance, rights and forced migration and the politics of water. Since 1991, she has conducted research on displacement and resistance in India's Narmada Valley. She has engaged in advisory work on issues concerning displacement, gender, dams and development with various UN agencies and the World Commission on Dams, and has also been active in advocacy and activist work on these issues with NGOs and social movements in Europe and India. She has authored *The Politics and Poetics of Water: Naturalising Scarcity in Western India* (2005), edited *Displaced by Development: Confronting Marginalisation and Gender Injustice* (2009) and co-edited *Forced Displacement: Why Rights Matter* (2008).

Rebecca Napier-Moore has worked on and in protracted refugee situations, and is especially interested in hostility from front-line workers in camps. Her work with forced migrants has been in the USA, Ghana, the UK and Uganda. She has an MPhil in development studies from the Institute of Development Studies, University of Sussex, and is currently at the Global Alliance against Traffic in Women in Bangkok, working with advocates on migrant rights and labour rights agendas, through regional and international lobbying, and feminist participatory action research.

Peter Newell is professor of international development at the University of East Anglia. He is a politics and international relations specialist in issues of environmental governance and development. He currently holds a UK Economic and Social Research Council Climate Change Leadership Fellowship, and is a trustee of the NGO One World Trust, which works on issues of accountability in global governance. He is the author of numerous publications on different aspects of environmental governance and development including most recently the books *Governing Climate Change* and *Climate Capitalism* and edited the earlier book in this series on *Rights, Resources and the Politics of Accountability*. He has conducted policy and consultancy work for a range of governments, NGOs and international organizations.

Steven Robins is a professor in the Department of Sociology and Social Anthropology at the University of Stellenbosch, South Africa. He has published on a wide range of topics, including the politics of land, 'development' and identity in Zimbabwe and South Africa; the Truth and Reconciliation Commission; urban studies; and most recently on citizenship and governance. His recent book, entitled *From Revolution to Rights in South Africa: Social Movements and Popular Politics* (2008), focuses on globally connected social movements, NGOs and CBOs that are involved in democratic struggles over access to AIDS treatment, land and housing. He has edited *Limits to Liberation after Apartheid: Citizenship, Governance and Culture* (2005), and co-edited *New South African Keywords* (2008, with Nick Shepherd).

Marcelo Saguier is a researcher at Argentina's National Science and Technology Research Council (CONICET) based at the Department of International Relations of the Latin American School of Social Sciences (FLACSO/Argentina). He also teaches international relations at Argentina's National Foreign Service Institute and in the MA programme of the Torcuato Di Tella University. Marcelo's research interests cover trade governance issues, and his work has focused on the formation of transnational coalitions of labour and social movements centred on trade and development issues; processes of regionalization in the Americas; and recently on the politics of regulation of transnational corporations. He holds a PhD in politics and international studies from the University of Warwick and an MSc in international relations from the London School of Economics.

Ian Scoones is an agricultural ecologist based at the Institute of Development Studies at the University of Sussex, UK. He is co-director of the Economic and Social Research Council's Social, Technological and Environmental Pathways to Sustainability Centre, and joint convenor of the Future Agricultures Consortium. His work focuses on the politics of policy-making in international development, with a particular emphasis on agriculture and rural development in Africa.

Julie Thekkudan has been working with PRIA for the last three years. Her doctoral thesis from Jawaharlal Nehru University, India, focused on the issue of gender and law. With experience in a range of positions in research, training and project implementation, her areas of specialization are gender and development, gender mainstreaming within organizations, gender and law, social accountability, participatory governance, citizenship, water and sanitation. She has written many articles on the issue of gender and citizenship in various journals.

Linda Waldman is a social anthropologist with experience in African poverty and the related issues of gender, racial classification, ethnicity and identity. She obtained her PhD at the University of the Witwatersrand, South Africa, where her research focused on indigenous identity and nationalism among the Griqua of South Africa. She joined the Institute of Development Studies as a fellow in the Knowledge, Technology and Science Team in 2004. Her recent research activities include an examination of how environmental issues are integrated into Poverty Reduction Strategy Statements and a comparative study of asbestos-related disease and its legal, medical and sociocultural dimensions in South Africa, the United Kingdom and India.

Index

accountability, 8, 20, 23, 80, 89, 122, 124, 133, 166, 176, 178, 185, 202, 207, 219; global, 9; of corporations, 93; transnational, 164
Achmat, Zackie, 65
Action for Southern Africa (ACTSA), 191, 205
ActionAid, 143, 151
ActionAid Brazil, 177
adaptation, 213, 224–6, 227
African Union Convention Governing Specific Aspects of Refugee Problems in Africa, 238
agency of citizens, 11
Agenda 21, 221
agrarian movements, transnational, 119–39 (emergence of, 121–4)
agrarian reform, market-led, 120
AIDS activism, in South Africa, 56–78
AIDS industry: epistemological standardization, 38; undermining health system, 36 *see also* HIV/AIDS
AIDS knowledge, contentious nature of, 61–3
AIDS Law Project, 60
Alliance for Rainforest Conservation, 217
Alliance for Responsible Trade, 169
Alternativa Boliviariana para las Américas (ALBA), 180–1
Amazon, 225–6; environmental issues in, 218, 219, 221
Amini, Abas, protest by, 243, 245
Andhra Pradesh, 82–4
Anna, AIDS activist, 67–74
antiretroviral therapy (ART), 64, 65, 72; access to, 59, 61; in Gambia, 45–6; in South Africa, 56; provided free, 58; 'revolution', 63; rural-based programmes, 66
apartheid, 194
Arbour, Louise, 247
asbestos, 14, 25; banning of, 185, 187, 199, 201, 205; externalization of costs of, 200; production of, 198–202 (state-sponsored in India, 206; subsidization of, 202); setting of standards for, 22; struggles against, in South Africa and India, 185–210
Asbestos Forum, 202–3
asbestos-related diseases, 14–15; mobilization on, 7
Asbestos Working Group (South Africa), 203
asbestosis, diagnosis of, 196
Asian NGO Coalition (ANGOC), 128
assessments, global, politics of, 96–115
asylum seekers, protests by, 18
Auden, W. H., 245

Babymilk Action Campaign, 82
Ban Asbestos Network India (BANI), 192–3, 197, 199, 200, 201, 206–7
Batmanian, Garo, 217
Beck, Ulrich, 140, 157
Behind the Label campaign, 82
Benetton, 177
bilateral trade agreements, 168
biomedicine, 19, 22, 34, 45, 52, 56, 59, 74; discourse of, 50, 61 (in vernacular forms, 75); global, challenging of, 62; resistance to, 76; suspicion of, 23
biotechnology, campaigning on, 177
Brazil, 23; environmental movement in, 7, 16, 19, 211–31; land reform

movement in, 133; plebiscite on FTAA, 173
Brazilian Forum of NGOs and Social Movements for the Environment and Development, 219–20
Brazilian Indigenous People's Programme, 218
Brot für die Welt, 218
Brown, Gordon, 151
Burkina Faso, HIV activism in, 34
Bush, George W., 176

Cadbury Committee, 81
campaign coalitions, 158
Cape plc, taken to court, 191
Capobianco, João Paulo, 215, 219, 225
Cartagena Protocol on Biosafety, 168
Castleman, Barry, 192
Central America Free Trade Agreement-Dominican Republic (CAFTA-DR), 165–6, 168, 170
Centres for Disease Control, 35
Centro Ecuménico de Documentação e Informação (CEDI) (Brazil), 218, 225
child labour, 150
Christianity, 75; and HIV/AIDS campaigns, 73–4
citizen agency, 205–7
citizen engagement, 3–30, 204; global, simultaneity of, 18
Citizens Trade Campaign, 169
citizenship, 26, 153; and displacement, 232–3; and exclusion, 15; and trade governance, in the Americas, 163; and transnational coalitions, 140–62; cosmopolitan, 9; definition of, 169, 233, 235–45; delinked from territorial boundaries, 4, 237; ecological, 180; education for, 154; feminist views on, 179; fragmented, 103–4; gendered, 180; global, 3, 9, 10–11, 24, 87, 154, 155, 163, 164, 245–9; health citizenship, 56–78 (mediation of, 59–60); horizontal and vertical workings of, 11–12; hybrid, 19; in claimed spaces, 172; meanings and practices of, 8–15, 25; multidimensional nature of, 4, 27, 140, 153; multiple, 237, 246, 247; national, 10; new forms of, 189; new spaces for, 123, 126, 135; new understandings of, 246; therapeutic, 34–5, 43, 47, 50; trans-scalar practices of, 176–7; transnational, 11, 178, 179; within invited spaces, 170–1 *see also* cyber-citizenship
citizenship, actor-oriented view of, 248
citizenship practices, everyday, 79–95
citizenship rights, campaigning for, 119–39
civil society, 20, 21, 37, 50, 99–101, 106–7, 125, 140, 145, 220, 221, 227–8; and globalization, 98–9; and privatization of land, 124; global, 107, 111 (free-floating, 145); interactions within, 130–3; role of, 107
civil society organizations (CSOs), 168, 169, 175; involved in trade policy processes, 170–1
Clean Clothes Campaign, 82
Clinton, Bill, 169
Clinton Foundation, 56
coalitions, around campaigns, 158
Coimbra Filho, Adelmar, 214, 215
collective farms, 120
Committee of Government Representatives on the Participation of Civil Society (CGR), 172
Commonwealth Education Fund (CEF), 151, 152
compensation, for asbestos diseases, 194, 195, 198, 200–1
Comprehensive Agrarian Reform Programme (Philippines), 125
Concerned People against Asbestos (CPAA) (South Africa), 194, 197, 202–3, 205, 206

condoms, use of, 70, 72–3
Confederación Parlamentaria de las Américas (COPA), 167
Confederation of Indian Industries (CII), 82
Conservation International (CI), 224
Conservationist Entrepreneur campaign, 223
Contentious Politics (CP) approach, 212–13
Convention on the Rights of the Child, 141
Convention relating to the Status of Refugees (1951), 233
corporate social responsibility (CSR), 81, 82, 84, 90, 93
Country Coordinating Mechanism (CCM), 36–7, 38, 42, 52, 59
credit, access to, for women, 80
crisis, global, 163
Cultural Survival, 219
cyber-citizenship, 107

Dakar Framework for Action on EFA, 142
delegates to international meetings, 151–2
democracy, 97, 167; deliberative, 109; democratization of, 111; global, 9; in era of globalization, 108; innovation of, 176–7; of trade policy, 173, 177, 178; top-down, 171
Democratic Kilusang Magbubukid ng Pilipinas (DKMP) (Philippines), 129
disempowerment, through biomedical industry, 75
displaced people: agency of, 13; mobilization of, 17; protests of, 241–4; regulation of, 7; struggles of, 232–52

e-mail, use of, 109, 134
ecological sustainability, 9
education, 143; as last outpost of the state, 141; governance of, 141–4; private, 143, 150; setting of standards for, 22; use of para-teachers in, 143
Education for All campaign, 12, 142, 146, 150, 157
Education International, 143, 148, 149
Egypt, refugees in, 17–18, 234, 241–2
empowerment, 51, 144, 154, 155: in biomedical knowledge, 57; medical, 66; of women, 19, 81, 85–7 see also disempowerment
emulation, 213, 217, 220, 222, 224, 227
English language, use of, 212
Environmental Coalition for NAFTA, 175–6
Environmental Defence Fund, 218
environmental movement, in Brazil, 211–31
Environmental Public Hearings (EPH) (India), 203–5
Everest company, 187–9
Everite company, 187–9
exclusion, 27, 33, 91–2, 174–6, 177
expose-and-oppose tactics, 136

farmers, interests of, 13
Fast Track Initiative of Dakar Framework (FTI), 143
Federação dos Orgãos para Asistência Social e Educacional (Brazil), 177
Federation of Free Farmers (FFF) (Philippines), 126–7
Feldmann, Fábio, 215
Food and Agriculture Organization (FAO), 120, 132, 133
Foodfirst Information and Action Network (FIAN), 132
Ford Foundation, 225
forest, Brazilian, conservation of, 216
Forest Stewardship Council, 223
forum-shifting strategies, 167
Fox, Vicente, 171
Free Trade Area of the Americas (FTAA), 165, 170, 172, 173–4
Friends of the Earth, 219
fund-raising, learning about, 216

Fundação Brasileira para a Conservação de Natureza (FBCN), 214–17

Gambia, 17; AIDS funding in, 39–42; HIV/AIDS in, 19, 20, 23, 33–55
Gates Foundation, 56
genitalia, naming of, 67, 68
global advocacy, 154–5
global authority, changing nature of, 186–7
Global Campaign for Agrarian Reform, 132
Global Campaign for Education (GCE), 7, 18, 20, 24, 140–62; Global Week of Action (GWA), 14, 17, 146–7, 150, 156
global citizenship *see* citizenship, global
Global Civil Society (GCS) theory, 212–13, 228
Global Environment Facility, 221
Global Exchange, 172
Global Fund to Fight AIDS, Tuberculosis and Malaria (GFATM), 6, 16, 17, 19, 20, 33–55, 56, 58, 62
Global March against Child Labour, 143, 149
Global Reporting Initiative, 81
Global Week on Education, 146
global-local relation *see* local-global engagement and processes
globalization, 185; and civil society, 98–9; and power of multinationals, 81; changing forms of power under, 3, 4, 163; creates new opportunities, 15; from below, 212; paths of, 211–31; resistance to, 4
Goemaere, Eric, 65
governance: changing nature of, 5–8, 35, 141; corporate, history of, 81–2; global, 26, 249 (growth of, 8); inclusive, 80–2; increased complexity of, 24; multi-level nature of, 80, 145; of education, 141–4; of trade, 163–84

Grameen Bank, 83
Greenpeace, 219, 222, 225
Greenpeace Bureau, 101

health, globalism in, 33
health and safety campaigns, 189, 204
health citizenship *see* citizenship, health citizenship
health governance: changing structures of, 35–9; global, 186–7
health mobilizations, around cancer, 65
health programmes, global, 13
healthcare, inequalities of, 61
health-related activism, 34
Hemispheric Social Alliance (HSA), 174
Hindustan Unilever Limited (HUL), 79–95; brand-building of, 92; product range of, 86–7
HIV-2+, 44, 46
HIV/AIDS: activism, in Burkina Faso, 34; 'African solutions' for, 57, 61; alternative forms of organization around, 52; awareness workshops, 68–9; death figures arising from, 61; dietary treatment of, 72; disclosure of status, 44–5; global epistemic community, 38; in South Africa, 16; myths about, 70; politics of, in South Africa, 56–78; hostility to scientific view of, 70, 74; in Gambia, 6, 13, 22, 33–55; in South Africa, 19, 22; pluralist therapeutic approaches to, 45; stigma attached to, 73; treatment of, 66, 74
HIV/AIDS Rapid Response Project (HARRP), 39–42
hybrid activism, 19, 211–31

illiteracy, 48, 198, 206
inclusion, 33, 91–2, 108, 174–6
India, 8; mobilization against asbestos in, 15, 18, 21, 185–210, 185
information society, 212

Instituto Socioambiental (ISA) (Brazil), 16, 211, 218–21, 227, 228; resources of, 221
Interchurch Organization for Development Cooperation (ICCO), 218
Intergovernmental Panel on Climate Change (IPCC), awarded Nobel Prize, 96
intermediation, politics of, 18–21, 126, 130–3, 202–5, 221–6
International Assessment of Agricultural Knowledge, Science and Technology for Development (IAASTD), 6, 13, 16, 19, 20, 22, 96–115
International Ban Asbestos Secretariat (IBAS), 187, 192, 205
International Conference on Agrarian Reform and Rural Development (ICARRD), 121, 130
International Covenant on Economic, Social and Cultural Rights (ICESCR), 141
International Federation of Agricultural Producers (IFAP), 20, 121, 126, 128, 130, 131, 136
International Fund for Agricultural Development (IFAD), 127, 132, 133; Farmers' Forum, 131, 136
International Labour Organization (ILO), Asbestos Convention, 186
International Land Coalition (ILC), 127–8, 130
International Monetary Fund (IMF), 143, 212
International Planning Committee for Food Sovereignty (IPC), 130
International Programme on Chemical Safety (IPCS), 186
International Union for the Conservation of Nature (IUCN), 214
Internet, use of, 84, 107, 134, 172, 212
intervention, politics of, 188
Ishii-Eiteman, Marcia, 99
Islam, 62

Jammeh, President, 34

Kamdar Swasthya Suraksha Mandal (KSSM) (India), 191–2
Kilusang Magbubukid ng Pilipinas (KMP) (Philippines), 129
Klabin, Roberto, 215, 222–3
knowledge, 26; alternative forms of, 105; democratization of, 212; local, 23, 99; pluralization of, 98; politics of, 21–4, 35, 45–6, 126, 133–7, 188, 189, 193–8, 223, 226 (in AIDS context, 56–78; in global assessments, 105–10); seen as neutral, 23; setting international standards for, 22
knowledge mediators, 24
knowledge-power interaction, 99
Kumara Mangalam Birla Committee (India), 82

land, hunt for, 121
land policies: alternative, 134; localization of, 124
land rights, 7; as citizenship rights, 12; campaigning for, 21, 23, 119–39 see also Philippines, land reform in
land sales transactions, 124, 125
land titling, localization of, 125
landless people, 125
Lara Mesquita, Rodrigo, 215, 216, 222
Lewis, Stephen, 62
liberalization of trade, impact on women, 174
Liberia, relation to United States, 243
local and global, mediation between, 20–1
local-global engagement and processes, 24, 33, 34, 42, 43, 46, 96, 99, 100, 144–5, 149–50, 152–3, 155–6, 213–17, 218–21, 224, 226; representation of the local, 102
localization of social movements, 119
Lusikisiki District (South Africa), 56

MacArthur Foundation, 215, 216
Malkki, L. H., *Purity and Exile*, 240
Mandela, Nelson, 64
Martin, Dan, 215
Martins, Eduardo, 217
Mbeki, Thabo, 57, 58–9, 61
Médecins Sans Frontières (MSF), 57; AIDS activities in South Africa, 58, 63–5; creation of, 63; in Lusikisiki, 63–7
mediation, 20–1, 26, 43, 46–50; of global medicine, 67–74; role of, 25
Medical Bureau of Occupational Diseases (MBOD) (South Africa), 190, 200
medicine: global, 68–74 (mobilization and mediation of, 56–78); traditional, 45, 46, 52, 61, 70; Western, distrusted, 59 *see also* biomedicine
Meirelles Filho, João Carlos, 216
Mercado Común del Sur (Mercosur), 165
mesothelioma, 185, 195, 196, 201
Mexican Revolution, 119
Mexico, 171; public hearings on trade negotiations, 167
microcredit, 80
Millennium Development Goals (MDG), 143, 146, 157, 159
Mishra, Haushala Prasad, 191
missionaries, 68; resistance to, 75–6
Mittermeier, Russell A., 213–17
mobilization, 26; against FTAA, 180; around trade, 165, 170–7; changing patterns of, 211–13; dynamics of, 188, 190–3; new forms of, 25; of displaced people, 241–4; over asbestos, 185–210; politics of, 15–18, 126–30, 126; trajectories of, 213–17
mobilizations, multi-issue nature of, 212, 227
Mouffe, Chantal, 111–12
Movimiento dos Trabalhadores Rurais Sem Terra (Brazil), 177
Mozambique, land campaigns in, 136

multi-stakeholder dialogues, 102, 105
multinationals, in asbestos market, 187–9
multivitamins, 62
muti traditional medicine, 70, 72, 74
My World environmental project, 224

Nansen, Fridtjof, 247
Nansen passports, 246–7
Narayana Murthy Committee (India), 82
nation-state, 103, 178, 233, 249; constrained, 8, 119; dissolution of, 237; role of, 4, 26; transformation of, 124
National AIDS Control Programme (NACP) (Gambia), 39
National AIDS Secretariat (NAS) (Gambia), 40–2, 49, 52
National Campaign on Dust-Related Lung Diseases (NCDRLD) (South Africa), 191
National Forum for Agrarian Reform, 133
National Institute of Occupational Health (NIOH) (South Africa), 192–3, 195, 196
National Network of People Living with HIV (Gambia), 48
National Union of Mineworkers (NUM) (South Africa), 191
National Wildlife Federation, 218
neoliberalism: crisis of, 163; resistance to, 164
Nestlé, baby milk marketing by, 82
network society, 212
new constitutionalism, 166
New Sahyadri Industries Ltd (NSIL), 204–5
New Social Movements (NSM) approach, 212
Nogueira Neto, Paulo, 214, 215
non-governmental organizations (NGOs), 34, 37, 42, 46, 47, 49, 50, 60, 63, 90, 106–7, 127, 131, 136, 142, 145, 148; harassment of, 57; preservation of brands, 151
North American Commission for

Environmental Cooperation (NACEC), 171
North American Free Trade Agreement (NAFTA), 7, 163, 165, 168, 170, 171, 175; and split in environmental movement, 175; Chapter Eleven, 166; gendered nature of, 174
Norwegian Church Aid, 218

occupational health, 7
Organisation for Economic Co-operation and Development (OECD), 142; Principles of Corporate Governance, 81
Organization of African Unity (OAU), Convention Governing the Specific Aspects of Refugee Problems in Africa, 234
Oxfam, 151

Pambansang Katipunan ng mga Samahang Magsasaka (PAKISAMA) (Philippines), 127
Pambansang Ugnayan ng Nagsasariling Lokal na mga Samahang Mamamayan sa Kanayunan (UNORKA) (Philippines), 129
Paraguay: consultations on FTAA, 173; mobilization in, 17
Participatory Research in Asia (PRIA), 192
Paryavaran Mitra organization (India), 204
people of the land, concept of, 137
Peoples of the Forest framework (Brazil), 219, 220, 227
Permanent Peoples' Tribunals on Transnational Corporations, 40, 176
Peru, health rights debate in, 167
petitions, signing of, 205
philanthrocapitalism, 8, 36
Philippines: land policy in, 8, 124–37; land struggles in, 21
Pilot Programme for the Protection of Tropical Forest in Brazil, 221

Political Process approach (PP), 212
polycentric social movements, 119
Pondoland, 17, 66, 69, 71, 75; antiretroviral therapy in, 65–7
poverty, reduction of, 80, 91
power: multi-tiered and complex, 25, 27; opaqueness of, 144
President's Emergency Plan for AIDS Relief (PEPFAR), 6, 34, 36, 56
prevention of parent-to-child transmission (PPTCT), 39, 40
Prieska (South Africa), asbestos mining in, 190, 194–5, 203, 206
privatization, 119, 166; of collective farms, 120
Programme for Private Natural Reserves (Brazil), 223
Project Shakti (India), 6, 79, 82–4

Quijano, Romeo, 99–100

rainforests: constructed as political issue, 214–15; destruction of, 222; preservation of, 223
Randeree, Ahmon, 191
Rath, Matthias, 62
re-embedding of economic actors, 170
Reaction to Conquest, 75
Reclaiming Public Water network, 166
Red Colombiana de Acción frente al Libre Comercio, 175
reflexive institutions, 110
refugees: Bhutanese, 243; Burmese, 235; Eritrean, 239; in concentration camps, 240; in Egypt, 17–18, 235, 241–2; Liberian, 239, 243; Palestinian, 236 (and right to return, 240); responsibility for, 233–5; rights of, 233; Sudanese, 242, 243, 244, 245, 248 (in Egypt, 17–18); Tibetan, 244
reviewers in assessments, 100–2; positionality of, 102–3, 105
Ricardo, Carlos Alberto, 218–20
rights, 8, 185; cosmopolitan,

grounding of, 179; global, 9; of citizens, realization of, 238–41; of displaced people, 232–52; to health, 167, 207; to healthcare, 60
rooted cosmopolitanism, 156
rootedness, importance of, 145

salaries of NGO staff, 40, 47, 48
Sanduguan organization (Philippines), 126
sangoma (diviner), 67, 69, 70
Santa Yalla (Gambia), 39
Santilli, Márcio, 220
Sarbanes Oxley Act (USA) (2002), 81
Satyam fraud, 82
Satyarthi, Kailash, 148
Save the Children Fund, 151
scale shifts, 16
Securities and Exchange Board of India, 82
Security and Prosperity Partnership for North America (SPP), 167
Self Help Group Federation, 91
self-help groups (SHG), 14, 79, 80, 83, 88, 89, 93
Senegal, response to HIV, 37
sexuality, 35; discussion of, 67
Shakti Amma (Empowerment Mothers) (India), 14, 82–92; opposition to, 92
Shakti Vani organization (India), 84
shingles, 74
Silva, Marina, 225
Sipho, AIDS activist, 68–74
social movements: and citizen engagement, 176; global, legitimacy of, 158
soft power, 22, 23
solidarity, 25, 103, 104, 130, 137, 147, 154, 164, 178; element of citizenship, 10; emergent, 107
SOS Rainforest (Brazil), 211, 213–17, 222–4, 227
South, voices of, 144–5
South Africa, 13; AIDS politics in, 56–78; anti-asbestos campaign in, 14–15, 17, 19, 21, 185–210; HIV/AIDS in, 23

South African National AIDS Council (SANAC), 58–9, 62
sovereignty, 57; going beyond, 111; national, 35, 61
stakeholders: interests of, 109; multiplicity of, 110
state: and definition of citizenship, 238; as ally of movements, 228; role of, 90, 163
state–civil society dichotomy, 213
structural adjustment programmes, 120
support groups, expectations and entitlements of, 46–50
Survival International, 219

Tarrow, S., 16, 19, 144, 145, 156, 157, 158, 212, 227, 228
Task Force Mapalad (Philippines), 127
techno-fundamentalism, 71
therapeutic citizenship *see* citizenship, therapeutic
trade governance, in the Americas, 163–84
trade unions, 198
transnational activism, 6, 164, 178, 228
transnational campaigns, building of, 144–5, 244–5
transnational coalitions, 140–62
transnational corporations, in Latin America, 176–7
transnational movements, 213; agrarian, 119–39
transnationalization of capital, 170
transparency, 166
Tratado de Comercio de los Pueblos, 180
Treatment Action Campaign (South Africa), 57, 60, 64–5, 67, 71, 75–6
treatment literacy practitioners (TLP), 66, 68
treatment support groups, 43–50, 51
trust, importance of, 147–8
Tshabalala-Msimang, Manto, 62, 72
twasa, 67

Unidad de Atención a las Organizaciones Sociales (UAOS) (Mexico), 171
Unilever, 14, 79, 90 *see also* Hindustan Unilever Limited
United Democratic Front (South Africa), 65
Universal Declaration of Human Rights (UDHR), 233
United Nations (UN), 97; treaties and conventions, 102
UN Children's Fund (UNICEF), 142
UN Conference on Environment and Development (UNCED), 216, 219, 221
UN Declaration of Human Rights (UNDHR), 141
UN Development Programme (UNDP), 39, 142
UN Educational, Scientific and Cultural Organization (UNESCO), 142, 143; Convention against Discrimination in Education, 141; Man and the Biosphere Programme, 214
UN Global Compact, 81
UN High Commissioner for Refugees (UNHCR), 234, 239, 241–2, 243, 245, 248
UN Programme on HIV/AIDS (UNAIDS), 56
UN Relief and Works (UNRWA), 234
United States of America (USA), involved in agricultural assessment process, 102
US Agency for International Development (USAID), 120

vertical approach, 5
Via Campesina organization, 7, 12, 17, 19, 20, 120–37; relations with other organizations, 130; Right to Land campaign, 135
view from everywhere, 110
Voluntary Counselling and Testing (VCT), 39, 40, 59, 64, 69

Walzer, Michael, 164
Watson, Robert, 98
witchcraft, 45, 62, 67, 73, 74
witnessing, 63
women, 47, 103; employment of, 90; empowerment of, 19; livelihoods of, in India, 79–95; political role of, 86; restricted to private realm, 91; rural, economic augmentation for, 84–5; self-help groups, 6, 14; unpaid labour of, 176; with HIV, 43 *see also* empowerment, of women
women's groups, 41
women's movement, 174–5, 176
women's tribunals, 177
World Bank, 23, 36, 49, 56, 97, 99, 120, 123, 127, 132–3, 134, 135, 142, 143, 150, 220, 212, 221; campaign against, 218; land policy of, 127; Multi-Country AIDS Programme (MAP), 6, 34, 36
world citizenship, 9
World Conference on Education for All (WCEFA), 142
World Health Organization (WHO), 35, 56, 186; Global AIDS Programme, 39
World Service Authority, 247
World Trade Organization (WTO), 99, 165, 170, 177, 181
World Wildlife Fund (WWF), 214, 216–17, 219, 222, 223, 225–6

Zapatista uprising, 170
Zuma, Jacob, 59